"This labor is a profound and life-giving ▮▮▮▮▮▮▮▮▮▮▮▮▮▮▮▮▮▮▮
shadow of death. Few people will escape the wrenching and sullen emptiness of depression or the exhausting ▮▮▮▮▮▮▮▮▮▮▮▮-yet there are is
▮▮▮▮▮▮▮▮▮▮▮▮▮▮▮▮▮▮▮▮▮▮▮▮▮▮▮▮▮▮ ▮▮ from ▮ ▮▮▮ al, neurological,
rel. ▮.▮.▮▮ ▮▮d spiritual viev, ▮▮int. Richard Winter offers not only decades of
wisdom and knowledge but the fruit of his own personal struggle with depression and anxiety. This is a tour de force of how to engage the reality of
our struggles in the bright light of our relationship with Christ."

Dan B. Allender, Ph.D., professor of counseling psychology and founding president,
The Seattle School of Theology and Psychology

"As a pastor for over thirty years, I must engage in my own personal battle
with depression and anxiety while seeking to equip others to fight this good
fight of faith. I have searched for a resource that is comprehensive enough to
cover the spiritual, physical, psychological and relational dimensions of depression while remaining readable and accessible, especially to one like
myself who faces depression. This is it! Dr. Winter has given his readers a
priceless tool. For those simply wanting to grasp the dynamics and difficulty
of depression or assist those who face it, here is a compass with which to
navigate these dangerously turbulent waters."

Joseph Vincent Novenson, senior teaching pastor, Lookout Mountain
Presbyterian Church, Lookout Mountain, Tennessee

"It is a special joy to be granted the privilege of recommending this excellent
book. Richard Winter has written the most wise and careful meditation on
sorrow, anxiety, depression and brokenness that I have ever read. His book
is full of deep reflection on Scripture, experience and the most up-to-date
scientific research on the troubles of the mind. Consequently, it will be a
wonderful resource for every pastor, counselor, psychologist and psychiatrist, or simply for anyone desiring to be a kind and helpful friend to those
who struggle with depression or severe pain and sorrow. Richard's sensitive
use of personal stories and his drawing on many years of listening to and
responding to deeply depressed individuals make this book come alive and
make it extraordinarily useful to the reader committed to trying to bring
hope to the hurting. His appeals to Scripture are never superficial but arise
from a deep understanding of the biblical story of creation, rebellion, redemption, and the expectation of consummation through which the Lord
desires to shape and direct our lives. This book will be a valuable source of

help for many years to come, both to those who are themselves troubled and to those who give their lives to serve the wounded heart."

Jerram Barrs, resident scholar, Francis A. Schaeffer Institute, and professor of Christian studies and contemporary culture, Covenant Theological Seminary

"Drawing on a wealth of experience in clinical psychiatry, counseling and biblical reflection, Richard Winter has produced a unique resource. It is worth the purchase price just for its carefully crafted inquiry into the role of the satanic. Depression in some form or other will almost inevitably come our way, either in our own experience or in the lives of those close to us. So read this book when the sun is shining and life looks good. Its practical wisdom will reduce the likelihood of these dark nights of the soul, and when they do come, provide a well-stocked toolbox for self-care, counsel, advice on treatment where needed and practical redemption. A must-have resource for pastors, counselors and all Christians who want to live well under God."

Glynn Harrison, Professor Emeritus of Psychiatry, University of Bristol, U.K.

"*When Life Goes Dark* is an excellent treatment of the full range of distressed mood. Dr. Winter clearly has the gift of comprehending the whole person and uses it to bring coherence to a part of our experience that is too often treated superficially and simplistically. He gives a balanced and thorough picture of both who we are and how we are in times of distress. There is no 'flavor of the month' here, but a true picture of the problem of being human and coping with emotion. In doing so he provides an accurate and integrated look at the complete human condition and its savor. I particularly enjoyed the various contemporary and historic examples of people coping with the world and all its brokenness: personal, biological, social, spiritual. It's good to know we are not alone but travel in a very real company who've experienced everything we do and lived on."

Mark Cundiff Johnson, M.D., Assistant Professor in Clinical Psychiatry, Washington University School of Medicine, St. Louis, Missouri

"Richard Winter's book, *When Life Goes Dark*, is a comprehensive and biblically based guide for finding hope in the midst of depression. It will be of great help to those suffering from depression and those who minister to them."

Siang-Yang Tan, Professor of Psychology, Fuller Theological Seminary, and author of *Counseling and Psychotherapy: A Christian Perspective*

RICHARD WINTER

WHEN LIFE GOES DARK

FINDING HOPE IN THE
MIDST OF DEPRESSION

IVP Books

An imprint of InterVarsity Press
Downers Grove, Illinois

InterVarsity Press
P.O. Box 1400, Downers Grove, IL 60515-1426
World Wide Web: www.ivpress.com
E-mail: email@ivpress.com

InterVarsity Press® is the book-publishing division of InterVarsity Christian Fellowship/USA®, a movement of students and faculty active on campus at hundreds of universities, colleges and schools of nursing in the United States of America, and a member movement of the International Fellowship of Evangelical Students. For information about local and regional activities, write Public Relations Dept., InterVarsity Christian Fellowship/USA, 6400 Schroeder Rd., P.O. Box 7895, Madison, WI 53707-7895, or visit the IVCF website at <www.intervarsity.org>.

All Scripture quotations, unless otherwise indicated, are taken from the THE HOLY BIBLE, NEW INTERNATIONAL VERSION®, NIV® Copyright © 1973, 1978, 1984, 2011 by Biblica, Inc.™ Used by permission. All rights reserved worldwide.

While all stories in this book are true, some names and identifying information have been changed to protect the privacy of the individuals involved. Other letters and stories have been used with permission.

Design: Cindy Kiple
Images: oil paintbrush strokes: © Qweek/iStockphoto
       black paintbrush strokes: © eva serrabassa/iStockphoto

ISBN 978-0-8308-3468-6

Printed in the United States of America ∞

Library of Congress Cataloging-in-Publication Data

Winter, Richard, 1945-
  When life goes dark: finding hope in the midst of depression /
Richard Winter.
     p. cm.
  Includes bibliographical references (p.   ) and index.
  ISBN 978-0-8308-3468-6 (pbk.: alk. paper)
  1. Depression, Mental—Religious aspects—Christianity. 2.
Depressed persons—Religious life. 3. Depression, Mental. I. Title.
  BV4910.34.W56 2012
  248.8'625—dc23
                                                              2012005247

P   20   19   18   17   16   15   14   13   12   11   10   9   8   7   6   5   4   3   2   1

Y   28   27   26   25   24   23   22   21   20   19   18   17   16   15   14   13   12

*"I . . . will make the Valley of Achor [trouble] a door of hope.
There she will sing as in the days of her youth."*

HOSEA 2:15 NIV **1984**

***

*For Jane, Johanna and John, Matthew and Anna,
Rebecca and Sam, Triona, Joseph, Eliza, Oliver, Rudy,
Margot, Zach and Martha—who give me great joy—
may they have hope and light in a world where there
is much sorrow and darkness.*

CONTENTS

ACKNOWLEDGMENTS

This book could not have been written without the constant encouragement and patience of Jane, my dearest companion in life. She has stood by me in times of weakness, shadow and darkness, and has allowed me to weep in her arms without shame.

My thanks go back over many years to Dr. Monty Barker, who initially encouraged me into psychiatry and taught me well. Thanks too to Dr. Francis Schaeffer, who prepared me for the battle of ideas and worldviews that I encountered in the arena of psychiatry and who also gave me a deep respect for the relevance, authority and trustworthiness of Scripture in relation to the whole of life. I have learned much from the friendship and wisdom of Dan Allender, who is a pioneer in the field of Christian counseling.

I am indebted to my friends and colleagues at the English L'Abri, with whom I initially shared and explored these ideas. I am also deeply grateful for the generosity of the administration of Covenant Theological Seminary who gave me sabbatical time to think and write, as well as to my faculty colleagues who encouraged and advised me when I asked. Thanks to Liz, Signe, Jeremy and Aaron, who patiently read and checked the manuscript, and to Al Hsu, my editor, who graciously pushed and encouraged me through the painful process of completing the work.

Finally, I owe much to my parents, who have contributed much to this book through their love and encouragement in my early years and in their faithful example of living out the truth of the Christian hope in a broken world.

And to those who have kindly given me permission to share their pain, you may never know how much it means to readers to know that others have been there before them.

INTRODUCTION

Severe depression is a profoundly crippling condition. It is associated with impaired work and relationships, greater physical illness and significant risk of death from suicide. And it's widespread. Approximately one in twelve people will experience a severe depressive episode in their lifetime, and unfortunately, more than 50 percent of people in the United States and Europe with serious depression do not receive or will not get adequate help. A friend wrote the following to me in a recent family newsletter after enduring a long season of depression that profoundly affected everything and everyone in his life:

> You need to know that it was dark for a long time. Days were eclipsed by weeks and then months . . . and even the years passed by with little light. The sun is shining now, which is why you are hearing from us again.

This book is written primarily for those like this friend, who find themselves—or their loved ones or the people they are counseling—vulnerable to depression. It is for those who want to find ways to resist the slippery slopes and vicious circles of confused emotions that so often end in depression. And it is for those who offer comfort and counsel to the depressed; it should help to provide a framework and perspective within which to evaluate the causes of depression in order to bring healing and hope.

When I wrote the first edition of this book in the early 1980s,[1] I had completed my training in medicine and psychiatry in England, where I had accumulated an enormous amount of head knowledge from many hours of study and much experiential knowledge from treating seriously depressed patients in the hospital and in outpatient clinics. I had also done some counseling and psychotherapy with people in a local church and at the L'Abri Fellowship, a Christian study center in the United Kingdom, where I had worked for many years. Personally I had been discouraged and sad in life but never seriously depressed—and hoped never to be. However, within the next three years after this book publication in 1986, my sister died in childbirth, my father-in-law died suddenly, my wife was diagnosed with cancer and my brother-in-law took his own life. In between all of this, a couple of good friends, with whom I'd worked very closely, moved to the United States, and simultaneously, I was thrust into heavy leadership responsibility in my church and in the L'Abri community. I was able to keep going, like the proverbial frog in the kettle where the water heats up all around him, but I was not dealing well with the grief and challenges that arose from all those losses and changes. I began to learn more about the subjective side of depression as I coped less and less well with conflict, lost most enjoyment in life, struggled with insomnia and became paralyzed by indecision. I was sad, discouraged, ashamed and slipping down into a serious depression. I talked to friends, mentors and counselors, as well as started taking antidepressants—all of which helped me through this dark valley in life.

It was ironic that all of this happened immediately after my book was published, almost as if God was saying, "You think you know a lot about depression, but let me teach you a thing or two." Twenty-two years later, I have experienced more grief and sadness but also much joy and encouragement. I am thankful that I have never been so deep in the pit of depression again and have learned to deal better with the inevitable times of anxiety and sadness that come to someone of my somewhat melancholic-leaning temperament. In a few times of major decisions, transitions and loss, I have felt my vulnerability to anxiety and depression taking over and manifesting as insomnia, tearfulness, early morning dread and a terrifying sense of my body and brain being taken over by an alien influence. In these times, I have felt like I was "going down" into a dark place, and indeed, the word *depression* is derived from the Latin word that means "pressed down." I am grateful that my "fall" was arrested before I slipped too far, but I feel profound sympathy for those who go much deeper into the darkness of depression for a long time.

Over the last forty years of my career, I have counseled many people whose struggle is somewhere on the spectrum between discouragement and severe depression. A large part of my calling as a psychiatrist and psychotherapist is to listen to people's stories. Almost every day I hear new stories from my students or clients of their struggles to deal with the pain of life. In each of their stories there is woven a unique tapestry of beauty and brokenness, of dignity and depravity, and many of these threads lead to an endpoint of deep emotional distress and depression. Each person's story is different but simultaneously absorbing, fascinating, disturbing and heart wrenching. There is no neat formula for recovery from depression, so I cannot prescribe some ready-made package of things to think and do or pills to take. Often, it takes many weeks of talking for some of the factors that have played into a person's depression to come out into the open—so hidden are they underneath layers of shame and fear. It then takes more time to understand the relative contribution of personality, attachment issues, early-life events, trauma, current stresses, genes and biology so that the client and I can work together toward turning a seeming "breakdown" into a "breakthrough" of new ways to see, believe and be. This is the privilege and wonder of counseling and psychotherapy, being able to walk alongside someone for a while and see God's gentle but persistent work of transforming and healing.

Since the first edition of this book, I have spent twenty years as a professor of practical theology and as the director of the counseling program at Covenant Seminary. I have worked hard to keep up with the ever-changing and fascinating scientific research on depression, as well as personally growing in my understanding of the relationship between scientific knowledge and biblical wisdom, and I have tried to communicate many of the ideas in this new book to men and women who have become pastors, youth workers, hospital chaplains and professional counselors. I also hope to give you some tools with which to understand and make sense of your own or your loved ones' experience of depression: the amazingly still relevant biblical stories and teaching about emotions, the current scientific research on the causes and treatment of depression, and the ways in which our brains can be changed by what we think and do.

So we will need to wrestle with some tough questions here. What is depression? Is it sickness or sin? Should we be concerned about regarding any and all unhappiness as a treatable disorder? And when it comes to relieving depression, do antidepressants really help? Are they a good thing? How do we relate the knowledge that comes to us from science, including brain scans and biochemistry, to the world of the Bible? What about all the different types of talking treatment? Are counseling or psychotherapy effective and useful?[2] Some Christians have a problem with secular psychology and others think the Bible is all we need.[3] Still others wonder, with all the benefits of psychology and medicine, if spirituality and, especially, the Bible remain relevant to the treatment of depression.

In order to answer these questions, we will need to define some differences between normal sorrow, discouragement and grief, and mild, moderate or severe depression. We will need to look at the causes of depression, including taking a look at current research on depression and deciding how we can think about the relationship between a Christian understanding of reality and the findings of medical and psychological science. But beyond understanding depression and its causes, I hope this book will help you find encouragement and insight into the many things that can be done to reduce vulnerability to depression, increase resilience and lift the darkness in order to have hope for the future. May the "valley of trouble" become a "door of hope" (Hosea 2:15 NIV 1984)!

Part One

THE ROOTS OF SORROW

NATURE'S EFFECTS AND NURTURE'S CHOICES

Cans't thou not minister to a mind diseas'd,

Pluck from the memory a rooted sorrow,

Raze out the written troubles of the brain,

And with some sweet oblivious antidote

Cleanse the stuff'd bosom of that perilous stuff

Which weighs upon the heart?

WILLIAM SHAKESPEARE, *MACBETH*

1

FALLING INTO DARKNESS

The Experience of Depression

That perilous stuff which weighs upon the heart.

WILLIAM SHAKESPEARE, *MACBETH*

*How weary, stale, flat, and unprofitable seem to me
all the uses of this world!*

WILLIAM SHAKESPEARE, *HAMLET*

Julie sat opposite me, staring at the floor. She spoke in a quiet monotone only when I asked her a question. Occasionally she smiled, but it was an empty expression since her eyes betrayed a deep sadness and perplexity. She could dimly remember times when life seemed to have some color, but now it was an effort to push herself from one day to the next. Her office work was the one thing that kept her going, providing a temporary relief from the negative thoughts that consumed the lonely hours before dawn or the long evenings when she wandered listlessly around the house or sat blankly in front of the television. *What is wrong with me?* she wondered. *Surely no one else is as hopeless and incompetent as I am?*

Julie did not realize that she was in the company of many people who have suffered from severe depression at some time in their lives. In *An Unquiet Mind,* Kay Redfield Jamison chronicles times when she felt "unbearably miserable and seemingly incapable of any kind of joy or enthusiasm. Everything—every thought, word, movement—was an effort. Everything that once was sparkling now was flat. I seemed to myself to be dull, boring, inadequate, thick brained, unlit, unresponsive, chill skinned, bloodless and sparrow drab."[1] Similarly, in his book *Darkness Visible,* William Styron attempts to describe the indescribable, writing that severe depression is an interior pain that is, "a veritable howling tempest of the brain."[2]

Despite the testaments of well-known writers, for many people the subject is often veiled in silence, disapproval or suspicion. Many, like Tony Lewis, speak of their shame at being depressed:

> I knew of a few people who had mental breakdowns but the term meant nothing to me. If anything I looked down on "them" as being weak, spineless people society would do well rid of. When a psychiatrist told me I was mentally ill, I was horrified. I felt ashamed of being ill—guilty, even. I told a constant stream of lies to cover up my visits to psychiatrists, my hospital attendances and my reasons for not being a student or holding down a proper job. . . . To feel a slow poison paralyze every faculty, to become gradually more and more helpless, and not to know how or why. . . . My own depressive illness grew from something mild and infrequent into a brutal scourge I believed I could only escape through death.[3]

Approximately one in every eight women and one in every sixteen men will at some time in their lives have such an experience of depression.[4] In 2007, 16.5 million American adults (approximately 8 percent of the population) experienced at least one episode of serious depression. Severe depression is being recognized as one of the major health concerns of this century. Antidepressants are the most frequently prescribed medicines, and the number of these prescriptions doubled between 1996 and 2005.[5]

Depression is associated with multiple health problems, and it increases the risk of heart attack and stroke, as well as likely undermining immunity to other diseases. Depression contributes to thousands of lost working hours, broken marriages and family dysfunctions, and many acts of folly and indiscretion. Its effects are more devastating in terms of years of being able to live an *active life* than AIDS, heart disease and cancer. Some have called depression one of the most devastating diseases known to humankind.[6]

In recent years approximately 33,000 people each year die by suicide in the United States. That is a rate of one suicide every sixteen minutes, and ninety suicides per day. What's worse is that for every death by suicide, there are an estimated eleven suicide attempts.[7] In more than two out of three suicides, depression that could have been treated was probably a contributing factor. In St. Louis, my home city in the U.S., three pastors took their own lives in one year.

Depression occurs in every culture, but it is often described in language different from our Western, psychological words. In many countries people complain of physical symptoms, such as headaches, back or stomach pain, or sexual difficulties rather than saying, "I am feeling sad or depressed." For these people, the stigma of depression is usually far greater than what we experience in the Western world, so they will suffer in silence.

WHAT IS DEPRESSION?

The word *depression* is used to cover a whole range of feelings— from a fleeting sense of unhappiness to profound, enduring, suicidal hopelessness. All of us have ups and downs each day that are usually related to the frustrations and disappointments of normal life. Sometimes a sense of dejection colors our thoughts and activities for hours or even days as we come to terms with a broken relationship, a failed exam, the lack of promotion at work, the loss of a job, or plans foiled by other unexpected circumstances.

Some people cycle in and out of moods of happiness and sadness with dramatic speed and intensity for all to see. Others, more placid by temperament, experience little outward variation in mood. There are people who reside at the ends of the spectrum—those who are consistently exuberant and enthusiastic, rarely appearing unhappy, while others are consistently depressive and melancholic, rarely seeming happy. But most of the time, most of us will live with a range of experiences of happiness and sadness, and we will rarely hit the dark places of despair and hopelessness or the wild excesses and disinhibition of mania.

However, in recent years, a concern has emerged that we are losing the subtleties of language that describe the middle range of emotions between extreme happiness and suicidal depression. With the common claim that depression and anxiety can be treated easily with a pill, it seems that any unhappiness may be defined as depression.

So when I am diagnosing depression, it is very important to explore the context and the meaning of the experience for the individual and his temperament before giving the label of "major depressive disorder" or "clinical depression." I have to ask "is this an appropriate reaction to the loss of a job or the breakup of a relationship or the death of a friend?" I need to explore the severity of the depression and how long it has lasted. Charles Barber comments on the difference between a fleeting experience of depression and major depressive disorder when he writes, "To confuse the two, depression with Depression, is to confuse a gentle spring rain with a vengeful typhoon."[8] Unfortunately, for many people who go to their doctor with symptoms of depression, they are prescribed an antidepressant before the situation has been discussed in detail.

Worse yet, there is often inadequate follow up or even appropriate advice about how to take the medication and deal with possible side effects. In one study, "43% of those prescribed antidepressants had no psychiatric diagnosis or any mental health care beyond prescription of drugs."[9] Not only is this an irresponsible use of medication, but recent research has shown that antidepressants do not work much better than placebo in mild and moderate depression. This fuels concern about the misuse of medication and the need for careful attention to what actually constitutes depression. It is possible that milder depressions are caused by psychological and social factors, whereas in severe depression, there is an additional biochemical factor that makes it more like a physical illness.

While most of us are probably more familiar with the middle range of emotions that include happiness and sadness, as well as periods of mild situational depression, we need to explore the less familiar territory of the extreme ends of human experience: here people can suffer from the pain and paralysis of severe depression (often called clinical or major depression) or the excitement, confusion and chaos of a manic state of mind—and some people will experience wild swings between these two worlds. One end is dark and desperate while the other is full of color and enthusiasm; but both are out of touch with reality. It is incredibly hard for those who have never been there to understand what it is like.

Severe depression. To give you a sense of the bleak experience of severe depression, here are quotes from several writers who have been "there." Sylvia Plath, who eventually took her own life, describes the inner world of Esther (the fictional protagonist of her novel *The Bell Jar*), a young journalist and recent winner of a fashion magazine contest:

> I wasn't steering anything, not even myself. I just bumped
> from my hotel to work and to parties and from parties to my

hotel and back to work like a numb trolley bus. I guess I should have been excited the way most of the other girls were, but I couldn't get myself to react. I felt very still and very empty, the way the eye of a tornado must feel, moving dully along in the midst of a surrounding hullabaloo.[10]

William Cowper, the poet and hymn writer of the eighteenth century, who suffered several bouts of severe depression, wrote to his cousin:

> You describe scenes delightful, but you describe them to one who, if he even saw them, could receive no delight from them, who has a faint recollection, and so faint as to be like an almost forgotten dream, that once he was susceptible of pleasure from such causes. . . . Why is the scenery like this . . . why is every scene, which many years since I could not contemplate without rapture, now become, at the best, an insipid wilderness to me?[11]

Severe depression is marked by several features, which manifest differently in each individual, and sometimes features that seem contradictory appear together at different times in the same individual. For example, severely depressed people often feel persistently sad and can be moved to tears at the most trivial events, sometimes crying excessively without good reason—*or* they may long to cry but be unable to do so, as if all emotion has been drained dry. Some people who are depressed will become restless, agitated, demanding, easily offended and difficult to please. They may be constantly irritated and experience occasional outbursts of frustration or rage. Others may withdraw, becoming very slow in their reactions to people and events, showing little emotion. Or they may appear quite normal because they can still cover their inner confusion with a smile and a joke.

For many struggling with severe depression, concentration becomes difficult, so settling down to anything or making even small decisions becomes an enormous burden. Simple tasks become enormous obstacles. Showing that depression is not a new phenomenon, nearly two hundred years ago, John Colquhoun vividly described these symptoms of depression in his "Nature and Signs of Melancholy in a True Christian":

> A man so depressed is utterly unable to exercise joy or to take comfort in anything. . . . He is always displeased and discontented with himself. . . . His thoughts for the most part are turned in upon himself. . . . He commonly gives himself up to idleness; either lying in bed, or sitting unprofitably by himself . . . daily harassed with fears of want, poverty and misery, to himself and to his family. . . . He is weary of company, and is much addicted to solitude. . . . His thoughts are commonly all perplexed, like those of a man who is in a labyrinth, or pathless wilderness. . . . He has lost the power of governing his thoughts by reason. . . . He can no more cease to muse on that which is already the subject of his thoughts, than a man, afflicted with a violent toothache, can forbear, at the time, to think of his pain.[12]

Constant feelings of inadequacy, failure, worthlessness, shame and guilt plague the mind, and it seems as though others are watching and critical of every action. Normally insignificant fears and anxieties become greatly exaggerated. William Cowper describes his churning thoughts and exaggerated fears at such times: "The terrors that I have spoken of would appear ridiculous to most. . . . I am hunted by spiritual hounds in the night season."[13]

In addition, constant tiredness is common and sleep patterns are usually interrupted so that waking at two or three in the morning is not unusual. William Styron writes: "Exhaustion combined with sleeplessness is a rare torture . . . my few hours of sleep were usually terminated at three or four in the morning, when I stared up into yawning darkness, wondering and writhing at the devastation taking place in my mind, and awaiting the dawn, which usually permitted me a feverish, dreamless nap."[14] For others, the day is too painful to face and there is a longing to sleep forever. So for these people, especially younger folks, the sleep problem may be an inability to fall asleep at night and a tendency to sleep long into the next day.

Furthermore, sometimes—and this is less common—there can be auditory and visual hallucinations or delusions, the latter of which are firmly entrenched, yet false, beliefs. For instance, Jamie believed that her body was giving off a horrible smell when nobody else could smell anything, and she was adamant that she had a serious abdominal cancer that the doctors could not find. This type of depression is often described as psychotic depression, where there is a severe break with reality, and delusions and hallucinations are present. Approximately one in four people admitted to the hospital with depression experience psychosis,[15] such as Joseph, who was convinced the CIA had bugged his room and was following him everywhere, or Marie, admitted for paranoid depression, who believed that she was being filmed for a movie that was being made about her life by the hospital staff.

Finally, in *any* kind of depression, the despair may become so deep that thoughts of suicide begin to invade the mind. At first it might be an occasional thought but then it can turn into an insistent pressure, as if someone were driving the depressed to self-destruction. My patient Judy had told me of her feelings of depression, but I did not realize how serious it was until she handed me a poem she wrote describing how much a burden she felt to everyone:

> I'm going off to die now, goodbye. Goodbye my dear loved ones. Shall I spend two years hugging each of you goodbye? No it suffocates and stunts and binds and, anyway, I must go.
>
> I must go. I cannot stay now. I am empty, ashamed, hollow and dead already. The death in me already smells. I can see

your noses wrinkling at the stink, and I love you all too much to cause you such discomfort.

Do not shake your heads and say too bad. This is best.

Those of us who do this really understand how broken we are: menaces.

This is my public duty. It's a favor to you all.

Exhale relief: one less broken life to cope with. Lift your hands and praise your Lord who has given you all life. I will bow before him and beg—my eyes down. Should he lend me his hand to stand I will sing a new song. If not I will crawl ever downward from his presence, understanding why.[16]

Criteria for major depression. To have an experience of depression considered "major depression," the person must experience depressed mood and/or loss of pleasure and interest in normal activities almost every day for at least two weeks. Even though people may not complain of feeling depressed, they might still be if they experience loss of pleasure and interest in the normal things of life. In a vivid memoir of his own depression, William Styron writes in *Darkness Visible*: "My brain had begun to endure its familiar siege: panic and dislocation, and a sense that my thought processes were being engulfed by a toxic and unnamable tide that obliterated any enjoyable response to the living world."[17]

In addition to this first criterion of depressed mood or loss of interest and pleasure, there must be at least four other symptoms or signs:

1. Appetite and weight disturbance. Often loss of appetite leads to weight loss or eating for comfort leads to weight gain. Sometimes there is a craving for carbohydrates.

2. Sleep disturbance. Older people tend to sleep less well, and if they're depressed, they may wake at 2:00 a.m. or 3:00 a.m. with all the anxieties of the world overwhelming them. Younger people tend to sleep later and, when depressed, may

sleep even longer, not wanting to get up and face the day.

3. Fatigue, loss of energy and lethargy. Andrew Solomon, author of *The Noonday Demon: An Atlas of Depression,* writes:

> Little has been written about the fact that depression is ridiculous. I can remember lying frozen in bed, crying because I was too frightened to take a shower and at the same time knowing that showers are not scary. I ran through the individual steps in my mind. You sit up, turn and put your feet on the floor, stand, walk to the bathroom, open the bathroom door, go to the edge of the tub. . . . I divided it into fourteen steps as onerous as the Stations of the Cross. I knew that for years I had taken a shower every day. Hoping that someone else would open the bathroom door, I would with all the force of my body, sit up; turn and put my feet on the floor; and then feel so incapacitated and frightened that I would roll over and lie face down. I would cry again, weeping because the fact that I could not do it seemed idiotic to me. At other times, I have enjoyed skydiving: it is easier to climb along a strut towards the tip of a plane's wing against an eighty mile an hour wind at five thousand feet than it was to get out of bed on those days.[18]

4. Agitation, restlessness, anxiety and irritability. Irrational worry and feeling that something awful will happen are often a part of the depression experience, so it is hard to know what to call this state of mind. A new category of depression has been suggested for the next edition of the *Diagnostic and Statistical Manual of Mental Disorders* (*DSM-V*) called "Mixed Anxiety/Depression."

5. Feelings of worthlessness and inappropriate guilt. Everything in the world is seen through a dark and pessimistic lens. There is a pervasive and powerful sense that the self is useless and the future is hopeless. Legitimate guilt over real events can lead to depression, but often when people are depressed, they drag up

minor things they may have done many years before—and they are preoccupied with how terrible they are for what they did. Even if they have confessed the wrongdoing in the past, they may feel that they have not been forgiven. Or worse, they may imagine they have done things that they have never done.

6. Slow thinking, indecisiveness and loss of concentration. In a later chapter, I will discuss the brain changes that happen in severe depression that correlate with this slow and laborious ("sticky") thinking. It can be hard for those struggling with severe depression to read a newspaper, let alone a chapter of a book, and decision making, especially for those prone to perfectionism, is like wading through molasses.

7. Thoughts of suicide. When the past seems terrible, the self feels worthless, and the future looks hopeless, then thoughts of an ultimate end to such terrible pain are not far from consciousness.[19]

Dysthymia. Dysthymia is chronic low-grade depression, wherein the person experiences a dark mood on most days for at least two years. This is usually accompanied by lethargy, irritability, self-criticism and hopelessness. Many people with this condition don't ask for help; it feels to them as if they have always been that way, and some are described as depressive personalities. Symptoms are less severe and last longer, but they are also prone to have episodes of serious depression. When this happens it is called "double depression."

DIFFERENCES IN DEPRESSION.

Between men and women. It is popularly claimed that twice as many women as men will experience major depression in their lifetimes. However, men *die* from suicide approximately four times as often as women, but women *attempt* suicide three times as often as men. So what are some possible reasons for these differences between men and women?

1. The hormonal factor: at puberty, after childbirth and again around menopause, women are more vulnerable. It is thought that changing estrogen levels enhance the risk of depression by affecting serotonin levels.[20] In addition, higher testosterone in men may protect them against depression. Before puberty and after menopause the rates of depression in men and women are the same.

2. Women seem to be more relationally sensitive than men and feel losses more intensely. One study found a number of differences between the brain scans of men and women under stress; this suggested that men's brains activated the "fight or flight" areas of the brain when they were under stress, while women's brains moved them to "tend and befriend."[21]

3. Women experience more sexual abuse and cultural oppression than men, and this has profound long-term effects.

4. Perhaps, most significantly, men express their depression in different ways than women do, so it may not be recognized as easily. Women usually experience many of the readily recognizable symptoms of depression that I described earlier, whereas men may have only a few of those symptoms. Men are often numb, withdrawn, self-critical, irritable, angry, frustrated and impulsive when they are depressed, so the depression may manifest itself most noticeably in marriage and job problems. And while women may feel less energetic, gain weight and be more anxious in depression, men are more likely to lose weight and be more agitated and obsessive.

In addition to reacting to depression differently, men and women also seek help differently. Women are more likely to talk to friends, a counselor or a doctor, but men more often feel ashamed by potentially being perceived as weak and will push themselves harder at work, abuse alcohol, drugs or sex to drown the pain, or ultimately even take their own lives. It is difficult for most men to get beyond the macho expectation that crying is weak and feminine (of course, there are some women who also find it hard to cry). Another intriguing factor in depression treatment for men is that males seem to respond to a different class of antidepressants than women, suggesting subtle differences in the brain that we do not yet understand.

At different ages. Depression is often disguised. The person experiencing it does not realize or say she is depressed, and others do not recognize it either. Depression may outwardly appear in the form of marriage conflicts, sexual problems or addiction, drug or alcohol dependence, chronic pain, aggression or violence, or in personality changes and problems.

Children and adolescents may become withdrawn or emotionally unstable, aggressive, phobic and generally antisocial without obvious sadness. In the last twenty years there has been increasing acceptance that even preschool children can be significantly depressed, which may show up as crying easily, having little joy in normal activities, and being irritable and whiny. Inside, these children often feel excessive anxiety, shame and guilt. Depressed adolescents may be unhappy, have physical symptoms such as migraines or stomach pain, and may live in fear of not achieving unreasonable parental expectations of academic performance. Older people may lose all joy in life, as well as have multiple physical symptoms, complaining of heart palpitations, restlessness, fatigue, dizziness, body aches and pains, difficulty with remembering things, and loss of interest and concentration. They are often restless and irritable, and they might become convinced that they have cancer or some other fatal illness.

Only through careful questioning does one discover that, with many of these problems, there are also other symptoms of depression. This happens across the world, in many other cultures where depression is felt and expressed in physical terms. Often the language itself does not have equivalent words to articulate depression and anxiety.

Depression and the Christian. The Christian's struggle with depression is often complicated, because the Bible can seem irrelevant, prayer a pointless exercise, forgiveness impossible and God far away—if he exists at all. Colquhoun wrote,

> Through his imagination he is disposed to aggravate his sin, or misery, or anger. . . . He thinks his days of grace are past and that now it is too late for him to believe, to repent or to expect mercy. He is perpetually apprehensive that he is forsaken by God and always prone to despair. . . . He is incapable to engage in secret prayer and meditation. . . . He dares not hope, and therefore dares not pray . . . and feels an uncommon degree of averseness from religious exercises. He is constantly troubled with hideous and blasphemous temptations against God.[22]

Although Colquhoun wrote this two hundred years ago, many of these experiences have even been described by David in the Psalms thousands of years ago. David was a man of strong emotions, of powerful joy as he danced before the Lord, and yet at times, he too descended into the depths of depression. "My tears have been my food day and night," he wrote (Psalm 42:3). He felt downcast and disturbed (Psalm 42); he was weak with sorrow, grief and groaning (Psalm 31). He felt utterly overwhelmed: "all your waves and breakers have swept over me" (Psalm 42:7). In Psalm 22, David bemoaned the fact that God seemed to have abandoned him, and he described many of the symptoms of depression.

We typically read or sing the psalms as if they were written quickly in a few hours, but perhaps some of them describe many weeks, or even months, passing through a time of darkness when faint hope is gradually being restored. Only Psalm 88 does not resolve within itself to a place of restored confidence in God:

"Darkness is my closest friend," David laments (Psalm 88:18). I am profoundly grateful for this psalm, as it stands as a comfort to many whose depression lasts a long time.

Similarly, the writer of Lamentations described his own vivid experience of grief, depression and feeling shut off from God, as he meditated on the sins of his people and the destruction of Jerusalem:

> I am the man who has seen affliction
>   by the rod of the LORD's wrath.
> He has driven me away and made me walk
>   in darkness rather than light; . . .
> He has made me dwell in darkness
>   like those long dead. . . .
> He has weighed me down with chains.
> Even when I call out or cry for help,
>   he shuts out my prayer. . . .
> I have been deprived of peace; . . .
> So I say, "My splendor is gone
>   and all that I had hoped from the LORD."
> (Lamentations 3:1-2, 6-8, 17-18)

Now these biblical writers were not necessarily suffering from clinical depression. In order to have some practical way of deciding how serious the problem is and what help is appropriate, psychiatrists and psychologists, who have observed countless depressed people, came up with certain criteria to define major depression,[23] distinguishing between what used to be called "reactive (situational) depression" from "endogenous (predominantly biochemical) depression." As psychiatrist Peter Whybrow writes: "What may have started as an appropriate response to a tragic moment extends into some sort of behavioral cancer, a malignant mood that invades and distorts the very nature of the self."[24]

If you are prone to depression, you are not alone. Many very

gifted, creative and influential men and women throughout history
have struggled with episodes of serious depression, including
Martin Luther, Abraham Lincoln, Emily Dickinson, Charles
Spurgeon, Winston Churchill, Judy Garland, Martin Luther King
Jr., Amy Tan, J. K. Rowling and Gwyneth Paltrow.[25] In a later
chapter, I will discuss how four of the central characters in the
Old Testament—Moses, Elijah, Job and Jonah—faced very different but extremely stressful, difficult circumstances, and all
came to a point of longing to die.

QUESTIONS FOR REFLECTION AND DISCUSSION

1. Has someone you've known experienced severe depression? If
   so, did their experience match any of the descriptions in this
   chapter? Which ones?

2. Where does your experience of depression fit on the spectrum
   of depressive mood—from feeling blue and a little discouraged
   to severe depression or dysthymia?

3. Do you think that there is still a stigma to being depressed?
   How does that stigma get played out?

4. How have you thought about people who have been seriously
   depressed? Do you feel sympathy, sadness, irritation, impatience, anger or some other emotion? Describe why.

5. What do you think about Christians who get depressed? Does
   depression mean that their faith is weak or that God is punishing
   them for something they have done wrong? Why or why not?

6. Can you think of other reasons why there might be a difference
   between men and women in the incidence of depression?

7. Do you know children, teenagers or elderly people who have been
   or are depressed? How could you tell they were depressed?

2

RISING INTO LIGHT

Bipolar Swings, Mania and Happiness

There is a particular kind of pain, elation, loneliness, and terror involved in this kind of madness. When you're high it's tremendous. The ideas and feelings are fast and frequent like shooting stars, and you follow them until you find brighter and better ones. Shyness goes, the right words and gestures are suddenly there, the power to captivate others a felt certainty. . . . Sensuality is pervasive. . . . Feelings of ease, intensity, power, well-being, financial omnipotence, and euphoria pervade one's marrow.

KAY REDFIELD JAMISON, *AN UNQUIET MIND*

The day before his admission to the hospital, Colin had felt on top of the world. In fact, he had never felt better. As he walked, or rather ran, down the street in the English village where he lived, he sang the few lines he could remember from an old Beatles song, mixed with some lines of his own. The village baker, whose last conversation with Colin two weeks earlier had been monosyllabic and gloomy, was amazed at the change. It was difficult to follow what Colin was saying because he seemed to flit from subject to subject, often throwing in a pun or a rhyme. He seemed almost larger than life as he breezed into the store:

Beautiful day! The race begins at 2:30 on Leading Lady. O'Grady says, "Run!" . . . Yes I'll have one bun . . . no half a dozen, Mr. Glacey, please. . . . How are you I'm fine . . . right on the line. . . . They'll be off soon. . . . I'll win a thousand grand. . . . I must fly, goodbye . . . bye . . . bye.

The police interfered when he started giving away five-pound notes in the street and walking out in front of the traffic. While he was detained at the police station as someone called a doctor, he amused everyone with a dance, a song, and a bout of anger and irritability at being misunderstood by the law. After all, he said, he had a right to entertain the public in the streets.

Some people, like Colin, who are vulnerable to severe depression can also experience times of being unusually happy, talkative, carefree, even euphoric. For three months prior to this episode, Colin had been severely depressed before swinging up into a "manic" phase. These swings can be relatively mild but can also be much more obvious, as in Colin's case.

Besides euphoria, in such a phase, there may also be moments of depression, tearfulness, irritability and anger. Mild overconfidence may later become a strong belief in being a messenger of God, a movie star, or a member of the royal family. Thoughts and conversations flow nonstop, often changing in midsentence from one subject to another. Little sleep is needed and sexual promiscuity or suggestiveness are common. All of this may cause considerable concern in relatives and friends.

Intense religious experiences, with claims of conversion, baptism in the Spirit, mystical rapture, or messages from God or Satan may confuse the situation. For example, Jo was normally a quiet, gentle person—often thought of by others in the church as very sensitive and spiritual. When she and her boyfriend broke up, she appeared to be taking it very well and was full of praise for God, but her friends began to get worried when they heard her singing in her room at four in the morning. The next day she stood up in the middle of the church with a message of judgment from God, and in the early hours of Monday morning, several people in the church received phone calls from her with mini-sermons about the sexual immorality in the church and rather suggestive comments. Finally she was arrested by the police for preaching incoherently on street corners and was admitted to a psychiatric hospital. This same reaction to stress occurred several times over the next few years, and each time, she needed medication and counseling to come to terms with the difficulties in her life and relationships. These recurrent manic episodes were usually accompanied by very little depression; it appears that she inherited a predisposition to break down this way when she was under certain kinds of pressure.

One of the most difficult problems in treating a person with mania is that they *feel* perfectly well and lack insight that anything is wrong. Years ago, before the discovery of modern tranquilizers, some patients with untreated mania died from exhaustion because of their ceaseless activity; similarly, some people with untreated depression starved themselves to death because they refused to eat—if they did not actively choose to kill themselves by suicide. People in states of mania or depression should be urgently treated by a psychiatrist before they do harm to themselves or others.

BIPOLAR DISORDER—MANIA, HYPOMANIA AND DEPRESSION

Most of us live in the middle range of emotions. Our temperaments and personality styles are a product of our genes, our early childhood experiences and our current relationships. While some people feel things very intensely, for others, feelings are muted and repressed. On the exuberant and hypomanic (less than full mania) end of the mood spectrum, life is full of vibrant color and energy, whereas on the depressive end, life is colorless, bleak and dark. When the brain gets out of control in true mania,[1] there is "often wildly exuberant mood, . . . expansive and grandiose thinking, cascading speech, phenomenally high levels of energy, little need for sleep, a frenzied tendency to seek out others, terrible judgment, and rank impulsiveness."[2] Often there are also delusions and hallucinations. Whether "high" with an apparent absence of any problems or cares in life, or "low" with the weight of the world on one's shoulders, both mania and depression involve a distorted view of reality.

Bipolar disorder and cyclothymia. Some people will have isolated manic episodes without ever becoming depressed, but more often, mania is accompanied by episodes of depression. About 20 percent of those who experience severe depression will also experience mania. This tendency to swing between extremes of mood—often staying either depressed or high for weeks or months at a time—used to be called "manic depression" but is now referred to as "bipolar disorder." It must be distinguished from the daily ups and downs that many of us experience, and from "cyclothymia," where periods of mild depression and excitement and mild euphoria may alternate regularly but fall short of bipolar disorder. Sometimes, and often adding to the confusion, bipolar disorder may present with both depressive and manic symptoms at the same time—this is diagnosed as a "mixed affective state."

Men are more likely to have more manic episodes; women experience more depression. About two-thirds of all cases of bipolar disorder start with a manic episode, and many adults who develop bipolar disorder will have had their first episode before the age of twenty-one. One in five report that a manic episode even occurred in childhood.

Kay Redfield Jamison, a psychologist and a world authority on bipolar disorder, describes her first experience of manic-depressive illness as a senior in high school:

I raced about like a crazed weasel, bubbling with plans and enthusiasms, immersed in sports, and staying up all night, night after night, with friends, reading everything that wasn't nailed down, filling manuscript books with poems and fragments of plays, and making expansive, completely unrealistic plans for my future. The world was filled with pleasure and promise; I felt great. Not just great, I felt really great. I felt I could do anything, that no task was too difficult. My mind seemed clear, fabulously focused, and able to make intuitive mathematical leaps that had up to that point entirely eluded me. Indeed they elude me still. At that time, however, not only did everything make perfect sense, but it all began to fit into a marvelous kind of cosmic relatedness. My sense of enchantment with the laws of the natural world caused me to fizz over, and I found myself buttonholing my friends to tell them how beautiful it all was.[3]

Her friends, exhausted by her enthusiasm, kept telling her to slow down, and eventually she did slow down into a depressed phase:

I was totally exhausted and could scarcely pull myself out of bed in the mornings. . . . I dreaded having to talk to people, avoided my friends whenever possible, and sat in the school library . . . virtually inert, with a dead heart and a brain as cold as clay.[4]

Some people are naturally exuberant and extroverted in their personalities. They are energetic, enthusiastic, cheerful and outgoing, and they rarely, if ever, dip into lower moods. Often they are very creative and productive people. Jamison claims that many "great scientists and scholars . . . tend to be enthusiastic, optimistic and energetic by temperament."[5] In her book *Touched by Fire,* she explores the link between bipolar disorder and artistic genius, claiming that 6 to 10 percent of American students have hypomanic or exuberant personality tendencies and some of these will eventually develop bipolar disorder.[6]

Hypomania. As noted before, there is a continuum of mood states on each side of the happiness-depression spectrum. Mania's extreme state of overactivity and disinhibition can be very dangerous to a person's health and safety because of the financial, sexual or physical risks they may take. In its milder forms, hypomania can lead to incredible creativity and productive energy.

Not all people who experience hypomania will go on into the extremes of full-blown mania. People who have experienced times of major depression with at least one or more episodes of hypomania are usually diagnosed with bipolar type 2 disorder, whereas people with experiences of full-blown mania and depression are diagnosed with bipolar type 1 disorder. Hypomania may be mistaken for just being in a very good mood, and if it follows an episode of depression, friends and family can often mistake it, just being delighted to see such wonderful improvement.

BIPOLAR DISORDER IN CHILDREN

In the United States, between 1993 and 2003, there was a startling and disturbing fortyfold increase in the number of children and teens visiting doctors with a diagnosis of bipolar disorder.[7] The average age at diagnosis for these young people was twelve, and many of them were treated with strong antipsychotic medications.

It is generally recognized that many children with bipolar disorder have a rapid daily cycle between highs and lows. In the morning they may be sluggish and slow to get going, irritable and withdrawn. In the middle of the day they may appear quite normal. After school they become euphoric, wired, very aggressive and explosive when frustrated, and this hyperactivity may continue late into the night. Parents are often at a loss to know what to do, and it seems like two different personalities are in the same child's body.

Researchers into bipolar disorder believe that many children are not getting adequate treatment for bipolar disorder, and they also believe that other children have been mistakenly given the bipolar diagnosis and are, therefore, receiving wrong treatments.[8] I am thankful that this mistake has been acknowledged, and the new label of Disruptive Mood Dysregulation Disorder will emerge in the *DSM-V* to be published in 2012. It remains to be seen whether this diagnostic mouthful will help the situation, as making the diagnosis is complicated, because many of these children also have symptoms of ADHD. But in any event, I am hopeful that there will be more care in diagnosis and that fewer children will be placed on large doses of medication.[9]

AN EXCURSION INTO THE HAPPINESS INDUSTRY: THE POSITIVE MIDDLE GROUND

After many years of neglect by psychologists, happiness has become a very popular research topic. There is now even a branch of psychology, called positive psychology, which focuses on generating happiness, wellness and resilience rather than treating illness and unhappiness. The results of the current research on this topic have been summarized and discussed in detail in academic and popular publications, and now many psychologists, counselors, and personal and business coaches teach the principles arising from this research.

By *happiness* I mean contentment and satisfaction rather than joy and euphoria. Everyone seems to have a happiness set point, which they return to pretty consistently throughout life, whatever their circumstances. If you win the lottery or get the job of your dreams, you will feel "happier" than normal for a while but soon will return to your set point. Negative events knock us down for a while, but we usually recover unless the consequences are severe and long lasting.

Psychologists presently debate how much we can learn to change our happiness set point, as we do have some control over attitudes and circumstances. For example, while approximately 50 percent of our happiness set point is temperamentally or genetically determined, and affected by the family in which life experience and expectations were shaped, the remaining 50 percent is a combination of our current life circumstances and our attitude toward them. It is this latter part that we might have some control over.

So what makes us happy? Here are some major themes that emerge from recent research:

- *Good health.* This stands out well ahead of all the others, as living with chronic illness makes many people unhappy.

- *Marriage.* Married people are generally happier than unmarried—especially if they have a good marriage and good relationships with family.

- *Community.* Friendships with neighbors and those around us are important.

- *Donating.* Helping others by giving time or money makes us feel good.

- *Religion.* People who attend religious services weekly or more are happier than those who don't.

- *Meaningful life purpose.* A sense of meaning and purpose is important.

- *Comfortable finances.* Money is helpful but only to the point where it allows a person to have all basic needs met (food, shelter, clothing).

The experience of "flow." Unfortunately, we as humans are usually not very good at predicting what will make us happy, because at whatever level we live, we usually think that having more will make us happier. In an article titled "If We Are So Rich, Why Aren't We Happy?" by psychologist Mihaly Csikszentmihalyi, he describes the sensation of being fully engaged and engrossed in some activity as the experience of "flow." He says that "the prereq-

uisite for happiness is the ability to get fully involved in life. . . .
Studies suggest that children from the most affluent families find
it more difficult to be in flow—compared with less well-to-do
teenagers, they tend to be more bored, less involved, less enthusiastic, less excited."[10] Perhaps the more affluent teens have not
learned the skills, or developed the internal resources, for dealing
with potentially boring situations because they have always had
the money for new distracting toys and entertainment.

With that said, it is not the things that we usually imagine which
give us the most satisfaction. Most people think that good food,
better sex, material comforts, exotic travel and toys—all the things
portrayed by seductive advertisements—will make us happy. And
if we can't afford those, we settle for television and a glass of alcohol.[11] These are, of course, enjoyable but the most rewarding activities are those that are not passive but active, where our minds
and often bodies are stretched to their limit "in a voluntary effort
to accomplish something difficult and worthwhile."[12]

This experience is described in Csikszentmihalyi's earlier best-
selling book called *Flow: The Psychology of Optimal Experience*,
where he details how he discovered the principles that can
"transform boring and meaningless lives into ones full of enjoyment."[13] He started out by asking people to wear an electronic
paging device for a week, and this pager sent them a signal eight
times a day to remind them to stop and keep a record of what they
were thinking and feeling at that time. His research team did this,
interviewing thousands of individuals in many cultures around
the world, from all walks of life. From all the material he has
gathered from this study and earlier studies over a thirty-year
timespan, he has discovered that there are moments in life that
seem to be the exact opposite of boredom and discontent. He called
this "optimal experience" of "flow"—the integration and harmony
of the body, mind and emotions—and, perhaps, the more we experience flow, the less vulnerable we will be to depression.

Flow is described in every culture as occurring during a variety of activities, but there are some common ingredients: there is a task (not necessarily physical) for which we have the necessary skills and competence to enable us to complete it. If it is too challenging and beyond our abilities, we feel anxious and threatened; if it is not stretching enough, then we feel bored, restless and unhappy. To be highly fulfilling, the task will demand intense concentration, as well as have clear goals and immediate feedback. There is such intense involvement that it is impossible to be aware of the normal frustrations and worries of life. When skills and challenges are almost perfectly balanced, there is a feeling of being in control that is rare in many areas of life. Often, at the time, there is no awareness of one's self at all, but afterward there may be a strong sense of self-confidence, satisfaction and identity. Csikszentmihalyi gives two examples:

> A rock climber explains how it feels when he is scaling a mountain: "You are so involved in what you are doing [that] you aren't thinking of yourself as separate from the immediate activity . . . from what you are doing."
>
> A mother who enjoys the time spent with her small daughter says: "Her reading is the one thing that she's really into, and we read together. She reads to me, and I read to her, and that's a time when I sort of lose touch with the rest of the world, I'm totally absorbed in what I'm doing."[14]

I can get completely absorbed in my work as a counselor. It is an amazing privilege to be allowed into the intimate details of people's life histories and inner worlds. Often it is difficult and painful to hear stories of disappointment, pain and abuse, but it is also wonderful to walk with people, patiently and slowly, as they begin to experience healing. Sometimes I sit in awe as I see the changes happening before my eyes. My brother-in-law is a surgeon, and his experiences of flow are very different. The results for him are much more immediate and tangible, and it is hard for him to understand how I could enjoy what I am doing. But we are both fortunate to find deep satisfaction in our work.

Interestingly, people report considerably more experiences of enjoyment at work rather than in their leisure time, but they also think that there is something wrong with this. To them, it seems like it ought to be the other way around. Surely play should be more pleasurable than work! "When engaged in leisure activities such as reading, watching TV, having friends over, or going to a restaurant, only 18 percent of the responses ended up in flow. The leisure responses were typically in the range we have come to call apathy, characterized by below-average levels of both challenges and skills. In this condition, people tend to say that they feel passive, weak, dull, and dissatisfied."[15] It is the active involvement and the use of highly developed abilities that is the key. We often think of active involvement as high-energy challenges, but sometimes taking time to enjoy slow-paced pursuits can be just as rewarding—as in the example of me compared to my brother-in-law.

As another example, cooking is a necessary part of life, but many find it very boring and easily opt for fast food. It takes time and effort to study cookbooks, to learn how to prepare different vegetables or meats, but there is satisfaction in working with the amazing variety of colors, textures and smells that go into producing a meal that gives pleasure to others. Besides the simple act of cooking and filling our stomachs with food, meals are places to spend time with other people, places for conversation about the day's events and challenges, places to share our stories, tears and laughter. This whole experience can be one of flow.

Indeed, this is the message of Ecclesiastes. The deepest satisfaction and happiness is found in the simple things of life. The author of the book tried all of the world's pleasures—houses, land, travel, women, sex—but none of them deeply satisfied. In the middle of this book that underlines the meaningless of life comes a refrain, though: "A person can do nothing better than to eat and drink and find satisfaction in their own toil. This too, I see, is from the hand of God, for without him, who can eat or find enjoyment? . . . I know that there is nothing better for people than to be happy and to do good while they live. That each of them may eat and drink, and find satisfaction in all their toil—this is the gift of God" (Ecclesiastes 2:24-25; 3:12-13). We will be most satisfied in living the way God intends us to live—in close relationship with him, being thankful. God does not promise happiness in this fallen world, where there are many painful experiences. As we will see later, there are many things we can do to reduce our vulnerability to depression, and these will also increase our experience of God-given times of deeper and more enduring contentment and joy.

This brief excursion into the psychology of happiness is part of a much wider examination of the range of human emotions. I have described the two ends of the spectrum in some detail—with severe depression and mania—though most people's experiences will fall somewhere in between the two. We all long for the secret to happiness and contentment. Being aware of the extremes gives us some idea about how seriously to be concerned about milder forms of depression or exuberance, and understanding what gives deep contentment and what contributes to times of deep satisfaction and joy helps us to live between the extremes.

On the depressive side of the spectrum it is important to ask a few simple questions: Is this a passing mood due to criticism from a friend? Is it a regular dark day or two before a menstrual period—predictable but sure to pass? Is it a complete change of character for someone who is normally coping well but over several weeks has become increasingly irritable, tired and pessimistic? Or is it a longstanding gloomy view of life that, at intervals, becomes worse and shows all the signs of severe depression? If it is more than a passing phase, help will often be needed, and in coming chapters, we will see how psychotherapy and medication, as well as other practical things can help to heal and prevent depression.

On the manic side of the spectrum it is important to be able to distinguish between normal happiness, enthusiasm and exuberance versus mild (hypomanic) or severe manic states of mind. We will see how medication and psychotherapy are very important in reducing the height and depth of bipolar swings of mood and also in reducing the frequency of these episodes. Without good treatment, depression and bipolar disorder cause much distress for the person and their family and friends.

QUESTIONS FOR REFLECTION AND DISCUSSION

1. Do you know anyone (a child or adult) who has experienced a manic episode? How have they described their experience, or how would you describe it as an observer?

2. Have you ever experienced anything like hypomania or mania?

3. Do you go up and down in mood, or are you predominantly more depressive or more exuberant in temperament?

4. Have you met Christians who have had profound spiritual experiences that may have been due to some degree of mania?

5. What do you think are the causes of bipolar disorder?

6. What makes you happy? What makes/made your parents happy?

7. What do most people in your culture think will make them happy? Do you think there are differences between cultures?

8. What do you think the Bible teaches about contentment and happiness? Does God promise that Christians will be happy and joyful?

3

A MIND DISEASED

Genes, Chemicals and Other Mysteries

Cans't thou not minister to a mind diseas'd?

WILLIAM SHAKESPEARE, *MACBETH*

The first questions we usually ask when attempting to help someone who is depressed are, "What's happened? What's gone wrong?" There is a widespread belief that sadness, misery and depression are caused by adverse circumstances, and for the vast majority of people, this is true. Just as stomach pains may be due to simple indigestion, appendicitis or, occasionally, cancer, so depression may be a symptom of a variety of problems in life—some easily cured, others more complex. A wide range of influences affect our moods, ranging from genes, brain chemistry, hormones, early childhood events, season of the year, loss of a loved one, lack of meaning, repressed anger, shame or guilt, or frustrations at work and in relationships. We are all vulnerable to depression in different ways in different circumstances. Two people, because of different temperaments, brain chemistry and life experiences, will react to exactly the same adverse circumstances in completely different ways—even if those two people were raised in the same family. One may become very depressed while the other remains calm and confident. For some, the genetic and biochemical factors are very significant.

John was found unconscious in his bedroom, and a note on the chair left no doubt that this was a deliberate attempt to end his life. He had swallowed a whole bottle of sleeping pills, but fortunately, he recovered from the overdose and was admitted to a psychiatric hospital. Over the following day or two, his story emerged. His wife had left him for another man. His normally successful business was declining under the pressure of the recession. When his wife was contacted, she described how, over the previous six months, he had become more and more difficult to live with, was occasionally very violent and seemed to have lost interest in everything. He did not talk much to her, and from the number of cigarette butts that she found in the ashtray, she thought that he had been getting up very early in the morning and sitting alone in the living room.

In the hospital, he remained very depressed, believing he was a total failure in life and convinced that his business was bankrupt. He was so preoccupied with these negative themes that it was impossible to help him to change his view of the situation. Antidepressants seemed to have little effect, and because he remained suicidal, he was eventually given a course of electroconvulsive therapy (ECT). After the third treatment, he began to see a glimmer of hope, and after the sixth, he had dramatically improved and was able to talk rationally about his business and his marriage. His wife became much more sympathetic to his situation and, after marriage counseling, she came back to him. He was even able to return to work with a much more realistic attitude toward his business.

Our bodies and minds are so closely interwoven that often we do not have a clear idea of how much depression is due to biology and how much is due to psychology, but biological and genetic factors do have considerable influence on our temperament and

personality. Take John, for example. His father had suffered from
bipolar disorder, but apart from a few ups and downs in adolescence, John had never been seriously depressed before—although
from this account, he appears to have inherited a *vulnerability* to
become depressed. Since his life was relatively unstressful, it was
not until his business began to decline that, under pressure, he
slid down into a pit of deep depression.

TEMPERAMENT AND PERSONALITY

Temperament is a "given" to a large extent; it is the basic inherited
building block of personality that is then shaped and molded in
childhood and adolescence. Some children are, physically and
emotionally, very sensitive to the world around them. They have
an acute awareness of colors, textures, smells, tastes and sounds.
They may have a lower pain threshold, may be very fearful, or may
be extremely sensitive to rebuke or encouragement, as well as to
the atmosphere of relationships, especially to what is going on
between their parents. This sensitivity is a great gift; it enables
them to deeply appreciate beauty, but it also leaves them more
vulnerable to the pain of ugliness and broken relationships.

One of the hardest tasks for parents is to help this sensitive
child be tough enough to cope with the real world, yet not lose
their sensitivity. Sadly many sensitive children are forced to retreat into themselves, either becoming very shy and withdrawn or
developing a couldn't-care-less attitude toward life, often building
a tough, aggressive exterior to protect the sensitive person inside.

Another child may be less sensitive and able to ride the inevitable ups and downs of life more easily. An easygoing temperament can be a great asset, but such a person may miss out on
experiences of extreme pleasure. Very often one sees the more
sensitive child being perceived as difficult and falling into a negative cycle of parental criticism and the resulting low self-esteem.
The more easygoing child tends to produce more positive re-

sponses from parents, but the tender plant usually needs more affirmation and help than the tough one.

It is probable that an inherited vulnerability to depression is partly due to temperaments that are more sensitive to rejection, loss or other difficulties in life. It is also probably expressed in chemical pathways in the brain that result in a lower threshold for stress.

BRAIN CHEMISTRY

We know that we can inherit a tendency to develop physical diseases like diabetes, so it is no surprise to find that some people can inherit a chemical vulnerability to depression. Currently, there is a large amount of research pointing to a biological component of depression, particularly in its more severe forms.[1] Sometimes our body or brain chemistry seems to dominate our minds. This can happen to anyone, like if you were to slip some LSD into my tea, I would be almost a different person, controlled by the chemicals in my body for a while. As another example, I remember being called to see Mrs. Gray when I was a psychiatric resident. She had just had a major operation, and the nurses on the ward were very distressed because she believed that they were putting poison in the injections they were giving her. When we did some tests, we found that her electrolytes were seriously abnormal and, once the balance was restored, she was back in her right mind.

A more extreme example of the way our brains may be affected by disease is seen in the process of senile dementia. My grandmother, a dear Christian woman, declined in her old age into a state of confusion and disorientation as the process of senile dementia destroyed her brain, so that she thought she was back in her early life in India. A failing body and brain apparently caged in the person that was my grandmother, though she was still visible as her normal self for brief moments. Finally, though, she was released by death and will, when Christ returns, have her body and mind completely transformed and renewed.

So if our bodies and brains can limit us and affect our interaction in the world in this way, it is important to have some idea about how significant the physical or biochemical factor really is when considering depression. In what follows, I will attempt to summarize the numerous genetic and biochemical studies in the medical literature without becoming too technical.

GENETIC STUDIES

Studies have found that anxiety and depression are more common in relatives of those with anxiety and depression than in the general population. This means one of two things: (1) that a genetic factor is at work or (2) that particular styles of dealing with stress are learned from other family members. Both are probably true. Our temperaments are partly inherited and partly learned. Studies of twins brought up in the same family and twins brought up in different families are helpful in sorting out what is commonly called the "nature-nurture" debate.

Identical twins who carry identical genes, whether brought up in the same home or adopted at birth and brought up in different homes, are more likely to suffer from the same emotional problems (50 percent risk or 1 in 2 chance) than nonidentical twins, who carry different genes, brought up apart or together (20 percent risk or 1 in 5 chance). Adopted children whose biological parents suffered from severe depression had three times the risk of developing depression as the biological children of their adoptive parents. Estimates of how much of depression is inherited are approximate and, as the research has improved, have fallen over the last twenty years.

Most studies show that the close relatives of someone with serious depression have a lifetime risk of becoming depressed that is two to three times the risk of the general population. The risk appears to be greater in female than in male relatives and in relatives of those who become severely depressed at a younger age. The risks are also higher for becoming depressed for relatives of those with bipolar disorder. A child with a bipolar parent has five times the risk of developing bipolar disorder than the child of parents who are not bipolar. These statistics may sound disturbing, but keep in mind that it is not inevitable that a child of a parent with depression or bipolar disorder will develop the disease himself, because many other factors are involved besides genes—a person is especially more prone if he has a history of childhood abuse or neglect or if he is experiencing significant life stress.

While the evidence for a genetic factor is certainly present, it is variable from person to person and family to family. There is a greater likelihood that a genetic factor is involved in severe depression, especially if that depression is associated with manic episodes. However, no specific gene for depression has been found; there are many genes involved.[2]

BIOCHEMICAL STUDIES

If we accept that there is, in some people, a genetic vulnerability that affects their temperament so that they are predisposed to depression, we assume that some of the genetic influence is on the chemicals in the body, particularly the brain. The function of the brain depends on the transmission of tiny electrical impulses along millions of chains of nerve cells aided by neurotransmitter chemicals (enzymes). Studies have demonstrated that the level of these enzymes is lower in depression, suggesting a reduction of the transmission of electrical energy in the brain in depression, and that the level of these enzymes increases as the depression lifts. However, this change is the result of a long chain of reactions that are not well understood.[3]

If severe depression remains untreated for a long time, there is some evidence that the hippocampus and frontal lobes (the parts of the brain responsible for emotional regulation) shrink. The size and number of cells is reduced, and neurogenesis (the birth of new cells) slows and may stop. Also the hormone cortisol is released in situations of stress to prepare the body for fighting or fleeing, and there is evidence that under chronic stress and the prolonged exposure to this cortisol, the hippocampus (where memories and emotions are stored) tends to shrink.

The important chicken-or-egg question is: does the chemical change in the brain come *before* the stressful event and make that person more vulnerable to depression, or does the stressful event *produce* the biochemical change? The answer seems to be that it is probably different for each individual. In one individual a genetic predisposition may be a strong factor, but then their reaction to stress produces further chemical changes, thus a biological vicious circle is initiated. In others, in whom there is no genetic predisposition, a prolonged depressive reaction to stress is likely the main trigger mechanism for the chemical change.

ANTIDEPRESSANTS VERSUS PLACEBOS

In a number of large drug trials, antidepressants have been compared with placebos.[4] In the treatment of *severe* depression, there is evidence that antidepressants work better than placebos in most people, so the antidepressant chemical does some good and more is happening than just taking a pill and believing it will work.[5] However, the placebo does often have helpful effects, and it is intriguing to discover that the placebo effect (in the United States) has doubled in the last twenty years. This could be because people have so much faith and belief in the effect of pills,[6] and some will argue that there is nothing wrong with taking advantage of the placebo effect if it appears to help.[7]

However, medication is not always needed, because even severe depression can have a variable course. Some will recover without medication in six to ten weeks, but others may remain depressed for nine to twelve months or longer. Recent research suggests that, "about half of an antidepressant's effect is due to the placebo effect, a quarter is due to natural fluctuations in depressive symptoms, and another quarter is the result of the active medication."[8]

How and why do placebos work? Nobody really knows how placebos work, but some intriguing research on pain throws light on this issue. In a study, volunteers were subjected to pain while their brains were being scanned. They were then given a pain-killing injection that was, in reality, just saline. Presumably because they believed they were getting a pain reliever, their brains responded by releasing endorphins that do actually relieve pain. Similarly, we assume that changes occur in the brains of depressed patients who believe enough in the medication and in the wisdom of the prescribing doctor. And, apparently, the more expensive the medication, the greater the placebo effect it has!

Another reason for the placebo effect might be that the pharmaceutical industry has been too successful in its marketing strategies! And recently, it has been disturbing to find that the pharmaceutical companies have published only the positive studies of the effects of antidepressants and have kept the negative studies under wraps. The reason these companies might do that is because, for a new drug to be approved, the drug has to be significantly better than a placebo in the so-called double-blind trials (where neither the doctors nor the patients know whether they are using the real medication or a placebo). Another interesting factor is that when the psychiatrists take a real interest in their patients and have a less distant therapeutic style, they get more positive responses with placebos.

How much of the therapeutic effect of antidepressants is really due to the medication and how much is due to the placebo effect is very hard to tell. Nevertheless, the more serious the depression, the less effective the placebo seems and the more effective the real antidepressant is. This seems to reinforce the view that milder depression is more psychological in origin, whereas severe depression has an increasing biological aspect to it, especially as it becomes deeper (whether the biological aspect precedes the depression or is a result of it). At this stage, depression needs to be treated to get the brain back to a level where it can think and feel accurately again so that it can respond to counseling and psychotherapy.

There is an increasingly strong view that antidepressants only really work in cases of severe depression, but there are still critics of the current research who believe that recent studies do not rule out a real effect of antidepressants in mild and moderate depression.[9] I have talked to many people who have found antidepressants to be helpful in both moderate and severe depression. There is evidence that antidepressants encourage confidence and reduce emotional vulnerability, thus making the brain more flexible and more responsive to counseling, so I certainly encourage clients to use them when they feel really *stuck* in their depression, whether it is moderate or severe.

How do antidepressants work? For many years the prevailing understanding of the biochemical cause of depression has been that, when a person is depressed, the substances that transmit chemical and neurological messages across the gap (synapse) between the billions of nerve cells in the brain have been depleted. So in order to increase the amount of the neurotransmitters it is necessary to inhibit its reuptake or reabsorption (hence the term "Selective Serotonin Reuptake Inhibitors," or SSRIs, as popular antidepressant medications). Some of these drugs work on serotonin, some on norepinephrine, others on dopamine, and some on all three. The main groups of antidepressants are SSRIs, Serotonin and Norepinephrine Reuptake Inhibitors (SNRIs), Dopamine Reuptake Inhibitors, Tricyclics and Tetracyclics. You may also hear occasionally about Monoamine Oxidase Inhibitors (MAOI) that block the enzyme that inactivates serotonin. Each of these groups of antidepressants has its own list of side effects, and a few have dietary restrictions as well.

Although, to add to the confusion, recent research has shown a drug that works by *reducing* serotonin levels, and it works as well as the current antidepressants that *raise* serotonin levels. So our current understanding of the biochemical causes of depression may have to be substantially revised in the future, as this is an area of controversy in the scientific community.

Various tests are being developed to ascertain which patients will respond to which antidepressant treatment, and to distinguish those in whom there is a significant biological component to their depression. Forty to fifty percent of people with severe depression will respond to the first antidepressant (usually an SSRI) they try—and usually within three months, though the peak effect is often felt around five or six weeks. Thinking becomes clearer, mood lifts and people are easier to be around. As one woman said, "Since I have been taking Prozac, you have all been a lot easier to get along with!" However, individual reactions to the antidepressants are extraordinarily variable, so it may take two or three tries to find a medication that works well. In more resistant depressions, a combination of antidepressants is more effective than one on its own. Herein lies a problem for large studies of the effectiveness of antidepressants: individual differences in the level of depression and in the response to medication are obscured.[10]

A few people (0.5 percent) have very strong negative reactions to antidepressants, which include agitation and anxiety. Side effects vary enormously, so prescribing doctors have to juggle therapeutic effects and side effects for each individual. SSRIs are the preferred first line of treatment, as they are less dangerous if taken in overdose. Common side effects are anxiety, nervousness, insomnia, drowsiness, nausea and weight gain. Again, there is great individual variation. Some people have minimal side effects while others are completely intolerant of one antidepressant, though they may have few side effects with another. Sexual dysfunction (decreased interest and arousal) occurs in approximately 50 percent of both men and women, especially in those over fifty when sexual drive is somewhat reduced anyway. In these circumstances, switching to Welbutrin, Remeron or Cymbalta may be very helpful because these have less adverse effect on sexual function.

Some people with recurrent depression may need to take antidepressants for life, and this is a reasonable option if other forms of treatment are not adequate or effective. Normally antidepressants have to be taken for six to eighteen months, and when it comes time to stop taking them, it is important to reduce the dose slowly over several weeks. If they are stopped suddenly about 25 percent of people will have very strong withdrawal symptoms, including dizziness, nausea, lethargy, headache, irritability, nervousness, crying spells, flu-like symptoms or "electric shocks" in and around the head. For most people who stop suddenly, these symptoms will begin within the first week and last only two or three weeks. These withdrawal symptoms are worse with Effexor and Paxil, which are quickly metabolized, whereas Prozac and the others have less pronounced and more delayed withdrawal effects.

One of the oldest drugs that has changed the lives of many people with severe and extreme bipolar mood swings is Lithium, a basic salt compound. First used in the 1940s, it helps reduce the number and the strength of the mood swings, thus decreasing vulnerability to depression. It has to be monitored for side effects but still remains a mainstay for the treatment of bipolar disorder. Various other mood-stabilizing medications (e.g., Depakote), anticonvulsants (e.g., Lamictal) and atypical neuroleptics[11] (e.g., Abilify or Risperdal) are also used for bipolar disorder and, increasingly, for severe depression that does not respond to antidepressants alone. The antidepressants discussed above are not usually recommended in the depressive phase of bipolar because there is a risk of precipitating a manic episode. Psychologist Kay Redfield Jamison writes:

At this point in my existence, I cannot image leading a normal life without both taking Lithium and having had the benefits of psychotherapy. Lithium prevents my seductive but disastrous high, diminishes my depressions, clears out the wool and webbing from my disordered thinking, slows me down, gentles me out, keeps me from ruining my career and relationships, keeps me out of the hospital, alive, and makes psychotherapy possible.[12]

ALTERNATIVE MEDICATIONS

The herb St. John's Wort has been prescribed for centuries as a folk remedy, and it is used widely in Germany to treat depression, anxiety and insomnia. It probably works by preventing the reuptake of serotonin. It seems to be as effective as other antidepressants in moderate depression, but its effectiveness has not been demonstrated in severe depression. It does interact with other medications, like birth control, so medical advice should be sought before using it.

The amino acid SAM e is another often used remedy for depression that seems to enhance the action of the neurotransmitters, and some have claimed wonderful relieving effects. However, it has occasionally precipitated mania, so more research is needed. Tryptophan and 5HTP are also sold over the counter in many countries and are marketed as cures for depression. There is *some* evidence of this, but without good quality research there is still uncertainty about the benefits because the placebo effect needs to be taken into account. Fish oil is still another over-the-counter remedy that is widely recommended for the heart and the brain, and it seems to increase resistance to disease and depression as well.

BRAIN SCANS

We have to admit that our understanding of the working of the brain is incredibly primitive compared to our understanding of, for example, the heart or kidneys. The living brain is heavily protected by the skull and very inaccessible. X-rays were discovered around 1900, angiography (showing blood vessels on X-ray) in the late 1920s, and the electroencephalogram was developed to record brain waves in the 1930s. Only in the last thirty years have we been able to get more accurate but still relatively primitive glimpses into the working of the brain with the advent of brain scanning technology. CAT, MRI, f-MRI, PET and SPECT scans are all increasingly sophisticated methods of creating beautifully colored images of the function of a living brain. We can now see which parts of the brain light up or die down with anxiety, depression or other mood states, as well as with different tasks or experiences. These scans can show what parts of the brain are over- or underfunctioning. We can also see the effects of antidepressant medications on the brain and which parts of the brain grow or shrink with different disease processes and treatments.

In relation to depression, early brain scans zeroed in on a small area of the brain located about two-and-a-half inches behind the bridge of the nose in what is called the subgenual prefrontal cortex, or area 25. This area seems to play a vital role in the control of emotions. Early scans showed that this area had fewer brain cells in depressed patients than in nondepressed patients, and this is the area that is targeted for deep brain stimulation (DBI) when all other treatments fail.

In severe depression there is increased activity in the emotion-related parts of the brain (amygdala and deep limbic system), and there is underactivity in the cognition-related areas (prefrontal cortex).[13] This fits with the subjective experience of the "pain" of depression, mood instability, and oversensitivity to stress and negative comments (which are all emotion related), as well as the tendency to experience guilt, to ruminate, and to have difficulty concentrating, thinking clearly and making decisions (which are all cognition related).

We saw earlier how some of the changes produced by placebos can have an effect on the brain's experience of depression. Another intriguing part of the story is that we can now show that psychotherapy and counseling produce changes in the brain as well. Until recently we always considered these to be purely psychological treatments that would not produce physical changes in brain pathways the way biological remedies do.

However, in several studies, patients with obsessive-compulsive disorder or depression were divided into two treatment groups. One group received cognitive behavioral therapy (CBT) or interpersonal psychotherapy, and the other group received the antidepressants Prozac or Paxil. Both groups improved, and PET brain scanning showed changes in the circuits of the brain in both groups!

An earlier study of Prozac and placebo in men suffering from depression showed similar brain changes in both groups, but those receiving Prozac showed additional brain changes, which seemed to be associated with maintaining improvement over time.[14]

In one of these studies of depressed patients in two similar treatment groups, Paxil damped down the limbic system and stimulated the frontal lobe, while cognitive behavioral therapy was associated with decreased activity in the frontal lobe and in the emotional parts of the limbic system (area 25). This means that the two treatments seemed to have partially opposite effects, but the patients improved with both. So it appears that the depression network can be corrected along various paths.[15]

Brain science takes us way beyond biological remedies. The structure and function of our brains is profoundly shaped by our relationships and attachments from the earliest moments of life, and recent neuroscience is helping us see the healing power of deep and caring relationships.

So while there is much more to be discovered about the brain, this is a glimpse of where our understanding is at this time. There are new discoveries every year, and our knowledge five or ten years from now may be quite different. Each era is limited in its understanding by the current science, values and philosophy of the culture in which it exists.

ELECTROCONVULSIVE THERAPY (ECT)

The advantages and disadvantages of electroconvulsive therapy have been fiercely debated over the years. It might sound barbaric, and in the past it was overused by psychiatrists and given to many patients who did not benefit from it. Although we have to admit that we do not know exactly how it works, recent research on rats has shown significant growth of new nerve cells after ECT, so it seems to have one of the same effects on the brain as antidepressants.[16] Indeed, ECT can be a very effective treatment for the type of severe depression where thought processes are so disturbed that the person may suffer from delusions and suicidal ideas, and it is often used when severe depression has not responded to medication. It is now the treatment of choice for approximately 100,000 patients in the United States each year.

Most people do not find ECT a painful or unpleasant experience. After the initial apprehension they are often surprised to find it no more upsetting than a routine visit to the dentist. Most people thought that ECT had helped them, and they would choose it again if recommended by a psychiatrist. Unwanted effects of ECT are largely confined to an effect on memory that is troublesome in approximately half the patients, where there is difficulty in remembering recent events and sometimes new information. This problem does not usually last more than a few days but may occasionally persist for a few months. Some have permanent loss of memory but only for events immediately around the time of the ECT. Treatment on one side of the brain (unilateral

ECT) has been found to be just as effective as treatment on both sides of the brain and with fewer side effects, so unilateral ECT is now being used more frequently.

Before antidepressant and anti-anxiety medications were available (in the 1950s), a trial of ECT dramatically demonstrated its effectiveness—at least in saving lives. The death rate, usually by suicide, among severely depressed patients in a large psychiatric hospital between the years 1900-1939 was found to be 16 percent in men and 14 percent in women. Between the years 1940-1948, it was found that, while the death rate remained as high in *untreated* patients, in the patients treated by ECT the death rate fell to 2 percent or less.[17]

Many people still believe that ECT is given as it was shown in the old movie *One Flew Over the Cuckoo's Nest*, with the patient being held down and having electrodes applied to his head while he is still conscious. Nowadays when ECT is given, the patient is given a brief (five or ten minutes) general anesthetic and a muscle relaxant to reduce muscle spasms. Electrodes apply a current to the brain to stimulate the equivalent of an epileptic seizure. It is normally given two or three times a week for six to twelve weeks, and in patients where it is used as a first treatment, it is 80 to 90 percent effective. Usually it is used after antidepressants have proved ineffective or if rapid treatment is necessary for someone who is actively suicidal or psychotic. Unfortunately, ECT is not particularly good at preventing further episodes of depression, and 50 to 60 percent will relapse within a year, which means that antidepressants and psychotherapy are necessary as well. There are also several newer experimental treatments, including transcranial magnetic stimulation (TMS), vagus nerve stimulation (VNS) or deep brain stimulation (DBS).[18]

Antidepressant medication or talking treatments will be adequate for many forms of depression, but ECT may sometimes be necessary. However, it is important to note that we find much evidence to suggest that antidepressant medication *and* psychotherapy are more effective in reducing symptoms than either treatment alone. Although, the less severe the depression, the more one can rely on talking treatments by themselves.

There is much research being done on pain-relieving chemicals, endorphins, that have been found in the brain. These endorphins are released in the body during exercise, and many doctors recommend running as a treatment for depression. Any form of exercise is beneficial for improving one's self-image, giving a sense of control, increasing fitness, and also causing a release of endorphins and raising the level of oxygen in the brain.

PHYSICAL ILLNESS

Physical illnesses can also make people more vulnerable to depression. For example, an underactive thyroid gland (hypothyroidism) or an overactive adrenal gland, producing too much of a stress hormone, can lead to depression. Low testosterone in older men may also cause depression. Deficiencies of vitamins B_6, B_{12}, folic acid and vitamin D have been linked to depression as well. Additionally, Alzheimer's, other dementias and brain injuries from strokes, traumas or tumors all increase susceptibility to depression. Finally, medications used to treat high blood pressure and cancer may trigger depression, whereas, on the flip side, steroids, antidepressants and treatments for Parkinson's disease or attention deficit disorder (ADD) can trigger mania in people with bipolar disorder.

When depression occurs after a physical illness or operation, there are usually a number of other factors that have made that person more vulnerable. For example, for a woman who has a difficult marriage and problems of low self esteem, to have a hysterectomy may seem like the final statement that she is not really much of a woman. Yet for another woman who has had a happy marriage, several children and then develops very heavy bleeding, this may not lead to depression and it might actually be a great relief to have a hysterectomy. So for each individual, a severe illness or operation will have a particular significance and meaning that will affect his or her reaction to it. It is rare for the biological factors to be the sole cause of depression, as there are usually many different influences interacting.

PREMENSTRUAL SYNDROME

Many women find themselves more vulnerable to depression in the five to ten days before their menstrual periods, describing a variety of physical and psychological symptoms, which include headaches, food cravings, thirst, nausea, dizziness, fatigue, breast tenderness and swelling, and abdominal cramps and bloating. Psychological symptoms—such as irritability, guilt, sensitivity to criticism, a desire to be alone, lack of concentration, depression or suicidal ideas—are often due to hormonal changes that affect the chemicals in the brain. If there are external stressors then these symptoms will be worse. For example, one woman described her desperate feelings of hopelessness and her strong desire to escape to bed just before her periods. She was struggling with conflicts in her marriage and difficulties in her work, but when the marriage and work problems were resolved, her premenstrual tension was much less noticeable.

Many extravagant claims have been made for different treatments for premenstrual tension, but few have stood the test of time and experimental research. Recognizing that the condition has a partial physical basis will be helpful in learning to live with it. When symptoms are mild, adequate exercise, small frequent meals, a daily multivitamin, reduction of salt intake, relaxation exercises, plenty of sleep, and elimination of caffeine and alcohol from the diet have been found to be helpful. Supplements of calcium, magnesium, vitamins B_6 and E, as well as some herbal remedies, may help. Ibuprofen, diuretics and oral contraceptives are also used to reduce premenstrual symptoms.

However, a few women are particularly disabled by the intensity of the psychological symptoms before their periods, and they may be diagnosed with premenstrual dysphoric disorder (PMDD). Antidepressants (SSRIs) are often helpful for this and may only need to be taken for the two weeks before menstruation. It is certainly worth consulting a doctor who can help each person find the best combination of remedies.

POSTPARTUM DEPRESSION
Depression after childbirth can range from very mild "baby blues" to extreme psychotic and suicidal states of mind. A good friend shared her story with me:

> After my first son was born, I was euphoric. But the joy of meeting him soon turned to extreme anxiety and insomnia. I could not calm down. I could not sleep. I would lie in bed for hours trying to fall asleep, more exhausted than I had ever been in my life, but I could not. Every peep he made sounded like it was coming from a megaphone. The days turned into weeks and I lived in a blur where time was suspended. I was constantly anxious and crying and, though I loved this new little one, I found myself even screaming at this poor little baby: "What do you want from me?!"
>
> I was irrational and afraid, which eventually turned into hopelessness. My husband was scared to go to work and leave me alone with the baby. I knew about postpartum depression, but I did not put two and two together. I thought my struggle was a reflection of my failure as a mom. I remember a lady at church coming up to me in those early weeks and saying, "Oh! Are you guys just having so much FUN?!" I wanted to hit her. At one point I was diapering my little guy and, in an attempt to try to calm him down, was singing "Jesus Loves

Me." I started sobbing and realized I needed someone to sing it to me. At his six-week checkup my doctor very insightfully saw I was *not* doing well and recommended antidepressants. I felt better within a few days.[19]

Not everyone feels better so quickly, and some struggle for a long time.

The interaction of physical, psychological and social factors is clearly seen in postpartum depression. Many women are much more vulnerable to depression in the months after childbirth because of the hormonal changes in the body and all the adjustments to the arrival of a new person in the family. Many women will experience anxiety, irritability and weepiness, peaking on the fifth day after childbirth—the so-called baby blues, where the mood seems to vary from hour to hour. There is often a feeling of despondency and inadequacy and some difficulty in concentration, but this *usually* disappears within a few days.

In 10-15 percent of women, though, the experience may be more severe, and depression may last for weeks and months after childbirth. Many of the symptoms of depression described in chapter one will be present, and there may be difficulty bonding with the baby. One person wrote to me with a plea for help: "I think my husband told you that I have been having a hard time since having Gemma. In the first four weeks postpartum, I thought it was the classic 'blues' symptoms. Some of the symptoms got better, but some also got worse—anxiety that would not go away, lack of appetite, loss of sexual interest, insomnia, lack of motivation, resentment toward Gemma for changing my life."[20]

In a few cases (1-2 out of every 1,000) women who have usually been well during pregnancy and had a normal delivery will suddenly, within a week or two of childbirth, become very confused, restless, sleepless, and may become severely depressed with thoughts of harming themselves and the baby, in addition to intense guilt and despair. Or sometimes they may become euphoric and overactive, and may appear to be hearing voices and seeing visions (hallucinations and delusions); there may also be paranoia. Sometimes the mood varies from day to day with both depression and anxiety. There is often the feeling of an inability to cope with anything, as well as an overwhelming tiredness. But although tired, there is great difficulty getting to sleep, and the rest of the family may be met with irrational bouts of frustration and anger. This form of illness is called postpartum psychosis. Admission to hospital for treatment with antidepressants is often necessary, and ECT can usually produce a complete cure within a few weeks.

These three forms of postpartum depressive illness—baby blues, postpartum depression and postpartum psychosis—are caused by a combination of factors, such as rapid changes in hormones (progesterone and estrogen levels fall quickly), blood volume and metabolism. Furthermore, sleep deprivation, anxiety about caring for a newborn, breast feeding problems, adjustment to changes in body image, changes in spousal relationships, a sense of life being out of control, and perhaps financial and housing pressures are enough to test the strongest person.

Women who do not have good support from their spouses or families, who have a history of previous depression or bipolar disorder, or who have experienced many stresses in past year are more likely to become depressed. It is important for such women to work with their doctors, because the small risks of taking antidepressants through the last months of pregnancy and during the time of childbirth may outweigh the risks to the health of the mothers and babies if severe postpartum depression occurs.

CONCLUSION

From the evidence that we have considered in this chapter, we can definitely say that there is a biological factor at work in severe depression and that sometimes antidepressants and even ECT are necessary to break a vicious chemical cycle. Some forms of depression seem to have a large biological element and some individuals are particularly vulnerable in this way; in others, social and psychological factors play a large part in causing depression. Needless to say, the treatment for depression will vary enormously according to the person and the situation.

QUESTIONS FOR REFLECTION AND DISCUSSION

1. Have you ever taken antidepressants? Did they help? Did you experience side effects or withdrawal symptoms?

2. Do you know other people who have taken antidepressants? What did they say about or did you observe of their experience?

3. Can you see how there might be a biochemical cause for depression? Why or why not?

4. Do you think there is a danger that our societies use antidepressants as a crutch or quick-fix remedy?

5. Is your opinion of antidepressants or their usage affected by the advertising of pharmaceutical companies? If so, how?

6. What do you think of ECT?

7. Have you or anyone you know well suffered from postpartum depression? What was it like and how long did it take to recover?

8. What other things have you or your friends and family found helpful in coping with depression?

9. How do these biological and genetic aspects of depression fit within a biblical perspective?

4

SOME ROOTED SORROWS

Childhood, Thought Patterns and Relationships

Cans't thou not . . . pluck from the memory a rooted sorrow, raze out the written troubles of the brain?

WILLIAM SHAKESPEARE, *MACBETH*

In sooth I do not know why I am so sad: It wearies me; You say it wearies you, but how I caught it, found it or came by it, what stuff it is made of, whereof it was born I am to learn. And such a want with sadness it makes of me that I have much to do to know myself.

WILLIAM SHAKESPEARE, *THE MERCHANT OF VENICE*

Back in the sixteenth century, the theologian Martin Luther struggled to help his wife with her anxiety and to deal with his own physical illnesses and tendency toward depression. He was acutely aware of the many different explanations of illness in his own day, and recognized the complex interplay between spiritual, social, psychological and physical factors:

> When I was ill the physicians made me take as much med- icine as if I had been a great bull. Alack for him that depends

on the aid of physic. I do not deny that medicine is a gift of God nor do I refuse to acknowledge science in the skill of many physicians but take the best of them how far they are from perfection. When I feel indisposed, by observing a strict diet and going to bed early I generally manage to get round again, that is if I can keep my mind tolerably at rest. I have no objection to the doctor acting upon certain theories but they must not expect us to be slaves of their fancies.[1]

CAUSES, CURES . . . AND CONFUSION?
A GLIMPSE INTO HISTORY

A brief scan of history takes us back to the Greek philosophers and physicians. Like us, they were conflicted over whether the cause of depression was biological (thinking that excess black bile caused melancholia) or emotional. Evil spirits and planetary influences were often blamed as well. Hippocrates described melancholia as a state in which fears and despondencies are long lasting.[2] John Cassian, a monk from the fourth and fifth centuries, understood the causes of depression in much the same way as we do today: "Of dejection there are two kinds: one, that which springs up when anger has died down, or as the result of some loss we have incurred or of some purpose which has been hindered or interfered with, the other, which comes from unreasonable anxiety of mind or despair."[3]

Don Duarte, king of Portugal in 1435, "lists six causes of depression: fear of death, dishonor and pain, anger, unfulfilled desire, . . . death of others."[4] In 1621 Robert Burton's famous *The Anatomy of Melancholy* vividly described the agony of serious depression, and he recognized that patients needed the help of a physician who can treat body and soul to recover.[5] Many physicians, from the Hippocrates to Burton and beyond, also recommend eating a healthy diet, getting enough sleep, doing meaningful work, talking with friends, listening to music and engaging in exercise as helpful for mental disorders.

The Puritan preacher and pastor Richard Baxter, in an article titled *The Cure of Melancholy and Overmuch Sorrow, by Faith* (1682), recognized three causes for too much sorrow or melancholy. First, extreme pain endured for a long time. This would have been much more common in his time, but even now, elderly people especially are much more prone to depression when they have chronic pain. Second, some people are more passionate in their feeling and expression of emotion than others, with what we call a sensitive temperament. They are, said Baxter, sad, discontent, easily troubled and not easily comforted. Third, a combination of sensitive temperament and vulnerability to biological depression are particularly difficult to treat. He wrote, "when the brain and imagination are impaired, and reason partly overthrown by the disease called melancholy, this maketh the cure yet more difficult; for commonly it is the foresaid persons, whose natural temper is timorous and passionate, and apt to discontent and grief, who fall into infirmity and melancholy; and the conjunction of both the natural temper and the disease does increase the misery."[6]

The Puritan John Colquhoun, like many of his contemporaries, saw a different quality to this severe depression and knew that the traditional psychological and spiritual remedies did not work so well. He wrote,

> In the case of some, melancholy through a bodily distemper produces dejection of mind; in others, it produces trouble of mind of spiritual accounts, especially if it is great, and of long continuance. Melancholy also increases trouble of mind, and trouble of mind increases melancholy. Where they both exist together, they mutually increase and confirm each other.[7]

Another Puritan pastor Thomas Brooks goes so far as to say, "The cure for melancholy belongs rather to the physician than the divine, to Galen [a Greek doctor] than to [the apostle] Paul."[8]

Amazingly these Puritan pastors describe an interaction between body and mind that is almost identical to the way we think about it today, although we now have more understanding of the biological aspect of depression.

We would all love to have some simple solution to depression, but there are few easy answers when facing the complexity of our lives in this world. Through the centuries, there have always been many schools of thought and as many different therapies for how to treat depression. This is because *biological, psychological, social* and *spiritual* factors usually all weave together, and several of the possible causes may be relevant at different times in different individuals. Sometimes it is easy to see the cause; at other times so many factors are involved that it is difficult to know where to begin.

We have already seen how some are *biologically* more vulnerable. Some are *socially* vulnerable because of the quality of their marriages or family lives. Chronic marriage dysfunction is both cause and effect of much depression. Living with ongoing work conflicts, job insecurity, poverty, disability, illness, unemployment, lack of good community support, economic crisis, political instability and war all increase vulnerability. How we react to these things will be greatly affected by our *psychological* vulnerabilities.

PSYCHOLOGICAL VULNERABILITY TO DEPRESSION

Psychological vulnerability arises from the interaction of our innate temperament and our relationships with our parents and childhood peers. We are made to find security and significance in relationships, creativity and work. Anything that undermines this will leave us vulnerable. So parental expectations and criticism may set up patterns of negativity and perfectionism, which will open doors to depression.

The importance of the early years. Over the years we have learned a lot about the vital importance of the pattern of attachment of a child to their mother and father. Anything that damages that bond may have significant consequences at the time and later in life. Soon after conception, at only a few weeks old, a baby within its mother's womb will respond to sound, light and painful stimuli. It is probable that the baby can, in some way, pick up the mother's emotional state, so that the baby may sense depression, anxiety, rejection or anger, as well as feelings of calm, joy and happiness while developing in the womb. There is a growing amount of fascinating research that suggests that babies in the womb react, as early as twenty-four weeks, to the mother's stress or relaxation, and that children subconsciously remember experiences in the first year or two of life.

As children grow they need not only food but warmth, acceptance and love. Babies given only food and deprived of touch and eye contact will fail to develop naturally, and many even die. The work of John Bowlby in the mid-1900s on *Attachment and Loss* has demonstrated the crucial importance of "bonding" between mother and child.[9]

Children are dependent on parental approval for their sense of achievement and self-worth. If love and approval are consistently given, there will be a growing inner sense of self-worth and significance that is less and less dependent on external events or relationships. If, however, a child grows up in an atmosphere where he is constantly undermined and criticized, accepted only when he performs well, he will probably become self-critical, frustrated and easily prone to depression. Of course, firm, consistent and loving discipline are also necessary for the development of a right sense of self-worth. When children do not receive love and affirmation, they will look for those things in the wrong places, and sadly, they often compound by their own choices the damage done by parental neglect, rejection or abuse.

Patterns of attachment. In the last thirty years, much research has been done on the patterns of attachment in early childhood.[10]

It is clear that, for our sense of security and identity, we need some relationships that are deeply in tune with our inner world. In one study of the first year of life, parent-infant interaction was assessed repeatedly during home visits by trained observers. At the end of the year, a twenty-minute "strange situation" test was done. The infant was separated from the mother for a while and immediate reactions were observed, as well as the infant's reactions when mother returned. The test findings correlated well with the observed relationship pattern played out between parents and the infants throughout the rest of the year.

According to this study, approximately 65 percent of children have a *secure* attachment, where the child will often cry when mother leaves but will settle quickly to play and explore, and then the child will greet the mother warmly on her return. Secure children actively seek renewed engagement with the caregiver. The parents of such children responded quickly and appropriately to their child's signals of needing attention and feeling safe. They were kind, patient and compassionate—not perfect but demonstrating a "secure enough" relationship.

The rest of the children had some form of an *insecure* attachment. Some children were *avoidant:* they were not distressed when the mother left the room and virtually ignored her when she returned. These mothers had demonstrated in the first year that they were not very sensitive to their child's needs and often ignored the child's distress signals. These children learned to expect little and to suppress their need for attachment. When these children got older, they were often described by their peers as controlling, aloof and unlikeable. Later in life they will lean toward being cut off from their childhood experiences, their feelings and their need for other people (often called a *dismissing* style of relating).

Some children with an insecure attachment were *ambivalent* (or *preoccupied*). Even before separation, these children seemed anxious, and on the mother's return, they were not easily comforted by her attention, remaining clingy and unable to play because of their uncertainty and insecurity. Parents of these children were erratic; sometimes they were highly sensitive to their children's needs and other times were detached and distant. In adulthood this ambivalent attachment style appeared in strong needs for other people and great anxiety about those relationships. There is difficulty for a person with this attachment style to develop a distinct identity, and her emotions are often entangled with another person's. Overall, they are insecure and anxious.

Some fitted a final category of a *disorganized* (or *fearful*) attachment style. These children looked terrified and distressed when their mothers returned, and they often seemed caught between clinging and pulling away. The parents of these children were often very frightening and detached, and they experienced a lot of anxiety themselves. This pattern was commonly seen when the parents were addicted to drugs. The child would be uncertain how to react because they were often traumatized by terrifying experiences of abuse or neglect; furthermore, they may dissociate in the face of impossible situations where they cannot escape from the threat. These children had more difficulty with relationships and emotional regulation, which had left them with a fragmented sense of self—the very opposite of the integrated self that was experienced by the securely attached child.

These children were followed for more than twenty-five years. Experiences in subsequent relationships obviously had some effect, but their relationship styles remained consistent with their early attachment patterns. Secure attachment has all sorts of good effects: emotional balance, good relationships, moral awareness, flexibility, empathy and less vulnerability to depression.[11] Secure attachment in childhood gives children resilience, greater awareness of their own and others' emotions, thus a greater ability to cope with life's challenges without being overwhelmed by anxiety or depression.

Early relationships shape our brains and our subsequent relationships in profound ways, but when damage has been done, all is *not* lost. Even if parents have not loved well, there may be someone else in a child's life—a sibling, a grandparent, an aunt or uncle—who can give some security and love. And later in life, a consistent friend, a spouse, a teacher, a counselor or a pastor can provide a relationship in which many of the emotional and relational challenges can lead a person to growth and resilience.

It has also been found in a structured research interview, called the Adult Attachment Interview, that the way we answer questions about our own childhood strongly predicts the type of attachment we will have with our own children, including the way we form relationships and process emotions. If a mother was rejected or traumatized in childhood, there is a high likelihood of the same thing happening between her and her child.[12] Without some intervention, patterns of child rearing tend to get passed down from generation to generation.

Nurture or nature? From the moment he was born, little Oliver was a difficult child. He would cry often, would wake all through the night and would not feed regularly or easily. His mother was anxious to be the best mother she could be and found this very confusing. There were many voices around her telling her what to do, and none of their suggestions seemed to work. She and her husband became more and more exhausted with sleep deprivation, and found themselves irritable and angry with each other and their new baby. Eventually Oliver settled into a sort of a routine, turning out to be a delightful but sensitive and anxious child. Critics of the attachment theory make a claim that these theorists do not take into account the different temperaments of the children and how that might affect the way in which the mothers react to them in the first year of life. Although we will look at some of psychologist Jerome Kagan's research on the significance of temperament in the chapter on anxiety, for now it is important to know that Kagan points out that there are relationships with other people in the household (besides the mother) that may have a significant impact on the child's security. It seems that both nature and nurture play a part in the formation of our fundamental sense of security.[13]

Critical incidents and relationships. Particular incidents in a child's life may deeply affect the child's view of himself. Many people have speculated about the cause of the artist Vincent van Gogh's depressive tendency, and it is interesting to note that, although Vincent was the eldest child, he was not the first. Exactly one year to the day before his birth, his older brother was stillborn. That child was called Vincent too and was often mentioned in discussion in the family. Every Sunday the young artist-to-be would have to walk past the grave of his dead brother. We know that he often wrestled with guilt and the feeling of being an "inadequate usurper," so perhaps he felt that he could never live up to his parent's expectations of the real Vincent.

Another example of how early childhood relationships can affect depressive tendencies is the story of Barbara. Some years ago, she came to see me for counseling. For as long as she could remember, her parents had argued and fought, and in her teens, each parent would pour out their problems to her with little awareness of the burden of care they were placing on her young shoulders. She felt pressure to keep the peace, and any needs of her own had to be forgotten because, in particular, her mother's needs seemed so much greater. While her mother often retired to bed with headaches, her father would usually be drinking too much to take his daughter's troubles seriously. Barbara tried to be perfect to please them but always failed, and now, in her mid-twenties, she found herself caught in a trap. She longed to leave home and live a life of her own, but felt very guilty because her parents needed her to be at home to make them happy. Not surprisingly, in her turmoil and depression, some of the memories of childhood began to flood back:

There are so many fears that haven't been voiced, that I've not allowed to surface—just trying to ignore the gnawing feelings. . . . Always feeling that it wasn't enough or okay to just be me—whoever that is. I won't be liked, approved of, loved. . . . It's scared me to look at a lot of this. I look back and "see" this little girl who covers up and hides what's happening and any pain from EVERYONE! What a task! And off to school goes this quiet, lonely little girl—wanting approval, to be liked . . . but so insecure and it really showed. So much fear holding her back, cruelty of kids and sometimes rejection. And I hurt for her, but it's still for "her"—not for me, as if they're two separate people. I'm really trying to keep this distant! Lots of pretending that everything was okay, the fighting at home was okay, lack of confidence and security was okay, but I'm seeing that it wasn't![14]

Such experiences, feelings and fears are very common in people who are prone to depression. Because they lack a deep sense of value and significance, they feel they always have to be earning other people's approval. Early childhood experiences color our reactions to people we meet as we grow up. The child in us lives on, and the memories and pain are hard to face.

Thought patterns. These kinds of early life experiences shape and mold our brain pathways to form what cognitive behavioral therapists call schemas, mind maps or templates. Many years ago Albert Ellis and Aaron Beck used the expression "automatic thoughts" to describe the so-called recordings in our brain that switch on as a reflexive response to certain situations. These unhelpful habits of thinking can deeply affect our moods and behavior. Beck believed that the self-defeating character of the depressed person is due to the illogical reasoning that she uses when faced with a difficult situation. Such a person's brain will twist the evidence, so that it produces an unduly gloomy view of herself and her worth. Beck described some of the primary assumptions and cognitive distortions that predispose people to depression, such as: (1) To be happy, I must be accepted by all people, at all times; (2) if I make a mistake, that means I am inept; (3) if someone disagrees with me, that means he does not like me; (4) my value as a person depends on what others think of me.[15]

Because of the absence of an inner sense of worth, such a person is dependent on the approval of others. Just as he needs food for physical survival so, for psychological survival, he desperately needs repeated assurances from others and enough success experiences to defend against the inner feelings of failure and uselessness. He is usually profoundly sensitive to things that might please or upset those around him, and he may react in one of two different ways: (1) in attempting to always please, he may never assert his own views or personality, which may lead to inner frustration and anger at being so dependent on other people, or (2) because of his fragile sense of self-esteem, he may overreact to any criticism or disagreement with dogmatism and aggression.

Perfectionism. Those who are very self-critical often set high standards for themselves and others, and this may be seen in their perfectionist approach to life. Some of us tolerate disorder and imperfection without anxiety; others have to have everything neat, orderly and clean before they can have any peace of mind. Some are perfectionists in just a few areas of life while able to tolerate imperfection in other areas.

In my book *Perfecting Ourselves to Death: The Pursuit of Excellence and the Perils of Perfectionism,*[16] I attempted to define the difference between healthy striving for high standards and unhealthy attempts to avoid any mistakes and to be perfect at everything. Unhealthy perfectionists tend to be all-or-nothing thinkers. They see themselves as either brilliant successes or total failures, so it is hardly surprising that they fear mistakes and overreact to failure. They tend to jump to the dogmatic conclusion that a negative event will be repeated endlessly: "I'm always making mistakes; I'll never get this right." They tend to be ruled by an overly critical conscience, with the tyranny of *shoulds* and *oughts* inevitably leading to enormous guilt and shame. The unhealthy perfectionist's whole sense of self-worth depends on achieving a perfect performance: "I did perfectly on this. This shows I'm okay. I deserve to feel good." Because they see themselves as inefficient and are likely to fall short of their unreachable aims, they are plagued by a sense of helplessness to achieve desired goals, and are thus more vulnerable to depression.

Perfectionism may be experienced in relation to appearance, performance or moral standards. It can also be primarily self-directed or directed toward others (expecting people to do things the way I think they should be done). The roots of unhealthy perfectionism often lie in attempts to be perfect in order to earn the acceptance and love of parents (especially if a parent's sense of self-worth was dependent on the child's success), and in attempts to control a chaotic world of conflicting emotions and insecurity. It can also be rooted in pride and the desire to be more important than others. Such unreasonably high standards and impossible goals will inevitably lead to self-defeat and depression.

Loss and separation. Many of the early studies of depression showed an association between the loss of a parent in childhood and the damage done to a person's basic sense of security. A study in Canada found that men were more vulnerable to depression in later life if they had lost a parent, particularly their father, before the age of seventeen.[17] A study in London found a link in women being more vulnerable to depression if they lost a parent before seventeen, and especially if the woman lost her mother before the age of eleven: "Loss of mother before 11 may have an enduring influence on a woman's sense of self-esteem giving her an ongoing sense of insecurity and feeling of incompetence in dealing with the good things of the world."[18] Another study demonstrated that separations between parents and children (children who are be-

tween the ages of five and ten), caused by parental illness or
marital discord, were associated with depressive problems in later
life.[19] But it is not only loss by death, as other studies have shown
the link to depression to be *stronger* if the loss is by separation
caused, for example, by the parents' divorce.[20] A possible explanation for this is that a separation is much less easily resolved in a
child's mind than death, because with separation, there is always
a glimmer of hope that the person will return.

The eighteenth-century hymn writer William Cowper's mother
died when he was just six years old. His whole sense of security
rested in her presence and, when she was gone, it was as if his
whole world was shattered. He never really got over this loss, because, for him, she was associated with that golden age when he
was absolutely happy. Forty-seven years later he wrote, "I can
truly say that not a week passes, perhaps I might with equal ve-
racity say a day, in which I do not think of her."[21] Cowper's grief
was compounded by the lack of a close relationship with his father
and by being sent off to a boarding school shortly after his mother's
death. Cowper attempted suicide several times in his late teens,
and although his conversion lifted some of the darkness and he
went on to write many wonderful hymns and poems, he continued
to experience episodes of deep depression throughout his life.

As mentioned earlier, cognitive psychologists focus on the way
in which depression arises from ideas and beliefs about life and relationships that are developed at an early age. Aaron Beck described
the vulnerability of the depression-prone person as due to a set of
"enduring negative attitudes about himself, about the world, and
about his future."[22] Although a child usually shuts away painful
memories in the unconscious, as well as repressing private feelings
of sorrow, anger or loneliness, these memories and feelings may
continue to influence both what the child thinks and how he feels.
So even though these attitudes are not obvious most of the time,
they lie in wait "like an explosive charge ready to be detonated" by

difficult circumstances.[23] Once the negative attitudes have been activated, they can dominate a person's thinking and will often lead to depression. However, the path to depression may vary in intensity, because it is not only loss by death or separation that may affect a child's sense of security but also the atmosphere in the house before and after the loss is also important. For instance, long-term tension in the home may make the reaction to the loss more complicated.[24]

Beck and the cognitive therapists focused primarily on intellectual insight and changing thought patterns with the popular form of counseling, cognitive behavioral therapy (CBT). This is very helpful, although we now know that, in order to heal the deep brain patterns from childhood thoughts, emotions and attachment patterns, the quality of current relationships in a person's life (not just the thought patterns) is very important too. Deeply attuned relationships can be powerfully healing in helping us to make sense of our life stories and current experiences; they also give us a different experience of secure attachment, which can undermine the effects of the earlier insecure experiences in childhood.

For many women, a good marriage is enough to cancel out the effects of an unhealthy childhood and thus reduce their vulnerability to depression. But a marriage characterized by "friction, hostility and lack of affection" is likely to lead to one partner becoming depressed. It is estimated that in 30 percent of marriage difficulties one partner is significantly depressed.[25]

Social and economic factors. A study of 235,000 American adults across most states found that in 2006 and 2008, 9 percent of the population met the criteria for moderate or severe depression in the two weeks prior to the survey. Depression was found to be more common in those who were women, were unemployed or unable to work, had no health insurance, had been previously but were not currently married, were black, Hispanic or of other minority races (or multiple races), and lived in the southeastern states.[26]

Disadvantaged social status is a strong predictor of mood disorders, addictions and criminal activity. In the United States and Europe, children in lower social classes feel that they have less significance, value and voice compared with children from higher social classes. This appears in lower motivation in school, worse grades, hostility to more-advantaged peers and less resilience in the face of difficulties. Such children have usually grown up in relative poverty, been emotionally deprived and have a greater chance of family members being addicted to alcohol or drugs, being depressed or being in jail.[27]

Childhood adversity. A large study of the impact of Adverse Childhood Experiences (ACE) demonstrates the strong relationship between early life trauma and mental and physical disease. In this study there were 17,337 participants with an average age of fifty-seven; 77 percent were Caucasian, 74 percent had attended college, 50 percent were men and 50 percent were women. There were ten categories of negative childhood experiences, which were subdivided into three major divisions: abuse, household dysfunction and neglect. To determine into which category a person fell, there were numerous questions, such as: Were you sexually, physically or emotionally abused? Did someone in the household kill themselves, go to prison, engage in crime and/or abuse drugs or alcohol? Was someone chronically depressed, institutionalized, mentally ill and/or suicidal? Did you witness your mother being threatened or beaten by a spouse or boyfriend? Did you feel loved, protected and well cared for?

Adverse experiences in childhood were very common. Only 33 percent had a score of zero, whereas 66 percent suffered some form of maltreatment and/or some family dysfunction during childhood. One person in six scored four or more (for example, sexual abuse, alcoholism, physical abuse and witnessing household violence). One person in nine scored five or more. Those with high scores like these suffered from more anxiety, panic reactions, anger control and sleep disturbances. They also had a much greater risk for all sorts of physical illnesses and disabilities, and were much more likely to become hooked on unhealthy self-soothing habits—like smoking, drinking, overeating, abusing drugs or engaging in promiscuous sex.

For example, the risks in terms of hard numbers are as follows: when the ACE score was four, their risk of being depressed was 4.6 times greater than for a person who'd scored zero; similarly, for these same people, the risk of alcoholism was 5 times greater and the risk of suicide attempts was 12 times greater. Males with a score of six were 46 times more likely to use intravenous drugs in adulthood than those with a zero score![28]

Learned responses. We also learn how to deal with stress and emotions by observing our parents. Some, when under pressure, always withdraw into a silent world of their own. Others, when angry and frustrated, set the whole atmosphere ablaze with their derisive, critical comments, and they often do considerable damage to any furniture, dogs or cats in the vicinity. In either scenario, those around them are left anxiously walking on eggshells. Later in life, we may find ourselves reacting in the same way as our parents did, and hating ourselves for it. However, learning may also work in a positive direction if our parents taught us by example, teaching us how to talk about our feelings to deal with emotions constructively, with a measure of self-control.

Another less common-sense aspect of learning is psychologist Martin Seligman's concept of learned helplessness. Dogs prevented from escaping from an electric shock eventually gave up trying and would just lie in the corner of the cage.[29] In a similar way, perhaps children or adults who are continually frustrated in their attempts to escape difficult situations will eventually give up, becoming hopeless and helpless. This is seen dramatically in the response of young children to prolonged separation: at first, there is much crying in protest, but this eventually gives way to hopelessness, despair and loss of hope.

The other side of this learned helplessness picture is that depression sometimes has rewards! After someone has been depressed for a while, they begin to appreciate (perhaps subconsciously, if not consciously) the secondary benefits of sympathy and attention from others who had previously ignored them. Depression may also provide an escape from the responsibility of living in a hard and difficult world, and there can be a sense of identity in a cynical and depressive life. The challenge is to help such a person find the hope and courage to break out of this defeatist pattern.

QUESTIONS FOR REFLECTION AND DISCUSSION

1. Can you think of ways that you might be vulnerable to depression?

2. How have your early years and your relationship with your parents helped to build your resilience or create your vulnerability to depression? How does the research presented in this chapter ring true to your experience?

3. Can you describe the attachment patterns that have been handed down in your family?

4. Can you identify certain thought patterns (all-or-nothing thinking, etc.) in yourself or in members of your family that might make you or them vulnerable to depression? What thought patterns have you noticed?

5. Are there people in your life who have helped you to understand your own emotional patterns and styles of relating? How has this helped you to deal with strong emotions more effectively?

6. Have you lived and/or worked in a deprived area where you could see evidence of the findings of the Adverse Childhood Experiences study? What effect did living that way or seeing that evidence have on you?

5

LOSS, SORROW AND GRIEF

Inevitable Pain in a Broken World

Everybody can master a grief but he who has it.

WILLIAM SHAKESPEARE, *MUCH ADO ABOUT NOTHING*

This grief hath crazed my wits.

WILLIAM SHAKESPEARE, *KING LEAR*

My grandparents died when I was in my teens after good, long lives. I missed them but did not feel deep sadness. I realize now that I knew little about grief until I was into my forties when my father-in-law died from heart disease, my sister in childbirth and my brother-in-law by suicide. All this happened over just a few short years, during some other very difficult life circumstances. Soon after that, we moved to the urban American Midwest from rural England, leaving behind family, friends, church, community, identity and England's gentle climate. When we arrived in mid-August to an old house with no air conditioning, it was humid and over 100 degrees, and I thought I had arrived in hell! I think part of my depression at that time was unexpressed grief from my accumulation of losses. I began to understand grief in a new way—from the *inside* out.

DIFFERENT TYPES OF LOSS

Sorrow and sadness invade our lives when we lose people or things that are precious and important to us. We usually think of grief in response to death, but we often experience some form of grief with other losses. It would be appropriate and normal for me to feel deeply sad if my house burned down, my pension evaporated in a recession, or if I lost the job that I have enjoyed and on which my family has depended. Other types of losses include these things that have happened to my friends: being paralyzed from the neck down in a gymnastic accident or having a mastectomy for breast cancer. Imagine a professional violinist losing a finger in a car accident with all the implications of lost identity, career and income.

Broken relationships. A lost friendship, a broken engagement, a chronically unhappy marriage or an eventual divorce are all reasons for sorrow and grief. In these instances, these things may be more difficult to come to terms with than death. The person is not completely gone, so they cannot be mourned the same way as if they had died. Yet, especially in divorce, there are multiple losses—dreams of a happy marriage, companionship and intimacy, shared parenting, a home, legal status and social standing.

Infertility. Some grief may not be openly acknowledged and is often borne silently behind closed doors. For example, many couples struggle with the pain of infertility. Each month they wait to see if they are pregnant, and each month they grieve again the loss of a dream of a child. It is a deeply distressing experience.

Others endure the pain of a miscarriage. Jean wrote this moving poem in response to her loss:

Tiny, tiny baby.
I called you Tadpole,
little frog in my belly. . . .
You came unbidden,
my answered unasked prayer,
And my body swelled with pride to hold you.
Then you left.
Bereft, my body bleeds.
Numbing pain swells,
expels the life that lives no more.
Now grieving. Grieving.
Bleeding. Bleeding.

Tiny, tiny baby.
Has the Father renamed you?
Remade the body that broke,
as you passed through mine?
Are you rocked in His arms
While mine lie empty?
My first, my only child,
little froglet,
His arms are best,
but I,
I was your mother once,
and I loved you then.
I love you still.[1]

In the weeks, months and even years after a miscarriage (or abortion), the parents may be touched by grief again as they are reminded by friends' children of how old their child might have been. Abortion carries its own particular complex grief, as there can also be shame, guilt and regret mingled with the grief of loss.

Chronic illness. Then there is ongoing, lasting grief after a child is diagnosed with mental retardation. Or when an adult is diagnosed with a slow progressing disease that takes away her strength and ability to enjoy life, or perhaps a disease like cancer with the roller coaster of hope and fear on the long road of tests, diagnoses, surgeries, chemotherapy, radiation, side effects—all while living with uncertainty and fearing the worst. Some have called this "the new grief . . . the gritty business of living with slow death."[2] Because of the advances of modern medicine, death can sometimes be held at bay for years.

Perhaps one of the most difficult situations is the ongoing, little-by-little loss involved in Alzheimer's disease. My mother-in-law died after ten years of slowly losing almost all her previous strengths: her excellent business sense, incredible memory, powerful intellectual arguments, canny tennis shots, stylish dress sense and, eventually, control of her own body. With each new loss, we all grieved. We were sad when she did die but were profoundly relieved that she would not have to go on suffering. While things like Alzheimer's are losses for the people the disease afflicts, we must not forget the huge toll those diseases can take on the caregivers of those who are dying slowly.

Living in the shadow of sin and the fall. Some grief comes to us just because we live in a fallen world, where bad things like cancer and earthquakes happen to good people. But there is also the sorrow and grief caused by other people's sin: the sorrow of losing a child killed by a drunk driver, the grief of living with the consequences of sexual abuse or rape, the agony of the wife who has an affair or the husband who turns to pornography. Trust (and much more) is lost and needs to be grieved and slowly rebuilt. And we are daily reminded of the heart-wrenching pain and loss caused by economic, social and political injustice, including war, around the world. But then there is the sorrow caused by our own sin against others—the big things we do and the small ways we offend each day—and the "godly sorrow" when we realize that we often break God's heart by our persistent rebellion.

Death. Our ancestors were probably better prepared for death than we are today.[3] For them it was a reality of their everyday experience. By the age of ten, most children would probably have attended several funerals of siblings or other relatives. They would have seen people dying in their own homes. Today, we are separated from this reality by the achievements of modern medicine. Although our children will have seen many thousands of violent deaths on television by the time they are ten years old, they are not prepared for the *reality* of suffering and separation by death. Death has become the cultural taboo and many live trying to deny its existence.

COMMON EXPERIENCES OF GRIEF

The pain of some of the losses above may not be as deep as the grief experienced after the death of a person, but they are legitimate and should not be ignored or repressed. In what follows, I will be discussing grief after death, but many of the same feelings are experienced after other losses as well. Also keep in mind that all sorts of circumstances can affect the intensity and duration of grief. We need to address the question of whether there is a "normal" pattern of grief.

C. S. Lewis, in his classic book *A Grief Observed,* wrote of the difficulty of neatly describing his experience of grief:

> I thought I could describe *a state*; make a map of sorrow. Sorrow, however, turns out to be not a state but a process. . . . There is something new to be chronicled every day. Grief is like a long valley, a winding valley where any bend may reveal a totally new landscape. . . . There are partial recurrences, but the sequence doesn't repeat.[4]

When death occurs suddenly and unexpectedly, people are often numb and unable to accept this new and very painful reality. When C. Everett Koop, previous surgeon general of the United States, and his wife, Elizabeth, lost their son in a tragic climbing accident on Mount Washington, they wrote:

> It is almost impossible to set down in writing how we felt.
> Even as we try to do so now, there is a recurrence of that first
> awful numbness, as well as the actual pain our bodies en-
> dured as we let the words of the dean race through our minds
> over and over again. It was absolutely impossible that David
> was dead; yet we were assuring one another that this was
> indeed the case.[5]

That initial stage of numbness may last hours, days or weeks.
Things have to be done, such as planning funeral arrangements,
and are done almost automatically, only vaguely remembered.

Passing through the storm. For most people it is not a long
journey through a deep valley of suffering but an oscillation in
and out of periods of sorrow and grief—an experience of the
waves of sadness followed by relief and even some happiness and
laughter. The psychiatrist Colin Murray Parkes put it well: "The
main characteristic of grief is not prolonged depression but acute
and episodic pangs . . . an episode of severe anxiety and psychological pain."[6] In fact, the ability to periodically smile and laugh
during mourning is a predictor of good recovery. Bonanno writes,
"Laughing and smiling give us a break, a temporary respite from
the pain of loss; they allow us to come up for air, to breathe."[7]

As those waves of feelings come and go with varying intensity,
many of the symptoms of depression are common: tearfulness,
lack of interest in food, sleeplessness, loss of energy, loss of concentration, anxiety, headaches, other physical symptoms of tension
and even suicidal thoughts. But unlike ordinary depression where
there may be no clear reason for the sadness, grief is related to a
deep sense of loss, of emptiness, of being torn apart inside.

Anne Lamott writes powerfully of her own grief: "Grief, as I
read somewhere once, is a lazy Susan. One day it is heavy and
underwater, and the next day it spins and stops at loud and rageful,

and the next day at wounded keening, and the next day numbness, silence." Later, as she moved through it:

> the more often I cried in my room . . . and felt just generally wretched, the more often I started to have occasional moments of utter joy, of feeling aware of each moment shining for its own momentous sake. . . . Don't get me wrong: grief sucks; it really does. Unfortunately, though, avoiding it robs us of life, of the now, of the sense of living spirit.[8]

The origin of the word *bereaved* is "deprived of or robbed," and that, for many people, is just how it feels. What is precious has been stolen and life is changed forever. There may be denial that the loss has really happened—waiting for him to come home from work, expecting her voice on the telephone. There is a deep yearning for the lost loved one and sometimes a sense of searching—thinking you see him on the street or in a bus. Hallucinations are not uncommon—hearing her voice or seeing his figure sitting in a chair or going through a door. As Parkes recounts, some people will say, "He is with me all the time. I hear him and see him although I know it is only imagination. I feel he is near me and at times I feel his touch. I cannot help looking for him everywhere."[9] Some people find that this sense of presence goes on for years and is strangely comforting, and some will continue to have (one-way) conversations with the one who has gone. Experiences of feeling ambushed by a song, a scent or a place that stir memories can precipitate tears and sadness.

When my children were younger, my wife and I used to read the book *Goodnight, Mr. Tom* by Michelle Magorian, and it often brought tears to our eyes as we read a chapter together each night. Will, an orphan from a very deprived background, had been adopted during the war by a wonderful man called Mr. Tom. Sadly, Will's best friend, Zach, was killed in a bombing raid on London, and Will, a talented artist, could not accept the reality of what had happened. Even in drawing and painting classes, he would sit and look blankly at the empty page in front of him, devoid of ideas. "I en't got anythin' left inside me," he would say repeatedly, for he felt that half of himself had been cut away—that life without Zach was only half a life and even that half was empty.

His art teacher gently encouraged him to talk about what had happened but:

> Will didn't want to hear. His eyes were blurred and his body hurt all over. He stumbled into the darkness . . . in the direction of the woods and river. . . . He felt again Zach's presence next to him, felt him staring up at the starry night and coming out with some strange fragment of poetry. "No, no," he whispered, shaking his head wildly. "No, no. You're not here. You'll never be here." With one angry sob he picked up a dead branch and struck it against a tree trunk until it shattered. Wildly he picked up any other branches he could find and smashed them, hurling the broken bits into the river. . . . He was angry that Zach had died. Angry with him for going away and leaving him.
>
> With an almighty force of venom he tore one tiny rotting tree up by its roots and pushed it to the ground. Catching his breath for a moment he stood up stiffly and looked up through the branches of the trees.
>
> "I hate you, God. I hate you. You hear me? I hate you. I hate you. I hate you." He stood, yelling and screaming at the sky until he sank exhausted and sobbing on to the ground.[10]

This was the beginning of healing for Will as he was able to openly express what he was only half aware of in that confused internal mix of yearning, depression, anger and loneliness.

Some will feel anger toward God for letting someone die, or toward the doctors and nurses for their apparent incompetence, or toward themselves for what they might have done, and or even anger at the one who has gone for leaving them so alone. And there may be guilt for the things they might have said that they now regret, or for the things left unsaid. Often the more complicated the relationship, the more complex will be these mixed emotions.

Initially the one who has died may be seen as perfect, and it may be difficult to imagine that she ever said or did anything wrong. This idealization is common during this time of grieving and reassessing the relationship. Then there may be a swing to the opposite extreme of remembering all the person's faults. Eventually, though, there will be a more realistic acceptance of good and bad, as well as an awareness that none of us are perfect.

As the days pass, reality slowly sinks in and the realization that this person is not going to return may lead to more waves of emotional withdrawal, crying, profound sadness, depression and times of despair. Familiar desires, routines and interests are disrupted. Concentration and decision-making may be difficult. Fatigue, an overwhelming desire to sleep, and difficulty getting organized in the daily tasks of life and work are common. These feelings may be at their worst some months after the loss, but will come and go. While the pain will never completely go away, for there is always a scar after the loss of a dear one, the intensity will fade over the coming months and years.

Gradually the stage of recovery, adjustment and a new reality takes over. Interests and activities are taken up again and new relationships are made. For many there is a time of saying goodbye and beginning to let go by getting rid of clothes and other possessions, perhaps rearranging the bedroom and making plans for a new and different life. This is a healthy sign of accepting the loss. In this process, there will be times of focusing on the pain but also times of focusing on a new future.

THE SHAPING OF GRIEF

Many other things affect the process of grief, for example, the age of the person who has died. We have seen how the loss of a child in the womb is deeply sad. Most parents recognize that a very early loss, when they are hardly aware of being pregnant is not so painful as a later loss when they may have seen the tiny baby (and the heartbeat) on an ultrasound monitor, felt the baby move and may have even decided on a name. A relationship has been formed and then broken. The longer and deeper the relationship, the harder it is to let go. From the beginning of pregnancy there is a human life and a little person (with great potential) has been lost. At the other end of the age spectrum, when someone dies after a long, good life there is sadness but an expectation and anticipation of death, so the pain is not so acute.

The mode of death also affects our grief. We used to pray that God would take my elderly grandmother to relieve her of her suffering in the confusion and loss of Alzheimer's disease. We were thankful when she—and later my mother-in-law, when she struggled with the same illness—passed away. We had been preparing for their deaths for months and years beforehand so there was relatively less sadness after they died.

When a death is particularly traumatic and difficult, there is more likelihood of a delayed grief reaction. For example, grieving death from suicide is much more complicated and is often a longer process.[11] There are so many mixed feelings about the one who has taken his or her own life—anger, betrayal, confusion, sadness and guilt. Rumination on "if only" thoughts is common, such as, "If only I had not said that before he left." Similarly, death from homicide is also complex and grief may be prolonged because of legal investigations.

After 9/11 and other disasters when there is no body to be found it is harder to come to terms with the reality of death. There is always some hope that maybe the person did not die after all and that, someday, they will turn up unharmed. When people disappear without a trace, it is hard to know if and when to have a funeral or memorial service.

The many faces of grief. Early writing and research on grief, especially the work of Elisabeth Kübler-Ross, described the importance of working through typical stages when facing death or when mourning after loss: denial, anger, bargaining, depression and acceptance. The negative aspect of this research is that people would sometimes feel guilty if they had not grieved well by following the prescribed experience. Recent research by psychology professor George Bonanno and others has challenged this expectation of predictable patterns of grief.[12] His research, based on studies of grief over many years and in all sorts of ordinary and extraordinary circumstances (after 9/11 and the SARS outbreak in Hong Kong), describes three main grief trajectories. In light of the older view, what is surprising is that most people (50-60 percent) recover relatively quickly and do not experience long periods of painful emotions ("resilience"). So in the face of loss, most of us are remarkably resilient and do not need to feel guilty if we do not experience deep emotions or suffer greatly. Some (20-30 percent), however, do become deeply distressed and disoriented for a while and then recover slowly ("recovery"), while others (10-15 percent) are overwhelmed by sadness and never really get over the loss ("chronic").

With Bonanno's three main trajectories of grief, he found that there is a fourth trajectory of "delayed grief or trauma," where there is little distress for some months but then grief symptoms begin to take over. This happens most often when the loss has been particularly traumatic.[13] Variations of the third and fourth trajectories are sometimes called "chronic," "complicated," "traumatic" or "prolonged grief," and are characterized by great trouble accepting the death, preoccupation and pangs of intense yearning, a sense of emptiness, meaninglessness and isolation, as well as a deep dependence on caregivers, which continue well beyond six months after the loss. In these stages, there is also a greater risk of using alcohol or drugs to dull the pain.

In another Bonnano study, this one of more ordinary loss (e.g., the loss of spouse from cancer), he and his colleagues show the striking variety of the experience of grief for men and women who have lost their spouses in their sixties and seventies.[14] In this study, some of the factors that affect the course of grief were demonstrated. For example, 49 percent of the survivors were described as "resilient," and they had long (forty-four years on average) and generally good marriages with low levels of (unhealthy) dependence. They generally coped well with life, had good social supports and believed in a just world. In their grief, they experienced minor levels of depression after losing their spouses, and this did not get worse over the following two years.

Some of the survivors (11 percent) were described as in "common grief." Their marriages were good, and they felt like they had generally coped well with the challenges of life. Many of their spouses had been ill for some time before they died so there was time to prepare. This group also had little depression before their loss, and their depression after the loss peaked at six months and then steadily declined.

Another 11 percent were described as in "chronic grief." These couples had good marriages but were very dependent on each other, and they had little outside support. Although there was little depression before their loss and the depression of grief peaked at six months after their spouse died, it remained high at eighteen months and was still significant at four years. They saw themselves as not coping well. Often their spouse had been taken ill very suddenly so there was little preparation for the loss.

For another 10 percent, they were described as "chronically depressed." They had difficult marriages, had been depressed before the loss and remained depressed afterward. For the final group (19 percent), they were described as "depressed-improved." They had high levels of depression before the loss that came down over succeeding months and the first few years, but after that they became depressed again. They had had difficult marriages and, after the loss, initially experienced some relief from dealing with chronic illnesses and complicated relationships. These people tended to be emotionally unstable and without good support.

This shows how the grief process is affected by a number of things: the level of support, personality, emotional coping mechanisms, mode of death (sudden and unexpected or slow and anticipated) and the quality of the relationship.

A theology of death and grief. Grief is also profoundly affected by our understanding of what happens after death. Many believe there is only oblivion after death since a person cannot live without a functioning brain. Others believe in reincarnation and the eventual dissolution of individual identity into the oneness of the cosmos. Others believe in life after death and do all they can to make that life comfortable and free of suffering by offering prayers or gifts on behalf of the dead. Christians believe that we go into the presence of God when we die but that our souls are separated from our bodies until Christ returns, when our bodies will be resurrected and reunited with our souls in a restored and renewed creation ("heaven"). So how does Christian belief affect how we respond to death?

Some Christians are so keen to emphasize our resurrection hope that they do not allow for the experience of the pain of separation and loss. But even Jesus wept and was "deeply moved in spirit and troubled" as he came to Lazarus's tomb (John 11:33-35). The Greek word for that experience implies that he was both grieved and angry at the fact of death—not at God, but at the abnormality of death. Death is an ugly intrusion into the world that God made; it came as a result of humans' disobedience and will one day be banished forever (Revelation 21:4).

Jesus was not only angry, but he was also sad as he wept for his friend Lazarus—so much so that those standing nearby said, "See how he loved him" (John 11:36). And we too, caught up in a broken world where separations and death are inevitable, weep at the breaking of relationships in such a violent way. Paul writes in

1 Thessalonians 4:13: "Brothers, we do not want you to be ignorant about those who fall asleep [in death], or to grieve like the rest of men, who have no hope." He is not saying "do not grieve" but rather "don't grieve as those who do not believe in a more wonderful life beyond the grave." Martin Luther wrote a lovely letter to a man called Dr. Benedict Paul whose son had recently been killed by a fall from the top of a house:

> Although it is nowhere forbidden in the Holy Scripture to mourn and grieve the death of a godly child or friend, nay we have many examples of the godly who have bewailed the death of their children or friends, yet there ought to be a measure in sorrow and mourning. Therefore loving doctor, while you do well to mourn and lament the death of your son, let not your grief exceed the measure of a Christian in refusing to be comforted.[15]

Paul and Luther both were warning of the temptation to self-pity or despair.

There is obviously a difference between losing someone through a tragic accident and having a close relative die after a long illness. For the latter, death is a release from pain and suffering, and can be seen in light of the fact that God prevented Adam and Eve from eating from the Tree of Life in the Garden of Eden "lest [they should] . . . live forever" (Genesis 3:22 NKJV). God knew that, when suffering became too great in a fallen world, death would be a release, but in the beginning, he intended neither an unexpected accident nor cancer. In cases like the latter, grieving often involves a mixture of emotions: thankfulness at the release from pain and sadness at the loss of a loved one. In either case, though, it is not wrong to feel two emotions at once. In untimely deaths we recognize the tragedy and weep, yet even there we can be comforted because God's grace reaches us and promises to bring good out of evil—and one day there will be no more death or tears (Revelation 21:4).

WEEPING WITH THOSE WHO WEEP

Many who are grieving think that it is weak, silly, immature or unspiritual to cry, because as children, they may have been punished or mocked for crying. My stoic, English, stiff-upper-lip heritage is not the best for processing grief. However, in many countries there is an accepted period of mourning when the culture gives the relatives permission to cry, and it would be seen as abnormal and lacking due respect and love if they did not.

Furthermore, there are *many* references in Scripture to crying: Abraham wept over Sarah (Genesis 23:2), the Israelites for Moses (Deuteronomy 34:8), mothers when their infants were killed in Bethlehem (Matthew 2:18), the women on the road to the cross (Luke 23:27), Mary at Jesus' tomb (John 20:11), Timothy at Paul's departure (2 Timothy 1:4), Jesus at the tomb of Lazarus (John 11:35) and over Jerusalem (Luke 19:41). King David also spent much time weeping ("My tears have been my food day and night," Psalm 42:3). He wept over the deaths of Saul and Jonathan (2 Samuel 1:17) and over his son Absalom (2 Samuel 18:33). Lament was very familiar to biblical writers. It is important to allow ourselves as individuals, couples, families, churches, communities and countries to lament loss and brokenness.

In Western culture, people who are grieving often feel very isolated, and because they don't know what to say or do, well-meaning neighbors and friends tend to avoid or try not to upset the one who is grieving. They are often more uncomfortable with the pain than is the one who is grieving. But it is important to try to seek good friends and to be a good friend; Henri Nouwen describes the friend or helper we all need:

> When we honestly ask ourselves which persons in our lives mean the most to us, we often find that it is those who, instead of giving much advice, solutions or cures, have chosen rather to share our pain and touch our wounds with a gentle

and tender hand. The friend who can be silent with us in a moment of grief and bereavement, who can tolerate not knowing, not curing, not healing and face us with the reality of our powerlessness, that is the friend who cares.[16]

After her fourteen-month-old child with spina bifida died, my sister found that one of the most meaningful things was when friends came and were able to talk about her daughter's death and to be there with her. Even six, eight and twelve months later, she had moments when she broke down in tears and felt the intense pain of the loss. So it is important for us to learn to "weep with those who weep" (Romans 12:15 ESV). Jesus said, "Blessed are those who mourn, for they shall be comforted" (Matthew 5:4 ESV). Mourning opens us up to comfort from God and others.

During the year or two after bereavement, it is vital to have a few people with whom we can share our grief. To be able to cry unashamedly, to talk about the one who has gone, to go over the details of the last months, weeks, days and hours helps to keep a right perspective by not burying the pain completely. Birthdays, holidays and other special days will often be sensitive and tearful occasions, as memories and associations come flooding back, and it is not unspiritual to feel upset at those times.

It is also important to have friends with whom we can laugh and play, to forget the pain for a while. The waves of sadness come and go, and we cannot be mourning all the time. Many of us will get through grief pretty well on our own or with the help of family and friends, and the more we can share with others, the better it will likely be, though some will need more intensive help from a pastor or counselor.

George Bonanno found, after following thousands of people after loss, that certain things seem to be associated with resilience: optimism, confidence, a belief that they have some control over their lives, fewer ongoing life stresses, the ability to be flexible as life changes, being able to express emotions or suppress them appropriately according to the situation, and "a broader network of friends and relatives on whom they can rely, both for emotional support and for helping with the details and demands of daily life."[17]

NAOMI'S TEARS AND GOD'S COMFORT

Last year I was working with an AIDS project in Ethiopia, and I was asked to do a Bible study for twenty women with AIDS, many who had lost husbands and been alienated from their families of origin. They were experiencing hostility from others because they had AIDS and because they had become Christians, so I told them the story of Naomi and Ruth—a story that their tears, smiles and nods showed me was very relevant for those who had experienced much loss.

The Israelite woman Naomi and her husband lived in Judah at a time when there was political and civil unrest and much corruption. Life was hard, but it became even harder when the rains did not come and there was famine. In order to survive they left their home, family and community and went to live in the pagan country of Moab, where there was more food, though they were likely discriminated against and perhaps persecuted. In the ten years they were there, her two sons married Moabite women, but then these sons, as well as Naomi's husband, died.

Having lost so much and feeling estranged in Moab, Naomi, a widow with no rights or protection, decided to return to her homeland because the famine had ended. On the way back, fearing more trouble for these young Moabite women, she encouraged her daughters-in-law to return to Moab to find new husbands. Orpah did go back, but Ruth remained with her mother-in-law, saying, "Where you go, I will go. . . . Your people shall be my people, and your God my God" (Ruth 1:16 ESV).

When Naomi reached her hometown of Bethlehem, nobody recognized her, asking, "Is this Naomi?" Presumably, she looked older and had suffered so much, so she responded "Don't call me Naomi. . . . Call me Mara [meaning bitter], because the Almighty has made my life very bitter. I went away full, but the LORD has brought me back empty" (Ruth 1:20-21). Naomi was courageously honest about what she was feeling. Her sadness and bitterness were understandably profound. She had been through so many losses, and now, back in her home community, she felt she had lost her previous identity and her confidence in God.

So Naomi and Ruth found somewhere to stay but did not have much to eat, so Ruth went out to find work gleaning (picking up leftovers) grain in the fields. The text says, "and she happened to come to the part of the field belonging to Boaz" (Ruth 2:3 ESV). Here was God's providential and guiding hand at work, protecting Ruth and providing for her and Naomi. Boaz was a fine man, and he made sure that his workers left some extra grain for her. He also instructed them not to take advantage of this vulnerable, single and, perhaps attractive, foreign woman (Ruth 2:9). Ruth was surprised and grateful to Boaz for his care, generosity and lack of racial prejudice. He responded, "All that you have done for your mother-in-law since the death of your husband has been fully told to me. . . . The LORD repay you for what you have done, and a full reward be given you by the LORD, the God of Israel, under whose wings you have come to take refuge!" (Ruth 2:11-12 ESV). It seems that Ruth now believed in God and was experiencing his tender care through this kind farmer. She and Naomi had been given the basics of food, water, shelter and work.

In a strange twist, they discovered that Boaz was a distant relative and, therefore, had some responsibility to help maintain the family line.[18] Naomi encouraged Ruth in her admiration and affection for Boaz, and it seemed that he was not disinterested in her. He was impressed by her integrity and strength of character, and he gave her a gift of extra food, saying, "Don't go [home] empty-handed" (Ruth 3:17). The God who seemed to have taken everything from Naomi was now filling her hands again through the kindness of Boaz to Ruth.

Eventually Ruth and Boaz married, and "the LORD enabled her to conceive, and she gave birth to a son" (Ruth 4:13). "Then the women said to Naomi, 'Blessed be the LORD, who has not left you this day without a redeemer, and may his name be renowned in Israel! He shall be to you a restorer of life and a nourisher of your old age, for your daughter-in-law who loves you, who is more to you than seven sons, has given birth to him'" (Ruth 4:14-15 ESV). Naomi's grandson was a great comfort to her, and out of this suffering and these ordinary events of village life came one who was to be the redeemer and comforter to millions. The child born to Ruth was the father of Jesse, the father of David, a direct ancestor of the promised Messiah.

In this story Naomi moves slowly but surely from a place of bitterness and emptiness to a place of trust in God's goodness, and then to a place of joy, gratitude and fulfillment through the love and kindness of Boaz and Ruth. I am sure the pain of losing her husband and two sons (and one daughter-in-law) never left her completely, but God brought others into her life to heal some of the wounds. Naomi seemed to have a deep confidence in God's love and grace that allowed her, in dark places of distress and confusion, to speak vividly and honestly to him and about him, without fearing that he would punish her or abandon her. In giving her sorrow words she found help and healing.

This is a story of loss and grief but also a remarkable story of how God uses ordinary people and situations to bring comfort and hope, just as he still does today, and in this story, we get a glimpse of how two regular people connected with God's bigger story of redemption.

CONCLUSION

In this chapter I have talked mostly about grieving the loss of a loved one, but there are all sorts of losses in life—relationships, jobs, homes, countries, dreams, innocence, reputation, marriage betrayals, precious possessions, pets, important people—and our experience may reflect some of the patterns of grief after a death. Being able to talk to someone about such loss enables us to makes sense of the loss and come to terms with it more easily. In counseling people with depression, grief is a very frequent theme. Many people are unaware of the many losses they have experienced, and they wonder why they feel chronic depression and a constant dull ache in their souls. They often need help and permission to name and express these repressed emotions. Macbeth wisely says, "Give sorrow words. The grief that does not speak whispers the o'erfraught heart and bids it break." Approximately ten percent of people who are grieving will go on to develop clinical depression. So professional help should be sought if the grief becomes prolonged and chronic—or if it turns into more serious depression.

QUESTIONS FOR REFLECTION AND DISCUSSION

1. As you think back over your life, make a timeline to show what significant losses you have experienced, including important people and even pets, possessions or places.

2. Describe what your experiences of grief have been like.

3. Have you felt guilty for not feeling sad or not "grieving properly" after loss? What do you think are the reasons you might have felt guilty or, perhaps, even not felt the loss?

4. Can you see the different patterns of resilience, chronic grief and slow recovery in family and friends who have experienced loss?

5. What has most helped you through your own periods of grief or sadness, including things you did or people you talked to?

Was it mostly family and friends who helped you, or did you get help from a pastor or counselor?

6. What biblical teaching helped you through loss and grief?

7. Have you experienced God's comfort in loss and grief through ordinary people and circumstances—as Naomi did?

6

SUICIDE

The Final Solution?

To be, or not to be, that is the question:
Whether 'tis nobler in the mind to suffer
The slings and arrows of outrageous fortune,
Or to take arms against a sea of troubles,
And by opposing end them? To die—to sleep,
No more; and by a sleep to say we end
The heart-ache and the thousand natural shocks
That flesh is heir to: 'tis a consummation
Devoutly to be wish'd.

WILLIAM SHAKESPEARE, *HAMLET*

just want the pain to go away and to be at peace."

"I can't stand living in this hell, and I can't stop thinking about ways to end it."

"They will be better off without me."

I hear such sentiments pretty regularly. Therapists inevitably have to deal with people who are struggling to find reasons to keep going, so we can't avoid this uncomfortable subject of suicide.

Although thoughts of suicide are common in serious depression, there are some Christians who are appalled to think that anyone could ever take their own life, and they regard it as an unforgivable sin. These people have usually never been seriously depressed themselves and find it hard to imagine such a state of mind. Others, living under the weight of considerable handicaps, may live for many years with the thought of suicide not far from their minds.

John Berryman was an American poet. From the age of ten, he lived with the possibility of his parents' marriage breaking up and with his father's constant threats of suicide. When John was twelve years old, his father shot himself outside John's window. As an adult, John's life was a constant struggle against alcoholism and depression, but in his poems *Eleven Addresses to the Lord* there is clear evidence of a time of real Christian commitment.[1] He wrote of God rescuing him repeatedly. Struggling to keep going, one of his last poems demonstrates his torment of mind, his faith and, perhaps, a sense of relief that his suffering would soon be over. He had decided to take the quick way home. In January 1972, at the age of fifty-seven, only a few years after having been acclaimed as a great poet, he jumped to his death from a bridge in Minnesota—leaving behind his wife and two young children.

Although it may be understandable to take one's life in the face of such suffering, I do not believe that is ever what God intended for us to do. Even as I write these words, I am aware that, for some people in the depths of severe depression, there is an appalling strength to the inner urge toward self-destruction. There are some who are so "sick" with clinical depression that they are no longer totally responsible for their actions. They may be experiencing irrational and pessimistic thoughts or even delusions so that they are out of touch with reality. Some feel a huge burden to others. Their view of reality is so distorted that there seems no other way out of their prison of pain. Only God knows what is going on in their minds in the minutes and hours before they end their lives.

For some the determining factors of biochemistry, perhaps the

repressed pains of early childhood and even the destructive influence of the prince of this world, Satan, may at the end over-
whelm the person's last island of resistance. Someone, like John
Berryman, who was a Christian, will be forgiven, but the solemn
reality is that those who take their own lives will have to stand
before God, the judge of all the earth, the One who gave them life,
and give account of their actions.[2] God knows and understands
the pain and suffering we experience, because he sent his own
Son to live and die in this world. But he also sent his Spirit to live
in us and his people to help us, so that we might have the strength
to cope with the struggles of this broken world. We must do all
we can to help those who feel so desperate that they wish to destroy themselves.

WHY DID THEY DO IT AND *WHO* DOES IT?

The risk of suicide is increased in those who are "mentally ill" or
addicted, especially with severe depression and alcoholism. It is
also increased in those with unstable personalities, in the lonely
and socially isolated—particularly after bereavement, the
breakdown of marriage, the loss of a job or a retirement possibility—and in those who have made previous suicide attempts.
The mind of the suicidal person is usually stuck in a sense of helplessness and hopelessness, a belief that her death will in some way
resolve uncontrollable and intolerable circumstances, while also
helping others. For others, they may not be thinking consciously
about suicide, but they are still desperate to find a way out of the
anxiety of feeling so trapped by their negative and sometimes
racing thoughts, so they may act on a fatal impulse.

Rates of suicide vary from year to year, but there are some recent
trends. In the United States in 2007 (the latest year available for
reliable stats), there were 34,598 suicides—a rate of more than
ninety per day, or one every fifteen minutes.[3] There are approximately eleven attempted suicides for every completed suicide.[4]

Women attempt suicide almost three times as often as men, but men end their lives almost four times as often as women.

Age ranges. The overall rate for suicide in the United States was 11.3 people out of every 100,000 in 2007. The highest rate of suicide (17.7/100,000) occurs in midlife (from ages forty-five to fifty-four)— the highest rate in this age group since 1977. The rate for those between fifty-five and sixty-four years old (15.5/100,000) showed the greatest increase in recent years and is at its highest rate since 1990. This midlife peak in suicides is probably a reflection of shattered dreams, broken families and loss of community.

The elderly. Typically the rate for the very old (who are eighty-five years old or older, and especially in white, non Hispanic men) is the highest of all, but in 2007 it declined slightly to 15.6/100,000, which is perhaps a reflection of greater awareness and prevention in recent years. Despite this recent decline, elderly men are still committing suicide at a rate that is seven times that of elderly women. Older people with serious physical illnesses are six times more likely to take their own lives than those without illness. Reasons why the elderly may be more prone to committing suicide are that, as people get older, they begin to lose their families and friends, they experience more illness, they may lose hearing and sight, and they often realize that they have not lived up to their youthful dreams of success in career or relationships—all factors which contribute to the possibility of severe depression. And unfortunately, depression in the elderly is sometimes misdiagnosed as the effects of aging or dementia, and treatment for clinical depression might well be very helpful.

Teens and young adults. In the years between 1950 and 1970, the suicide rate increased dramatically among those in the fifteen to twenty-four age group, but since then, it has leveled off and has even been decreasing in recent years to 9.7/100,000 in 2007. However, in that same year, young adults between the ages of twenty and twenty-four had almost twice the rate of suicide (12.7) of adolescents between the ages of fifteen to nineteen (6.9). And again, young men died by suicide five to six times more often than young women did.[5] A survey in 2006 found that nearly 10 percent of college students said that they had seriously thought of suicide, whereas only 1 percent attempted it.

In this discussion, we must note a rising epidemic of self-harm among young people that must be distinguished from suicide attempts. Someone cutting their wrists may be a serious suicide attempt, but often cutting or burning the skin of one's forearms, thighs or stomach is a means of releasing tension (especially repressed frustration and anger), of relieving emotional numbness and feeling something, even pain, and perhaps of asking for help. This kind of cutting is often followed by a sense of calm but then shame and guilt, and since the person does not have the intention of harming herself in order to die, it should not be considered a suicide attempt.

Ethnic and cultural variables. Within the United States, the highest rates of suicide are among Native Americans and Alaskan natives, followed closely by non-Hispanic whites. The lowest rates are in Hispanics and non-Hispanic blacks. Internationally there are very high rates in some Eastern European countries and in the Russian Federation. In the latter, approximately 30 out of every 100,000 commit suicide, and six times as many men as women take their own lives, whereas in the United Kingdom and in the United States, the rate is seven and eleven, respectively, out of every 100,000—and more than three times as many men as women, which is usually because men tend to use more violent means, especially guns. Women, on the other hand, most commonly choose overdose as their method. The overall suicide rate in the United States has remained constant since 1965, though there has been a recent upturn, which may reflect the economic recession and unemployment.

WILL SHE DO IT?

When assessing the suicide risk of a seriously depressed person, professionals usually look for the following signs. The more of these signs, the greater the risk:

• withdrawal from social situations

• strong mood swings and changes in personality

• giving away valued belongings to friends and family

• neglect of home, finances or pets

• use of alcohol or drugs

• recent major losses

• having a plan

• buying a gun, pills, rope, razor blades, pipe, etc.

• frequent thoughts of death and thinking they would be better off dead

• threats of suicide or talk of wanting to die

• family history of suicide

• previous suicide attempts

It is important to know that after someone has made a decision to end her life she may become more cheerful and less preoccupied and tense. Relatives and friends may be deceived into thinking that the person is recovering, so they may become less watchful. Also there has been recent controversy about whether starting to take certain antidepressants is associated with an increased likelihood of suicide. It is possible that, in some individuals, starting to take such medication might stimulate them out of depressive apathy and indecision, without lifting their mood, to a point where they have enough energy to act on their self-destructive and hopeless thoughts. Much research has addressed the question of whether antidepressants increase the risk of suicide, especially in young people, and the conclusion is that there may be a *slight* increase. Often one has to weigh the risk of not treating with an antidepressant in severe depression against the relatively small risks of treating.

Impulse and suicide. In the vast majority of suicide attempts (approximately 85 percent), there are symptoms of chronic depression—much of it untreated. But the signs I have enumerated above are not always present, as some people make very impulsive and last-minute decisions to end their life without giving those warning signs. Two of the most lethal methods are guns and jumping from high bridges. Scott Anderson summarized his investigation of impulsive suicides for the New York Times:

> In a 1985 study of 30 people who had survived self-inflicted gunshot wounds more than half reported having had suicidal thoughts for less than 24 hours, and none of the 30 had written suicide notes. This tendency to impulsivity is especially common among young people—and not only with gun suicides. In a 2001 University of Houston study of 153 survivors of nearly lethal attempts between the ages of 13 and 34, only 13 percent reported having contemplated the act for eight hours or longer. To the contrary, 70 percent set the interval between deciding to kill themselves and acting at less than an hour, including an astonishing 24 percent who pegged the interval at less than five minutes.[6]

Scott interviewed survivors of a jump from the Golden Gate Bridge and commented:

> What united all the survivors . . . was a sense of having been utterly transformed by their experiences that, in essence, they had become different people. . . . One aspect of the survivors' personalities that appears to have been left behind is whatever mind-tumble caused them to try to kill themselves in the first place. Since their attempts, none of the survivors

I spoke with had experienced another impulse toward suicide. Nor had they spent much time seeing psychologists or hanging out in support groups.[7]

It seems that none of these impulsive jumpers really wanted to die, but they were desperate to escape the inner struggle and pain. Having faced the reality of a near-death experience, they found new meaning and purpose in life.

Suicide may appear to be a final solution, but if the person is not a Christian it is especially distressing, as they will go into eternity without God. Even if the person *is* a Christian and even though responsibility may be diminished in severe depression, there is a sense in which it is a selfish act because it leaves many problems for relatives and friends. I have met a number of people who have been haunted by their father's or mother's suicide, unable to get it out of their minds, unable to forgive them for abandoning their children and spouse, and often fearful lest they too may become so depressed as to do the same thing. A suicide may hang over the family like a dark shadow. It may also leave behind unresolved guilt in those who were trying to help or in relatives who may have ignored that one desperate telephone call out of the hundreds they had had in the previous year. Therefore, it is important for the survivors to talk about it openly with family and friends, difficult as this may be.

HOW CAN I HELP?

What can you do to help someone who appears depressed and gives hints of wanting to end it all? It is important to take all talk of suicide seriously and not to be afraid to discuss it openly. Even jokes about it may be half serious and should not be dismissed lightly. If people make references to feeling trapped or wanting to get out of the situation, don't be afraid to ask them what they mean and if they have planned to do anything. It is often a help to be able to share such thoughts with someone else. It should be obvious that simplistic solutions like, "Come on, pull yourself to-gether; you'll feel better in the morning," or some variant of, "Be-lieve in Jesus and he'll take all your problems away," are very unhelpful. If they have already made plans (for instance, pur-chased a gun, pills, razor blades, rope or a flexible pipe to put through a car window), then the situation is potentially more se-rious. They may need to allow someone to hold onto the pills or to take the gun away, or they may need someone to stay with them until the crisis is past. In any situation, encourage them to get professional help from a doctor or counselor. If there is a serious death wish then they may need to be admitted to the hospital (sometimes against their will) for their own protection.

Some people who have considerable difficulties in relationships may use threats of suicide as a form of blackmail. It is an ace card that it is difficult to ignore or respond to without giving in to all the person demands. In such situations, it is very important to know a lot about the person and to have discussed the problem with a professional counselor before ignoring such a threat. There is always a risk that the attempt will be successful, even if only because of accidentally taking too many pills or not realizing how strong they were.

Those who are severely depressed may need both medication and counseling to help them overcome their hopelessness and self-destructiveness. Others who are not severely depressed but who have longstanding difficulties in coping with life may go from one crisis to another—at times willing to receive help and at other times unwilling to receive help or to help themselves. There may be little that a helper can do in such a situation, except to reassure the person that you are willing to help when he or she is ready for it. Although it is true, in an ultimate sense, to say that a relationship with Christ is the answer, we must also recognize that we still live in a fallen world, where even for Christians there is much struggle, pain and suffering in this life. It is hard for most people in the depths of suicidal despair to grasp the relevance of the gospel, and even when they do, there will still be problems in their lives as they learn to apply the truths of Scripture to each situation over time.

If you are struggling with thoughts of suicide even as you read this, please tell a friend and seek help from a counselor, doctor or pastor. Just sharing with someone else can help to relieve some of the loneliness, hopelessness and despair. And you may need practical help, regular counseling and, perhaps, medication for depression. If you have no one to turn to, you can call the National Suicide Prevention hotline (1-800-784-2433 or 1-800-273-8255), or you can look for local hotlines on ‹suicidehotlines.com›. In the next chapter we will explore the stories of three heroes of the faith who reached the point of wanting to die—each in very different circumstances. I have found great comfort in these stories and I hope you will too.

QUESTIONS FOR REFLECTION AND DISCUSSION

1. Do you have family or friends who have thought about, attempted or completed suicide?

2. How did you react to that information?

3. Have you ever thought about suicide yourself?

4. How would you assess the risk of suicide in a friend? What questions would you ask?

5. How would you help someone who is suicidal?

6. What biblical stories might be helpful in thinking about suicide?

Part Two

COPING WITH THE DARK AND MOVING TOWARD THE LIGHT

It's like in the great stories, Mr. Frodo. The ones that really mattered. Full of darkness and danger they were. And sometimes you didn't want to know the end . . . because how could the end be happy? How could the world go back the way it was when so much bad had happened? But in the end, it's only a passing thing . . . this shadow. Even darkness must pass.

SAM, IN *THE LORD OF THE RINGS: THE TWO TOWERS*

7

BREAKING POINTS AND SUICIDAL SAINTS

If this is how you are going to treat me, please go ahead and kill me.

MOSES, NUMBERS 11:15

I have had enough, LORD. . . . Take my life.

ELIJAH, I KINGS 19:4

There was a time in my life when I reached a breaking point. Some days I imagined running the car into a wall or a tree to escape the pain. My concentration was poor, I cried easily, decisions were appallingly difficult, sleep was restless, and I felt very ashamed of my weakness in a position of leadership. I had known little failure in life, and now I did not know how to deal with it. I kept going but inside felt more and more desperate. This was the end point of the combination of grief over several major losses, relationship difficulties and work burnout that I described in the introduction. At that time I found great comfort in the biblical stories of desperate leaders. I even preached a sermon on this topic! It was a comfort to know that other men, of far greater faith than mine, had walked that way before me.

Many of us admire the great heroes of the Bible and imagine they did not have many struggles. But look with me at two men, Moses and Elijah, and notice the very different circumstances that led them each to a common point of despair and longing to die. In walking through these stories, you should find that there are ways in which you can relate, and I hope this will help you understand more of your own heart and also of the heart of God toward you. We can learn much about dealing with life's dark moments from the stories in Scripture.

These men were certainly depressed and deeply discouraged. This is sometimes called "reactive situational depression," as opposed to clinical, or major, depression. These men were humans just like us who were coping pretty well with life but who ran into times when things just got too overwhelming. They recognized that life is God's gift and that they had no right to take their own lives, but in their own way, they each said, "Lord, I've had enough. I'm in so much pain. Take my life." If they had remained in that state of mind for too long, they might well have begun a downward spiral of hopelessness and despair, leading to biochemical changes in their brains and serious clinical depression. So in these stories, there will be important lessons for us in reducing our vulnerability to depression in such painfully stressful moments of life when there seems no way out, and there will also be profound warnings and, I hope, wonderful encouragements.

In exploring these two biblical stories, I want to try to help you see how we can use such stories to find insights into the character of God and into our own hearts, as well as to discover principles for dealing with difficult situations that push us to the desperate edge of our coping abilities. For those familiar with the Bible, this may feel like a sermon you have heard before, but I am asking you to listen again with new ears. And for those who don't know the Bible well, I hope this will help you to see the relevance of these ancient dramas to our lives in the twenty-first century.

Remember, in the biblical drama, Moses and Elijah were two of the greatest men of God. Both had been through their own incredible mountaintop experiences of encountering God and having victory over enemies, but here we find them in deep valleys of crisis, difficulty, doubt and depression.

MOSES

Moses is described as a very humble and faithful man who had intimate communication with God (Numbers 12:3, 7-8). But in an incident described in Numbers 11 we find Moses feeling the heat and pressure of leadership. The people for whom he was responsible (about 600,000 men; some have calculated that this meant about 2 million people . . . some congregation!) were whining and complaining about their hardships (Numbers 11:1) and about the monotony of the manna they had to collect each day for food. They looked back at the good food that they had in Egypt, a diet that would be the envy of any dietician—fish, cucumbers, melons, leeks, onions and garlic—and we can imagine them chanting, "We want meat; we want meat" (Numbers 11:4-6). As so often happens, a small discontent and complaint nurtured in the heart quickly grows into sinful coveting and lustful craving for something more. The collective dissatisfaction and bitterness spread very quickly in this crowd.

Moses was worried because he was caught between the strong anger of God on one side and the people frustrated, wailing and complaining on the other (Numbers 11:10). With this tremendous pressure, you can imagine him going back to his tent, tossing and turning, waking at 3:00 a.m., thinking, "What on earth am I going to do? How can I deal with this situation?" So he talked very frankly to God,

> Why have you brought this trouble on your servant? What have I done to displease you that you have put the burden of all these people on me? Did I conceive all these people? Did

I give them birth? Why do you tell me to carry them in my arms, as a nurse carries an infant, to the land you promised on oath to their ancestors? Where can I get meat for all these people? They keep wailing to me, "Give us meat to eat!" I cannot carry all these people by myself; the burden is too heavy for me. If this is how you are going to treat me, please go ahead and kill me—if I have found favor in your eyes— and do not let me face my own ruin. (Numbers 11:11-15)

Why? What? Where? How audacious! I cannot help admiring Moses' brazen honesty and courage. It says something, perhaps, about his trust in God and about the honesty that we need to cultivate in our own relationships with God—even with the difficulties and struggles that we have.[1]

Here Moses, the great leader, is on the edge of burnout—a common problem for people who minister to others, especially pastors and therapists. Three things often contribute to burnout: pressure of responsibility, fear of failure and stress of conflict.[2] The pressure of responsibility and the conflict are clear. Moses was caught between the opposing, conflicting demands of his loyalty to God and his loyalty to the people. Given enough pressure of this sort, anyone will crack. Moses was obviously very afraid of failure and the loss of reputation this would involve when he says, "Do not let me face my own ruin" (Numbers 11:15). Those in leadership, especially, find the shame of failure almost unbearable and will go to any lengths to avoid it. Shame is a powerful emotion that often moves men and women to self-contempt. Moses probably felt he would be letting God and the people down, in addition to not living up to his own dreams of being a good leader for the people. His sense of self-worth was pretty low at this point, and he wanted a way out. Death seemed preferable to continuing in this seemingly impossible situation.

However, it is encouraging to see God's response to Moses. Yes,

God was very angry with the people, and we might have expected him to zap Moses with a sharp rebuke: "Pull yourself together, man. What are you doing getting so depressed and fearful? Have you no faith? Get down on your knees. Pray more. Read the Scriptures more." But no, God was very gentle and compassionate, as well as intensely practical. He told Moses that he was not the only one who could do this task, and Moses must share the responsibility of leadership (Numbers 11:16-17). Like many gifted and conscientious leaders, Moses seemed reluctant to delegate. He knew how everything should be done, and he probably didn't want to be bothered with any staff who would not do things as well as he would! Moses should have learned this lesson before when his father-in-law, on a previous occasion of great pressure and responsibility, had warned him that he would wear himself out—telling him that he would be able "to stand the strain" if he delegated some of the work (Exodus 18:18-23).

Nevertheless, notice that God dealt severely with the people for their grumbling and coveting, but he dealt amazingly graciously with Moses and lifted some of the burden of responsibility from his shoulders.

ELIJAH

Turning to another leader of God's people, we find the prophet Elijah with, not so much the weight of the people of God on his shoulders, but the weight of the world's evil. In 1 Kings 19, Elijah was in a state of exhaustion and fear. Presumably he had been in a state of exhilaration and excitement after all that had happened during the triumphant defeat of the 450 prophets of Baal on Mount Carmel when his fervent prayers for rain were answered, ending a three-year drought. First Kings 18, after describing these amazing and dramatic events, ends: "The power of the LORD came upon Elijah," and presumably flushed with victory, "he ran ahead of Ahab all the way to Jezreel." We have the first hint of how physically fit Elijah was because Ahab had to cover the distance in his chariot, about twenty miles (1 Kings 18:46). Once Ahab arrived, he told Jezebel what had happened, of the terrible slaughters on Mount Carmel and of the rain, and we can only imagine her rising fury! If Jezebel had had a phone she would have gotten right on it to pronounce, "I will make mincemeat out of you, young Elijah! Wait till I get my hands on you for what you did at Mount Carmel. I am leaving right now to get you."

What the story actually records her saying is, "May the gods deal with me, be it ever so severely, if by this time tomorrow I do not make your life like that of one of them" (1 Kings 19:2). So after Elijah's incredible triumph on Mount Carmel, he runs for his life. In a typical fight-or-flight decision, he chooses flight— due south to get as far away from the troubles in the north. He would have done well in a triple marathon or in the Iron Man, for the distance was about ninety miles to Beersheba. Then he went a day's journey into the desert alone, without his servant. Spending too much time alone is a dangerous thing to do when you are feeling so depressed and afraid, because the solitude allows things to get completely out of perspective. While it is good to spend time alone with God, we also need each other at such times of crisis and anxiety.

It is here that we find Elijah collapsed, exhausted, disillusioned, close to breakdown, utterly preoccupied with everything negative about his situation and in the grip of despair. All memory of the recent triumphs of faith and prayer had somehow mysteriously evaporated from his mind, and there was a drastic loss of perspective. He cowered before the threat of one angry woman. Now, mind you, she was one *very* angry woman, and Elijah knew her ruthless reputation as a prophet slayer so there would be no mercy. In fear, anxiety, depression and panic, this spiritual giant, prayer warrior, man of God was caving in completely under the pressure—or so it seemed. He collapsed in the shade of a tree: "'I have had enough, LORD,' he said. 'Take my life. . . .' Then he lay down under the bush and fell asleep" (1 Kings 19:4-5).

So how did he get into this state of mind? First, he was clearly physically and mentally exhausted, the classic situation after a great victory. He needed sleep, food, drink and personal touch, and that is exactly what the angel of God brought to him—twice, a double prescription. Sometimes we need sleep, not a sermon, when we are under pressure or in a crisis (1 Kings 19:4-7). In a crisis like this is when we will come to the end of our own resources and have to rely more deeply on God. But it is often not until we are truly "fed up" that we are open to God feeding us.[3]

Second, he may have been experiencing something like the typical psychological slump after a spiritual high. Many have experienced this when coming back to reality after a conference or retreat, or after an evangelistic outreach or mission trip.

Third, there was the cumulative effect of a prophetic ministry. Few of us are called to such a grand ministry as Elijah, but perhaps we can bring it into our context. There is little status or significance in Christian work in the eyes of the world, and it is all well and good when we are among other Christians, encouraging each other. But in the eyes of the world, we are often seen as arrogant Bible-thumpers, fundamentalists or even weaklings who need the "crutch" of religion. King Ahab had accused Elijah of being a troublemaker (1 Kings 18:17), and similarly for us, Christians are sadly not seen as people of peace, love, good news and justice but rather as troublemakers who merely challenge the relativism, atheism and idolatry of our culture. It is much more comfortable to tell people what they want to hear, that they will prosper and be accepted by God if they live the good life. You won't run into trouble nearly as often if you promise health and wealth, or that God will meet all people's needs and give them total happiness if they turn to Christ.

Fourth, Elijah was in the grip of a great sense of failure. His dreams and hopes were shattered. He had run back to Jezreel with tremendous strength, confidence and joy that the battle was won, and he ran straight into the concrete wall of Jezebel's death threat. He thought everything was done, he had completed his job, and God's victory was assured. But he could not cope with the sudden switch in the direction of events, and he swung to the opposite extreme of panic, depression, hopelessness and fear: "Take my life; I am no better than my ancestors" (1 Kings 19:4). Elijah's sense of self-worth reached an all-time low, a dramatic drop that is not uncommon in times of major stress, overload and depression. He felt that he had failed in the task that God had given him, basically saying, "I've been exceedingly busy in your work, Lord; now I am the only one left, and they are out to get me." You can see the seeds of anger, self-pity and even some paranoia that are beginning to grow in his heart. He had an inflated view of his own importance in the battle against evil, and when things did not go well, he swung to the other extreme of feeling useless, like a complete failure. Author and psychology professor Terry Cooper writes, "If I search around long enough, I'll find insecurity beneath my grandiosity and arrogant expectations beneath my self contempt."[4] Our hearts hold such complex extremes of emotion.

For Elijah, evil appeared to be winning again, and the reality of the battle against the world and the flesh and the devil was too much for him. He had had enough. There was more than a trace of anger with God. He had put all he could give into the Lord's work, he had been exceedingly busy, and it seemed as if God was finally letting him down: he led him on with wonderful victories and then dropped him into the hands of the enemy. Elijah's trust in God was shaken. Doubts and bitterness began to creep into his mind and heart. His faith weakened. He felt grievously betrayed by God.

By this time Elijah had traveled forty days and forty nights, and had reached Mount Horeb—probably an alternative name for Sinai—another 400 miles south in the blistering heat of the desert and mountains. This man had gone a long way to get away from the pressure.

Running from conflict and difficulty is not uncommon in depression—anything to escape the pain! After his painful conflict, my client John sank into a dark place of bitterness and hopelessness. Impulsively he ran from the situation and took a flight from London to Los Angeles with little money and just the clothes he was wearing. He ended up in a homeless shelter where he met a man who came alongside him in his distress and helped him back to belief in God—and to the point of returning to his family and being willing to start marriage counseling.

Why did Elijah go to Mount Sinai? Was he curling up in a sort of spiritual womb, a place of security and safety, in the cave on a mountain where he knew others had encountered God? There he had another night's sleep, and God came to him. The wonderful Counselor, the master of the open-ended, nondirective question (the most basic of counseling skills), asked him: "What are you doing here, Elijah?" (1 Kings 19:9). God told him to stand in his presence for "the LORD is about to pass by." Surely this is what we long for most at those moments of intense pressure—an experience of God's presence, of his love, of his favor, of refreshment and renewal. *Lord, show me yourself, show me what I should do, give me a vision of your presence, a sense of your love and approval will solve all my problems.* That is often our prayer. We passionately want to feel his arms of affection and to hear his word of approval, but in deep depression, God often feels far away and prayer seems useless. So you may identify with Elijah's sense of despair and having no sense of hearing God's voice or feeling his presence.

But then came the drama of the wind, the earthquake and the fire, yet God was not in those. He was not in the sensationalism of the signs and wonders, of the dramatic touches of the Spirit. He was not in the symbols of judgment, *but* he was in the gentle whisper, the still, small voice. The quiet work of God in Elijah's heart and mind was beginning. In the more ordinary stresses and strains of life, we may sometimes sense the soft voice of the Spirit of God, reminding us of truth and bringing comfort and hope—as Elijah did. Yet the still voice of God is much harder to discern when we are caught in the darkness of serious depression.

So God comes again, repeating the question, "What are you doing, Elijah?" It is interesting to reflect on why God asked that sort of question. It seems to me that this good and loving question exposed Elijah's heart. It forced him to ask himself, "Why am I running? What are my motives for being here?" It showed his arrogance, anger, self-pity, loneliness and fear; "I've been doing all this," says Elijah, "and what have you been doing, God?" Elijah needed to stop and listen, so God allowed him to examine himself and gave time for his own answers to sink in before God gave his perspective. As with Moses, there was no sharp rebuke to Elijah for his fear and faithlessness, but a loving response of gentleness and faithfulness. Perhaps in his shame, Elijah wrapped his face in his cloak and listened as God told him to go back and get to work. Like with Moses, God told him to delegate responsibility to certain individuals who were ready to help him. In Elijah's arrogance and stress-induced amnesia, he thought he was alone, but God reminded him that there were 7,000 others who had not bowed to Baal either and that the work of judgment would be completed (1 Kings 19:15-18). God restored Elijah's perspective, confidence and hope. He gave him the facts, and there was no open rebuke or punishment for his momentary cowardice and lack of trust.

WARNINGS AND ENCOURAGEMENTS

As we look at these men and women (including Naomi) of God, we can see the extraordinarily different circumstances that they faced. In their reactions to these circumstances, we can see both warnings and encouragements. These situations force us to ask ourselves similar questions: *What am I doing here in this place and at this point in my life? What are my priorities? What are my fears? Where is my faith?*

There are warnings about the danger of lack of trust and lack of faith, of self-pity, pride, unrighteous anger, unwillingness to forgive, perfectionism, fear of failure and blaming God. There is also a positive warning that we need to be protected, to put on the whole armor of God against the attacks of the evil one. These incidents are examples of the reality of the battle against the world, the flesh and the devil in the midst of the difficult and stressful circumstances of life.

But there is deep encouragement as well. These people are like us, and we are so like them in their reactions to difficulties and in their passions and sinfulness. There will be moments in our lives of burnout, fear, loss, confusion and anger where our character will be tested to the limit. Yet we can be honest with God. We can pour out our hearts—our anger, frustrations, longings and fears. God, in his fatherly gentleness and grace, will help to restore our perspective and to change what needs to be different. Like the father who holds the child in his arms until the tantrum is passed, so God holds us in these moments of frustration and despair. He is ready to deal with us patiently and gently when we need it, firmly when we need that too; and to me, this is an enormous encouragement. In none of these situations does God judge these men, who we might have expected to be more mature in their reactions, blasting them out of the way in his displeasure and impatience! No, there is a gentle but firm love and compassion; there may be rebuke when needed, as well as an exhortation and encouragement to "get up and go on"!

We find in these stories that suffering and difficulty emerge from different life circumstances and from our reactions to those circumstances. Our perception of the situations will affect how we react to them. In a crisis, we need to keep a clear head, and that is often done with the help of a friend. We need to ask with David,

"Why are you cast down, O my soul?" (Psalm 42:5 ESV), as well as these questions: *Is what I am feeling normal sadness or grief at the loss of a loved one? Is it deep disappointment? Is this depression a result of physical exhaustion? Is my anger righteous or unrighteous? Am I unwilling to forgive? Is this self-pity sinful self-protectiveness? Could this be Satan's influence? Is my fear of failure realistic or a result of my perfectionism? Am I taking on too much responsibility while being unwilling to delegate?*

We also find that these biblical characters have reluctantly landed on the divine psychoanalyst's couch, and they have been faced with some searching and penetrating questions that have exposed their hearts and prompted repentance and change. They have also experienced the wonderful Counselor's comfort and encouragement. God is in covenant relationship with them and will not let them go.

We have seen brief and dramatic moments in their lives. In the Psalms we have much longer sessions of divine psychotherapy recorded for us. David and the other psalmists are so confident of their relationships with this covenant God that they can let the worst hang out in his presence: anger, frustration, confusion, depression, shame, guilt, longing and fear. When we do this too our attitudes begin to change, our perspective is restored and our trust is renewed so that we can resist despair and self-destructive thoughts in order to keep going for another day.

Nowadays, God uses the people around us to do the things he did more directly with these biblical characters. As we saw in the story of Naomi and Ruth, God used ordinary people to help them, and today he will often use family, friends, counselors, pastors and others to support us, to challenge us with good questions, to help restore perspective and to encourage us through the breaking points of life.

Finally, like these characters, we need courage. We need to be reminded that we are not alone in the battle—God and others stand with us. These stories are about human beings just like us, but more important, their stories are about their (and our) God who is faithful and gracious. Our story is part of a much bigger story of God rescuing his people, including us, from the grip of sin and all its effects. He is a God who, in coming to live among us in the person of Jesus, has experienced the worst of life's pressures and crises, so we do not come to a God "who is unable to empathize with our weaknesses, but we have one who has been tempted in every way, just as we are—yet he did not sin. Let us then approach God's throne of grace with confidence, so that we may receive mercy and find grace to help us in our time of need" (Hebrews 4:15-16).

Up to this point, we have been predominantly considering the emotions of sadness, grief, depression and despair. In the next few chapters we will explore other emotions—anxiety, anger, guilt and shame—as these are often involved in the genesis of depression. Depression may be the presenting problem, but under the surface, often there is a tangle of other difficult emotions.

QUESTIONS FOR REFLECTION AND DISCUSSION

1. Have you ever felt like Moses or Elijah—or, perhaps, Naomi? With whom do you identify most?

2. What were the circumstances that led up to your point of despair and hopelessness?

   What helped you to get out of it?

3. What heart attitudes and idols did God expose through that crisis?

4. Do you wish that it had never happened?

8

COPING WITH ANXIETY, WORRY AND FEAR

Of all the base passions, fear is the most accursed.

WILLIAM SHAKESPEARE, *HENRY VI*

Our doubts are traitors
And make us lose the good we oft might win
By fearing to attempt.

WILLIAM SHAKESPEARE, *MEASURE FOR MEASURE*

I woke up early this morning worrying about whether we would have enough money for the future. The economic recession is eating away at pensions and savings, and many have similar anxieties and fears. Others here in the United States have worries about medical insurance. They can't afford the health care premiums, and if they get pregnant or sick, they could end up in huge debt. Several years ago, in the aftermath of 9/11, we all lived in fear of imminent terrorist attacks. Others in the inner city live in fear of being shot, their children using drugs, being raped or getting AIDS. In many parts of the world, the main concern is how to get enough food and water to survive another day.

There is considerable overlap between depression and anxiety. In clinical depression there is often much anxiety, as well as sadness or loss of pleasure, but anxiety can also be one of the causes of depression. Just as we can experience appropriate sadness and discouragement without suffering from clinical depression, so we will see that there is appropriate anxiety and abnormal anxiety. I will use the words worry, anxiety and fear somewhat interchangeably, although there is a spectrum of severity from mild worry through anxiety to extreme fear.

WHAT MAKES US ANXIOUS, AND IS IT WRONG?

The body's normal response to a threat is to prepare to fight or to flee: the sympathetic nervous system speeds up the heart, focuses the mind, sends blood to the muscles and puts the whole system on alert. When fighting or fleeing are not possible, we usually panic and freeze. Chronic anxiety and stress will lead to overstimulating the fear centers in the brain and to overproducing the stress hormone cortisol. Over time, repeated stressful events drain the reserves of body and mind to be able to deal with such stressors—especially when there is an ongoing sense of losing safety and control. When circumstances do not change significantly, then our bodies may chronically overproduce cortisol, which may eventually exhaust the system and lead to physical symptoms, such as exhaustion, headaches, palpitations, insomnia, depression and burnout.

Most of us are amazingly resilient, but for various reasons, some people will reach a point where handling the stress will be too much. It is almost as if we can cope for a while, but each person has a point at which he or she will break down. We often find unhealthy ways to deal with anxiety: by obsessive worrying (thinking it will somehow change things) or by escaping—into alcohol, video games, movies, TV, drugs, sleeping pills, obsessive exercise or work. We'll do anything if it will help avoid the low-grade, nagging anxiety or gnawing, gut-wrenching, mind-preoccupying, paralyzing fear. Anxiety may cause depression, and depression may exaggerate or even produce anxieties and fears.

If we take some of the biblical texts out of the context of the whole Bible, we might think it is wrong to be anxious. After all, the Bible says repeatedly, "do not fear," "do not worry," "do not fret," "the Spirit of God did not make us timid," and "do not be anxious about anything."[1] However, we need to understand these verses in their context and in the context of the whole biblical story.

It is important to make a distinction between healthy and unhealthy anxiety or fear. If I am facing an exam, some anxiety and adrenaline is a good thing to push me to prepare. But too much anxiety could lead to panic or paralysis. In a world where there are real dangers, it is appropriate to feel fear that should lead me to take evasive action. If my child is running toward a busy road, I should be afraid! In these cases, it is easy to see that some anxiety is healthy in a fallen world, but some is also sinful. I will attempt to tease out which is which when we return later to the biblical teaching on anxiety. But for now, we'll look at some of the research and contemporary psychological thinking on this topic.

TEMPERAMENT AND ANXIETY

Research has clearly shown that some children, from a very early age, are more prone to anxiety than others. Psychologist Jerome Kagan's research exposed 500 infants at four months old to colorful mobiles, tape-recorded voices and a balloon popped behind them. (Not all at once!) He found that 20 percent of the infants cried and became distressed at the sights and sounds. Another 40 percent rested, babbled happily or laughed. The other 40 percent were somewhere in between. He tested them again at fourteen months and twenty-one months with novel but not too threatening situations. He found those children who had shown little negative reaction before were fearless, and those who had reacted strongly were now very fearful.[2] He writes:

> We observed these children at ages 1, 2, 4, 7, 11, 15 and 18, and found that the infants' tendency to become easily distressed or to remain placid in the face of unexpected change endured for many, but not all, children. As teens, more high-reactive children reported a number of unrealistic anxieties over confronting crowds, strangers, unfamiliar cities, riding a subway, and the future. The low-reactive children have few such worries, and were likely to approach new situations and people with gusto. Relatively speaking, life was easier for them.

None of the latter were phobic or fearful. There are some people who seem to fear very little in life—especially those who indulge in extreme sports, like sailing single-handed in the fog, storms and icebergs of the Southern Ocean on their way around the world, or others who climb vertical rock faces for thousands of feet without ropes!

It is highly probably that children who are high-reactives will not grow up to be "outgoing, bold and exuberant" as adults. Later brain scan research has shown that many of these "high-reactives" had an overactive, "excitable" amygdala. A proneness to anxiety seems to be partly biological and genetic.[3]

However, imagine the compounding effect of raising a temperamentally fearful child in an insecure or abusive home. Many of us know from our own experiences with our own children how different each child can be from another—even in the way they move in the womb before birth and especially in how they react in the early years. Some children are laid back and easygoing, some a bundle of energy and nerves, and many are in between. Our temperaments are shaped by a combination of our genes, by the example of how our parents coped with anxiety or the lack of it, and by our life experiences. The way we react to anxiety is a result of both nature and nurture.

In addition, shy and fearful children are more at risk for depression and social anxiety in a country like the United States, which values outgoing extroverts, than in many Asian countries where shyness and introversion are regarded as acceptable or even praiseworthy.

EXTREME FEARS

Some people who are prone to anxiety end up dealing with crippling fears, such as phobias, panic attacks, obsessive compulsive disorder and posttraumatic stress disorder. These are the so-called anxiety disorders, and although the Bible says a lot about anxiety and fear in general, we will struggle to find much in Scripture about these extreme manifestations of our fallen minds and bodies.

Even if we do not have a phobia (e.g., of flying, snakes, enclosed spaces, heights, blood, public speaking), we almost certainly know someone who does. People develop fears of all sorts of things, and there is a long list of phobias with complex Latin names, like aphenphosmphobia (the fear of being touched) and dystichiphobia (fear of accidents).

Panic attacks are common manifestations of anxiety as well. If you have had one you will recognize the intense experience of fear with dizziness, heart palpitations, chest pain or tightness, a sense of choking or difficulty getting your breath, and tingling in your hands and feet. You were probably convinced you were dying or going crazy. Once people have had a panic attack, they become terrified of having another one, and that alone raises anxiety and may bring about the very attack they fear. If the panic attack has occurred in a crowded place, like in a supermarket or on a plane, they may develop a secondary phobia of public spaces (known as agoraphobia) or fear of flying. Most phobias and panic attacks are relatively easy to treat by a specialized therapist—though some people "cure" themselves by pushing through the fear and desensitizing themselves.

Others may suffer from another form of anxiety disorder—generalized anxiety disorder (GAD). For Lois, who is not obviously depressed and has been anxious for some months, everything in life is threatening in a particular way. For example, storms mean that the electricity will be cut off, her house will catch fire, and her husband will be killed. Any physical symptom must mean that she has cancer or some other disease. She is also a perfectionist and tends to see everything in all-or-nothing terms, so a small difficulty becomes a complete catastrophe. She goes through each day filled with exaggerated worry, even though there is little reason for it.

OBSESSIVE COMPULSIVE DISORDER (OCD)

In the movie *The Aviator* the story of millionaire Howard Hughes is dramatized, and as his obsessive compulsive disorder takes hold, he retreats from society and lives in a sterile environment in order to escape any germs that may come into contact with his body. For some people with OCD, they will wash fifty or a hundred times a day, or they will clean their houses repeatedly, all in an attempt to escape the fear that something terrible will happen if they don't obey their compulsive thoughts. Other people will check that they have locked the door many times before they are able to leave the house or get to sleep at night. In the TV series *Monk*, the detective uses some of his OCD to good purposes to solve crimes, but he needs a nurse therapist to keep the negative aspects under control.

Obsessions are repetitive thoughts, ideas, impulses and images. Compulsions are repetitive and rigid activities that the person feels compelled to do. Approximately one in fifty people suffer with OCD, and accompanying the disorder is often a problem with perfectionism where personal security depends on looking just right or doing things in just the right ("perfect") way.

John Bunyan, the author of *Pilgrim's Progress*, battled with intense scrupulosity and OCD for at least a two-year period of his life. He continually questioned whether he was saved and whether he had committed the unpardonable sin. He found all sorts of blasphemous thoughts invading his mind, which caused him great anxiety and paralyzed him in his daily activities: "All my comfort was taken from me; then darkness seized upon me; after which, whole floods of blasphemies both against God, Christ, and the Scriptures, were poured upon my spirit, to my great confusion and astonishment."[4] Some would say that these intrusive, unwanted thoughts were caused by the devil or by some sin Bunyan had committed, but they bear all the marks of classical OCD that can, nowadays, often be greatly helped with medication, behavioral therapy and counseling.

POSTTRAUMATIC STRESS DISORDER (PTSD)

The wars in Afghanistan and Iraq have brought this disorder into our everyday life now, as we hear how many soldiers are affected by the damaging complications of PTSD, with high rates of alcoholism, divorce, depression and violence. And even closer to home, many people have experienced muggings, severe car accidents, rapes, hurricanes, earthquakes, floods, terrorist attacks and other life threatening situations, which can leave them wounded and scarred. Most people experience some signs of traumatic stress after such terrifying moments, but if the symptoms continue beyond a month, then we call this PTSD.

For instance, a stranger raped Susan at gunpoint in a terrifying attack that seemed to come out of the blue. Months later, she was still experiencing flashbacks and nightmares. She had to move out of the house where it happened, and she avoided going anywhere near that part of the city or having anything to do with something associated with the attack. She also found herself very distrusting of men and was very wary of being in their presence alone. She became withdrawn, depressed and detached, saying that she could not feel much at all. Her mind was so hypervigilant that sleep was restless, she could not concentrate on her studies, and she was anxious and easily startled. Thankfully, she found a good therapist who helped her to work through this by having her tell her story little by little, and who helped her manage her strong emotions and move toward healing and recovery.

As another example, Sean came to see me after he fell flat on the sidewalk when a helicopter flew overhead. Working his way through graduate school as a school janitor, he had considerable debts, and he worried over his teenage children when he had to confiscate a gun from a student at school. This incident was the final straw that broke him and precipitated the start of his PTSD. Sean had been in Vietnam twenty-five years before, and most of his time, he told me, was incredibly boring apart from two major, terrifying battles where his two best buddies were blown to pieces beside him. He was still struggling with unresolved grief and a burning rage at the president and his advisors in the White House who had, at the time, not supported what they were doing. When he came home, it was not to a hero's welcome but to antiwar demonstrators. He, as well, was able to work through his grief and anger, although it left longer-term scars that were difficult to heal.

Current research and treatment of PTSD. Much research is being done to find ways to help people heal from PTSD. Considerable progress has been made in recent years, as our understanding of the effect of PTSD on the brain has increased greatly. It seems that, in situations of great fear, the two halves of our brain become partially disconnected. The emotional ("implicit") memory of the event is stored in the right side of the brain, which deals in images and feelings. The left side of the brain is the realm of logic, verbal language and literal thinking, and this is the side that makes sense of experience and tells the story ("explicit" memory) of what happened.

Traumatic situations arouse strong emotions and, if there is no possibility of fighting or fleeing, freezing is the only option. In that situation, the only conscious escape from fear is to disassociate and think about something else completely different in order to survive the experience. The emotional memory becomes seared into the brain but is disconnected from the logical (factual) memory, and this creates a state of disconnection and disintegration. At this point, we are at the mercy of the emotional memories that invade our consciousness in moments of flashbacks, nightmares and panic, which can make us feel completely out of control. The only defense is to rigidly avoid anything or anyone that triggers those experiences. The more profound the sense of helplessness, feeling trapped or out of control in the original experience (a rescue worker trapped in a burning building, a rape victim), the deeper the wounds of PTSD. If there is guilt about things done or not done—such as soldiers who have killed innocent children—this strengthens the repression of the trauma because of the fear of bringing the shame and guilt back into awareness.

In the research, what is remarkable is that we do not *all* have PTSD after traumatic incidents; we are amazingly resilient. Psychology professor George Bonanno followed the victims of 9/11 and the SARS epidemic in China, while also examining the research on the nuclear explosions in Hiroshima and Nagasaki in World War II. In relation to the latter, he reports, "Only a small percentage of those who endured the devastation remained depressed or exhibited other types of enduring psychiatric symptoms."[5] In relation to the attack on the Twin Towers, he wrote, "Four months after the attack, the prevalence of PTSD in the New York area had dropped to just a few percentage points, and by six months it was almost nonexistent."[6] But for those who had lost loved ones and had witnessed the attack, one third experienced symptoms of PTSD. Another third had some symptoms but they did not last long. "And yet just as many people who had experienced this same horror—one in three—had no trauma reaction at all."[7] The panic of the SARS epidemic affected a large number (approximately 40 percent) with PTSD symptoms, but note that 60 percent were not affected seriously enough to be given this diagnosis.

This shows us that many will have amazing resilience after trauma, but some, because of an anxious temperament, insecurity in early relationships and a history of previous trauma, are more vulnerable to PTSD. Efforts to promote healing of PTSD focus on providing a safe place in relationship for the person to talk about what has happened and to make sense of it. As the person begins to face the feelings and tell the story little by little with a safe person in a safe place at their own pace, the intense feelings and facts begin to make sense and the fear becomes less crippling. Therapists have devised various techniques to enhance the reintegrating of the left and right side of the brain, the logical and emotional memories.

Through all the research on PTSD, we have recognized that many children have been traumatized by their families and are suffering from the effects of chronic trauma and disrupted attachment. This has, to put it very simply, damaged their brains and nervous systems so that there is profound disintegration at every level of being—emotions from thoughts, body from mind, and self from others—which results in greater vulnerability to anxiety, depression, relationship difficulties and a host of other problems. We previously thought of this damage in very psychological terms, but beneath that is actual disruption and damage to the brain itself. We used to think that physical damage to the brain and its connections was irreparable, but now we are finding that both medication and psychotherapy can produce the healing and reintegration of the synapses, circuits and chemical systems of the brain. Techniques that promote emotion and body awareness, as well as right and left brain integration, increase tolerance to stressful situations so that these individuals are more able to resist the common tendencies to the extremes of rigidity (depression and avoidance) or chaos (anxiety, agitation, rage).[8] These techniques help afflicted people become more balanced and whole.[9]

THE REALITY OF ANXIETY IN A FALLEN WORLD: BIBLICAL WISDOM

We must turn now to ask what the Bible teaches about anxiety and fear. How do we relate all this brain science and psychology to the teaching of Scripture? It seems that the apostle Paul was no stranger to anxiety. His friend Epaphroditus nearly died, and Paul wrote of his relief from anxiety when Epaphroditus recovered (Philippians 2:28). Paul spoke of physical exhaustion and being "harassed at every turn—conflicts on the outside, fears within" and "daily . . . concern for all the churches" (2 Corinthians 7:5; 11:28). He even confessed that he came to Corinth "in weakness with great fear and trembling" (1 Corinthians 2:3). And it is said of Jesus in the Garden of Gethsemane that he "offered up prayers and petitions with fervent cries and tears" (Hebrews 5:7), fearfully longing not to have to go through what was ahead of him: crucifixion. So anxiety is a reality in many circumstances in a fallen world, and it is obviously not always sinful. Loss, transition, threat, challenge or even the potential of these things will prompt anxiety in most of us.

In the Old Testament, David was often fearful and anxious in the face of threats and attacks from Saul and other enemies:

My heart is in anguish within me;
    the terrors of death have fallen upon me.

> Fear and trembling come upon me,
>   and horror overwhelms me.
> And I say, "Oh, that I had wings like a dove!
>   I would fly away and be at rest. (Psalm 55:4-6 ESV)

At the end of that psalm, David had worked through his emotions and was able to say, "But I will trust in you" (Psalm 55:23 ESV). So what did he do in the face of these threats? He poured out his heart to God in prayer, not pretending that he was not afraid but, with a wonderful honesty and transparency, slowly moved to a place of being able to trust God for the future.

Jesus' teaching on worry and anxiety. In the Sermon on the Mount, Jesus addressed the ordinary and common fears that we face from day to day—not the things we should be afraid of for our own safety. So in Matthew 6:19-34, he first challenges our priorities, knowing that our tendency is to value our possessions too much. It is not wrong to have things, but he says that we often try to serve God and money at the same time, which lays us open to greater anxiety because moths, rust and thieves can easily take those things from us. He continues with this radical teaching:

> Therefore I tell you, do not be anxious about your life, what you will eat or what you will drink, nor about your body, what you will put on. . . . Look at the birds of the air: they neither sow nor reap . . . yet your heavenly Father feeds them. Are you not of more value than they? And which of you by being anxious can add a single hour to his span of life? And why are you anxious about clothing? Consider the lilies of the field, how they grow: they neither toil nor spin, yet I tell you, even Solomon in all his glory was not arrayed like one of these. But if God so clothes the grass of the field . . . will he not much more clothe you, O you of little faith? Therefore do not be anxious, saying, "What shall we eat?" or "What shall we drink?" or "What shall we wear?" For the Gentiles seek

after all these things, and your heavenly Father knows that you need them all. But seek first the kingdom of God and his righteousness, and all these things will be added to you.

Therefore do not be anxious about tomorrow, for tomorrow will be anxious for itself. Sufficient for the day is its own trouble. (Matthew 6:25-34 ESV)

Jesus was strongly affirming the most basic principle from the beginning of the book of Proverbs, "The fear of the LORD is the beginning of knowledge" (Proverbs 1:7). All through the Old Testament there are many exhortations to fear God. In other words, if you rightly fear[10] God, you don't need to be paralyzed by fear of other things. Again and again throughout Scripture comes the reassurance not to fear because he is with us and for us: "Even though I walk through the valley of the shadow of death, I will fear no evil, for you are with me" (Psalm 23:4).

But back to the Matthew text, Jesus was encouraging us to reflect on the ultimate truth about reality: we don't need to worry, because God exists, and if he cares for birds and flowers (and he does), then how much more does he care for us? He has, of course, given us the responsibility to care for the world, to work for our food each day and to make sure our children have clothes, so when he says not to be anxious about what we will eat or drink, this does not mean that we should do nothing. There is a difference between the care that drives us to responsible action and anxious, preoccupied care that paralyzes us with fear.

Furthermore, Jesus was challenging priorities and exposing the competing treasures of the human heart—and the lack of faith and trust in the One who is in control behind the scenes. For example, if our appearance and the type of car or house we have become too important, as we compare ourselves with our neighbors or friends, then we are more vulnerable to anxiety. Jesus was not saying that we should not care at all about dressing well or having quality possessions, but he was warning us not to become too obsessed with these things. Our anxieties can often reveal our idols by showing us the things and values that have become too important to us that give us primary significance and security in life. As the proverb reminds us, "Better a little with the fear of the LORD than great wealth with turmoil" (Proverbs 15:16).

Paul's practical suggestions for dealing with anxiety and fear. Probably the most well-known text about anxiety is Paul's teaching in Philippians 4:6-7 where he says, "Do not be anxious about anything, but in everything, by prayer and petition, with thanksgiving, present your requests to God. And the peace of God, which transcends all understanding, will guard your hearts and your minds in Christ Jesus." Paul's exhortation not to be anxious may feel like a "just stop it!" command, and we know that is unrealistic. But we should note that Paul does not just say "don't do it"; he gives us reasons not to worry and things to do to replace the anxious worry. For instance, he had just reminded the Philippians that the Lord is near, which is good reason in itself not to be anxious. But then he exhorts them to bring their anxious thoughts to God in prayer, with thanksgiving. In the next verse, Paul further encourages them (and us) to positive thinking with "Whatever is true, . . . noble, . . . right, . . . pure, . . . lovely, . . . admirable . . . think about such things" (Philippians 4:8). Finally he exhorted them (us) to put into practice the things they had learned, and he promised, "The God of peace will be with you" (Philippians 4:9). As we trust that God is really there, pray to him and act in faith, then we will experience the peace of God guarding our hearts and minds.

It is intriguing to note that one of the fathers of cognitive behavioral therapy (CBT), the atheist psychologist Albert Ellis, developed a scheme that has close parallels to the apostle Paul's anxiety "therapy." Ellis called it rational emotive therapy, though others call it cognitive behavioral therapy. It works like this: in response to an activating event or situation, such as (A) losing the

car keys, our dysfunctional beliefs (B) often lead us to "catastro-
phize" and think in all-or-nothing terms: "If I can't get to work on
time, my boss will be furious and I will lose my job, and that
means I can't pay the mortgage and my children will not be able to
continue to go to private school and my husband will think I am
very careless and stupid and want a divorce!" The consequence
(C) is that we feel anxious, agitated, afraid and frustrated. So we
need to learn to dispute (D) by confronting reality and asking,
"What am I saying to myself? Is it true? What evidence is there for
this belief?" Creating a new belief, then, has the effect (E) of creating happier emotions. CBT counselors train their clients in this
process of testing their irrational thoughts, disputing them, and
training themselves to break old worry habits and practice new
thinking.[11]

If we pursue biblical principles further, we are called to obedience and repentance of faithless worry with repeated exhortations throughout Scripture: "do not fret . . . trust . . . be still"
(Psalm 37), "take captive every thought . . . to Christ" (2 Corinthians 10:5) and "cast all your anxiety on him because he cares
for you" (1 Peter 5:7). Many of us may feel that our faith is
stretched to a breaking point in trusting God in our particular,
difficult circumstances. But I wonder how we would comfort a
believer living in Darfur, with the constant terror that she will be
raped or killed if she goes out of her village to get firewood or
water, but knowing her family will die if she does nothing. The
glib, super-spiritual answer would be to tell her to just trust God,
but this needs more explanation.

First, we would probably have to acknowledge that most of us
have no idea what this situation must be like, but in the face of the
ultimate threat, there is only one promise to fall back on. While
God has not guaranteed to protect us from poverty, starvation,
illness, torture, rape or, even, death—although he sometimes does
do that in mysterious and miraculous ways, and we can certainly

pray for deliverance—he has promised us that, even through death, he will never desert us or let us go and beyond death is a wonderful deliverance. Paul writes in Romans 8:18: "I consider that our present sufferings are not worth comparing with the glory that will be revealed in us." He then reminds us that, even while we groan in this broken world, the Spirit "intercedes for us with groans that words cannot express," and Christ himself also intercedes for us (Romans 8:26, 34). More than that, Paul says, "Who shall separate us from the love of Christ? Shall trouble or hardship or persecution or famine or nakedness or danger or sword? . . . No, in all these things we are more than conquerors through him who loved us. For I am convinced that neither death nor life, neither angels nor demons, . . . nor anything else in all creation, will be able to separate us from the love of God in Christ Jesus our Lord" (Romans 8:35, 37-39).

So the Bible gives wonderful, practical principles for dealing with anxiety, but it does not give specific descriptions or treatment suggestions for the more extreme anxiety disorders. Here we have to turn to the sciences of medicine and psychology to see if there are any valuable ideas and techniques that do not conflict with a Christian perspective and worldview. Phobias, panic attacks, generalized anxiety, OCD and PTSD all have specific behavioral, psychotherapeutic and medical treatments that are usually very helpful. With the more ordinary, day-to-day anxiety and worry that we all experience, there are some common grace/practical wisdom[12] tips to add to the clear teaching of Scripture. These practical suggestions are recommended by non-Christians and Christians in most self-help literature.

Practical wisdom/common grace. As with depression, research has shown that exercise helps to relieve anxiety since it uses up some of our excess adrenaline and cortisol. Exercise then helps us to think more clearly, sleep better at night and feel better about ourselves. Taking time to walk in green places among flowers, trees and birds can also be restful to the spirit. Listening to music can be relaxing and healing. Calming the body and mind with controlled and rhythmic breathing and muscle relaxation exercises helps to undermine worry. Mindfulness techniques can help us be more aware of our feelings and thoughts, and learn to deal with them more effectively.[13] These techniques need to be practiced at least daily to be effective—in situations of calm at first, so that later they can be used when things get tense and difficult.

Rest and recreation are important too. God gave us a sabbath day of rest for our good, and we ignore it at our peril. A sabbath should be a time of rest from work, a time of worship and a time of celebrating the good things that God has given us to enjoy in this world—food, nature, friendships, music, books and so on. Sometimes it is helpful to take a fast from the news, as feeding ourselves a diet of stories of murders, sexual assaults, accidents, recessions, storms and disasters does not help us to keep a right perspective on risk. Rather, it teaches us that we are all in great danger all the time and should be fearful!

Some of us who have a tendency to work very hard and feel responsibility to care for others may need to learn to say no to overload. Counselors, therapists, social workers and pastors often find great pleasure in caring for others, but they may have a deep need to be needed, which may feed their sense of value and identity in an unhealthy way that can lead to burnout. Furthermore, it is important to be part of a community of caring people. We all have our own burdens that we should carry, but when we are carrying an extra load, others can be there to help just as we can be there for them (Galatians 6:2, 5).

Finally, however, if someone has serious anxiety, they should have a medical examination to check for any physical cause. They may be taking medication for other conditions, and a side effect may be anxiety. They may have a disorder of the thyroid gland, a heart problem or some other physical illness that can produce symptoms of anxiety. It is also important to discern whether the anxiety is part of an episode of serious depression, because we have seen that heightened anxiety may come as a result of or be a cause of depression, so it needs to be helped in that context.

QUESTIONS FOR REFLECTION AND DISCUSSION

1. What typically makes you anxious?

2. How did your parents teach you to deal with anxiety? Was this by word or example?

3. What difference do you think temperament makes in how people experience anxiety? Do you think anxiety is mostly inherited or mostly learned?

4. Are there circumstances in your life that might make you more vulnerable to anxiety in certain situations?

5. When do you think worry, anxiety and fear become sinful and unhealthy?

6. What does it mean to fear God but not be afraid?

7. How do our worries and fears expose our heart's idols?

8. What practical things help you to deal with anxiety?

9. What are the lessons you have learned from the Bible about dealing with anxiety?

10. Have you experienced severe anxiety in the form of phobias, panic attacks, GAD, OCD or PTSD, and what have you found helpful in dealing with it (or have you found help to deal with it)?

9

ANGER AND THE STRUGGLE TO FORGIVE

Oft have I heard that grief softens the mind, And makes it fearful and degenerate; Think therefore on revenge and cease to weep.

WILLIAM SHAKESPEARE, *HENRY VI*

In your anger do not sin.

PAUL, EPHESIANS 4:26

Anyone can become angry—that is easy. But to be angry with the right person, to the right degree, at the right time, for the right purpose, and in the right way—this is not easy.

ARISTOTLE, *THE NICOMACHEAN ETHICS*

You may be asking, *Why is there a chapter on anger when we are talking about depression?* Well, the answer is that depression and anger are closely linked. Here is a letter that one of my clients wrote to his parents in the early days of trying to deal with his powerful and potentially destructive emotions:

Dear Mum and Dad:

What I'm asking for, in this my first time to ever show or even know my anger in its depth (so "disrespectful" it was for us to get angry around our place), is simply honesty on your part. For you know my weaknesses . . . I've not hidden them. However, what absolutely infuriates me is that—after suffering a major, seven-year ordeal of depression, at times a clinical one, and at others, subclinical—you roundly deny any significant mishandling of my upbringing??!! I will not allow such a denial to go unchallenged. I have tried the peace-at-any-cost route for twenty-seven years to no avail, being tolerant and keeping my mouth shut. But I am almost beside myself with anger, and it is justified. I will tell you my anger in hopes that you change, also realizing my own problems and imperfections too. However, if you both continue such a denial of significant mishandling of my upbringing, don't expect me to expose myself to such abuse in the future. I won't be so masochistic as to hang around you much, though I love you very deeply.

Sincerely, Jack[1]

Was this a helpful way to write to his parents? While it is good to be honest about what we are wrestling with, I think there are better ways of trying to move toward reconciliation. So often people who come to counseling for depression are struggling with a difficult relationship, and more often than not, it is a relationship with a spouse or parent. As I work with them, I often ask them to write a letter to that person and to be completely honest about what they think and feel. This letter is *not* to be sent. I use it to help the client explore his heart and to bring real feelings and thoughts out into the light, which can be a revelation to the person writing. "I sat down to write," said Jack, "and nothing came for a long time, and then I started and it just poured out onto the screen for the next two hours. I never knew I had so much bitterness inside me." This experience opened the door for several sessions of talking about the biblical principles that govern our anger and push us toward forgiveness. Later he sent another more carefully expressed letter to his parents.

ANGER—THE UMBRELLA EMOTION— AND WHAT IS UNDERNEATH

So often our anger is the superficial emotion, but underneath it are more complex feelings that need to be brought to the surface. In counseling people who are angry and depressed, I help them to explore the feelings behind the anger, which are often hurt, sadness, disappointment, fear, shame or guilt. For example, when my pride is hurt or I feel ashamed because I have failed at something, I may protect my fragile ego with an outburst of anger or irritation. The situation may be the same when I am frustrated that other people don't do things just the way I think they should be done, or when I am afraid and feel out of control, or when I am envious that others are more gifted or have things that I covet. The apostle James exposes these deeper heart motives when he says: "What causes fights and quarrels among you? Don't they come from your desires that battle within you?" (James 4:1). Even our legitimate, God-given desires for good things can easily become demands: I want what I want when I want it, and I will make sure that I get it!

In Galatians 5:16-26, Paul elaborates on our inner battles, saying that hatred and fits of rage arise from our sinful nature, so he says that to deal with unrighteous anger, we are to take responsibility for our part in the conflict, put off the old nature, break out of old habits and vicious circles, and establish new patterns of thought, feelings and behavior—thus not giving the devil a foothold. It takes a conscious, willing choice to cooperate with the Spirit of God.

Anger's disguises. As we come to terms with past relationships and face frustrations in the present, we often have to deal with a mixture of anger and love, as expressed in the last sentence of Jack's letter. His long-suppressed anger was a cause of his years of depression, and this is a common cause for depression—especially when it is turned against oneself with self-blame and self-contempt. If the anger is directed against others, it tends to simmer within for a while like a grumbling volcano, though spurts of steam or hot lava will escape at intervals, which are expressed in a number of different ways.

Irritable, critical, silent and uncooperative behavior is a sure sign that anger is near the surface. Other less obvious disguises that anger hides behind are impatience and boredom. Physical symptoms, such as backaches, headaches and fatigue, may be caused by suppressed anger: "A calm and undisturbed mind and heart are the life and health of the body, but envy, jealousy, and wrath are like rottenness of the bones" (Proverbs 14:30 Amplified Bible).

It is often mild-mannered, gentle people with much self-control who, when repeatedly provoked, finally erupt with devastating anger and then feel terrible guilt and depression afterward. On the other hand, those who often lose control may feel too *little* guilt. Sometimes when we cannot accept responsibility for our own anger, we blame others for being angry with us first. We often criticize in others what we hate most in ourselves. Self-destructive urges in the form of drug-taking, alcohol abuse, self-injury or even suicide attempts often arise from anger that has been turned inward against oneself.

Sometimes when a feeling of anger is very frightening and unacceptable it is repressed into the unconscious with rather unexpected consequences. I vividly remember my first day in a psychiatric clinic when a woman was sent to see a psychiatrist because she had a terrible fear (phobia) of kitchen knives, which was so disabling that she could hardly enter her own kitchen. As we talked it became clear that this gentle, mild-mannered lady was being seriously abused by her husband. One day, the thought of killing her husband with one of the kitchen knives crossed her mind. She was so horrified at the thought and so afraid that she might lose control of herself that she forgot (repressed) her anger and was only aware of a great fear of knives. Our minds can deal with anger in amazing ways.

So how *should* we deal with anger? Is it right just to let it all out? The so-called ventilation school, or "exploders," would have us believe so: shout, scream, hit a pillow, break a few plates, anything to get it out of the system. Others say that we should suppress or control it. Still others say that it is a sin for a Christian to ever be angry. As Christians we are called to be "holy," to be like God, to put off our old nature and put on the new, so we need to step back a little and look first at God's anger.

GOD'S ANGER

Is God's anger an unfortunate lapse, a moment of self-forgetfulness in an all-loving and all-accepting God? Is the anger expressed in the Bible just a projection of the writer's character, making God in his own image? It is very difficult to believe so when we read of God's judgment on unbelievers: "He let loose on them his burning anger, wrath, indignation, and distress" (Psalm 78:49 ESV), or "The wrath of God is being revealed from heaven against all the godlessness and wickedness of men who suppress the truth" (Romans 1:18). This strong language expresses God's hatred of sin and evil. To think of God like this is offensive to many but a great comfort to those who have been victims of great evil and injustice.

With his own people, the Israelites, we find that, "the LORD is slow to anger, abounding in love and forgiving sin and rebellion" (Numbers 14:18). The Bible says that he "disciplines those he loves" (Hebrews 12:6), and "his anger lasts only a moment, but his favor lasts a lifetime" (Psalm 30:5). The purpose of his loving discipline is to keep us safe and draw us back into relationship with him.

In Christ, we see the living demonstration of God's character. His anger is not capricious or out of control; it is appropriate to the situation. His fiercest anger was reserved for the religious teachers, the hypocritical, legalistic scribes and Pharisees, denouncing them publicly as "hypocrites," "blind guides," "snakes" and a "brood of vipers" (Matthew 23). He took a whip to those who desecrated the house of God (Matthew 21:12), and many other incidents are recorded when Jesus rebuked, charged, commanded or spoke strongly to the Pharisees, evil spirits, the crowds and the apostle Peter. In the final judgment, those who have stood against him will have to face the "wrath of the Lamb" (Revelation 6:16).

However, a very different expression of anger is seen in Jesus' arrival at the tomb of Lazarus. When he saw Mary crying, "he was deeply moved in spirit and troubled," and as he approached the tomb, he was upset again (John 11:33, 38). The Greek word for "deeply moved" can mean to snort with anger, like a horse going into battle. "It invariably suggests anger, outrage or emotional indignation."[2] This time, his anger was not at hypocrisy or hardness of heart but, presumably, at the brokenness of the world and at the results of sin—including sickness, injustice, death and separation.

So we cannot say that being angry is always wrong. As our purpose is to become more and more like Jesus, we should seek to understand when anger is justified and how to express it in the right way.

OUR ANGER

What does the Bible say about *our* anger? The basic principle is simple, "In your anger do not sin" (Ephesians 4:26). There *is* a possibility of anger without sin—righteous anger. But our anger can be sinful or righteous in two dimensions: in relation to *what* I am angry about and to *how* my anger is expressed.

What should we be angry about? God expresses anger at injustice, cruelty, greed, arrogance and hypocrisy, so I should be angry about these things too. Men like William Wilberforce and Lord Shaftesbury channeled their anger at injustice into fighting for legal reform in the abolition of slavery and in protecting young children from working in factories. Surely we should feel angry about child pornography, abortion on demand, racial intolerance, sexual slavery, ecological irresponsibility and other gross injustices around the world. These issues move the heart of God and so should move us. God says to his people:

> Is not this the kind of fasting I have chosen:
> to loose the chains of injustice
>   and untie the cords of the yoke,
> to set the oppressed free
>   and break every yoke?
> Is it not to share your food with the hungry
>   and to provide the poor wanderer with shelter—
> when you see the naked, to clothe him,
>   and not to turn away from your flesh and blood?
> (Isaiah 58:6-7)

We are not called to be tolerant toward evil and injustice, but we do need wisdom in how we express our anger. I should not go out and shoot the people responsible for child pornography or abortion. Or while anger has its place in loving discipline of children and I might be angry with my child for lying to me or directly disobeying me, I should not curse and shout or hit her. In a parent-child relationship of strong affection, friendship and respect, there may be moments of hot displeasure that lead to appropriate discipline. But, as with God and the Israelites, we should be slow to anger, and our anger should last "only a moment" (Psalm 30:5). If our anger festers for hours or days and leads to a critical and resentful spirit, it will breed an attitude of deep bitterness and rebellion in the child. Anger should motivate us with the appropriate balance of reason and emotion—not losing control nor suppressing so much that we become ineffective.

How should we be angry? There is also a place for occasional expressions of righteous anger in relationships, in marriage, between parents and children, between children and their parents (children may be rightfully angry with parents), between friends or in work situations. This is a difficult area because our anger is so easily self-protective and unrighteous. Paul describes sinful expressions of anger as "bitterness, rage and anger, brawling and slander, along with every other form of malice" (Ephesians 4:31). In both Colossians and Ephesians, the emphasis is on the fact that we are all sinners and that we must do all we can to help each other fight against such expressions of our sinful nature. Not only are we commanded to avoid unrighteous anger but, in the same passages, we are told to be humble, patient, gentle, full of self-control (1 Corinthians 13:4-7), to speak the truth in love, to recognize each other's gifts (Ephesians 4:15-16), to be kind and compassionate, and to forgive one another (Ephesians 4:32). It is not just getting rid of anger; it is an active replacement of negative feelings and actions with positive ones (Ephesians 4:20-24).

Bottle or blow? What then does the Bible say to the two extremes of those who tend to bottle their anger and those who blow up and let it all hang out? The Bible has more to say to those who blow. Two of the fruits of the Spirit mentioned in Galatians are "patience" and "self-control." Because we are so prone to unrighteous anger, which is the easiest, most downhill route to take, we have to apply the brakes very firmly. We have to stop to take time out and to regain our rationality, which is so easily overwhelmed by powerful emotions. The book of Proverbs gives some rich images: "Like a city whose walls are broken down is a man who lacks self-control" (Proverbs 25:28). "A fool gives full vent to his anger, but a wise man keeps himself under control" (Proverbs 29:11). "Starting a quarrel is like breaking a dam; so drop the matter before a dispute breaks out" (Proverbs 17:14). In the heat of the moment, we are just one word or phrase away from either intimacy or war.

Modern brain science shows that when we are very upset and angry, our rational cortical functions become less connected to the emotional and physiological functions so that we literally "lose it" or "flip our lid." We lose our temper as we let go of healthy control and integration of different parts of our brain, especially the prefrontal cortex.[3]

Until twenty years ago, many psychotherapists and counselors belonged to the cathartic, or ventilator, school of anger, believing that all anger must be let out. Some therapies encouraged any form of releasing aggression (shouting, kicking, hitting—usually not a person but a cushion or some other inanimate object) to "get in touch" with feelings. But research has demonstrated that, far from defusing anger, this technique may inflame it. Children encouraged to get rid of pent-up feelings by kicking furniture and playing with violent toys or "shoot-em up" videogames tend to become more aggressive, not less.

At the other end of the spectrum are those who tend to bottle their anger. They may have an unhealthy inhibition about ever being angry—to the point where they have trouble asserting themselves or speaking strongly about anything. These people are especially vulnerable to depression. For them any form of self-assertion feels like unrighteous anger. They are normally oversensitive to others' opinions, always anxious to please, and find it difficult to express their own opinions or disagree with others. Often such people have experienced repeated putdowns or abuse from others in a more powerful position, and they have had to repress their anger at such injustices because there was no response that would not have brought down more anger on their heads. Such a person will wrongly blame himself for the situation and as psychotherapist Anthony Storr says:

By repressing his destructive hostility, he has at the same time deprived himself of those positive features of aggression which would allow him to assert himself when necessary, stand up to other people, initiate effective action, "attack" difficult problems, and make his mark upon the world. I said that helplessness and hopelessness march hand in hand [in depression]: let us add hostility to make a triad of "h's."[4]

Depression might be thought of as frozen passion. When anger is bottled up for long periods, we are often hardly aware that it is present, and when it is "frozen" within us, other emotions are often inhibited as well. The thawing process can be very painful. In order to love others truly, we may have to face the reality and depth of our anger, and as we bring that to God, we will be set free to assert ourselves appropriately, to express anger in a righteous way, and also to love more fully and freely.

SELF-CONTROL

Back to those who tend to let anger explode. Working toward self-control can be achieved by learning to recognize the body tensions that often accompany anger, learning relaxation techniques or going for a brisk walk, and also by actively changing one's thinking about the person with whom they are angry. One way to do the latter is to learn to reinterpret events that are apparently provocative, and be prepared to believe the best, not the worst, about the other person. To that effect, the apostle James writes, "Everyone should be quick to listen, slow to speak and slow to become angry, for man's anger does not bring about the righteous life that God desires" (James 1:19-20). Furthermore, revenge is often the first instinct, and this impulse needs to be retrained, as the apostle Paul writes, "Love is patient, love is kind. . . . It is not rude, it is not self-seeking, it is not easily angered, it keeps no record of wrongs" (1 Corinthians 13:4-5).

For those who tend to bottle up their anger, there is not such detailed advice in the Bible, but there are many principles to learn from. "'In your anger do not sin': Do not let the sun go down while you are still angry" (Ephesians 4:26). While I don't think this is to be taken literally, it is still a good general principle. The second word for anger in this verse is a stronger word that implies bitterness and resentment, so anger should not be held inside for long or it will become poisonous. If we know we need to, it is best to deal with anger on the same day. We are encouraged not to hold hatred in our hearts, for "whoever hates his brother is in the darkness" (1 John 2:11; see also 1 John 3:15). Honesty and "speaking the truth in love" (Ephesians 4:15) are qualities of spiritual maturity. Either repressing anger or losing one's temper is obviously an unrighteous way of dealing with anger, but it is the particular *style* of dealing with the anger that is wrong, not necessarily the anger itself.[5] Anger quickly becomes unrighteous because of *how* it is handled or expressed!

In order to exhibit self-control over anger, I believe the first stage is to slow down, taking time to think and pray, being aware of our own responsibility in a conflict and our own faults—the possible "plank" in our own eye (Matthew 7:4). Of course, nobody is perfect and every day we probably hurt people who are close to us in a number of ways. Perhaps in that context is where "love covers over all wrongs" (Proverbs 10:12), so for instance, a married couple will not need to talk about every angry thought or feeling. However, when the anger remains as a consistent theme in a relationship, then we need to try to talk calmly and rationally about it, confessing our anger and trying to see the other person's point of view—seeking to rebuild the relationship peacefully. We speak the truth in love when we ask for forgiveness and are ready to forgive. We long for reconciliation, not revenge. Where these principles do not work, then help may need to be found by working with a pastor or counselor.

ANGER FOR THE PAST

What about anger that is rooted in past injustices and relationships? Is it possible to untie the knots of hurt, resentment and revenge that are embedded deep within our hearts and minds? Because we are made in the image of God, with his concern for justice in the world, anger may be justified when we were hurt and wounded in childhood. That was the theme of the letter at the beginning of the chapter.

That was also the case for Toby, whose father never wanted him. His mother had tried desperately to get an abortion (before it was legal) but had failed. From the time he was born, he was neglected, punished for being upset, abused, criticized and eventually, at the age of seventeen, told to leave home. Not surprisingly he had unconscious reservoirs of (forbidden) anger but was unaware of these when he sought help for depression.

Sometimes events in the present may trigger deeply buried emotional memories. For instance, a man being criticized by his boss may feel overwhelmed by anxiety and shame as the experience reverberates with the many times his own father told him he was useless and "profoundly disappointing." Or a newly married woman whose husband is sexually demanding and insensitive may trigger an emotional reaction of terror because of incidents of sexual abuse in childhood. These emotions often turn to anger.

Knots untangled. It is not wrong to be angry at neglect, abuse or injustice, but as we face the anger and acknowledge it, we have to be prepared to deal with it in appropriate ways. It may take hours of patient talking with a friend, counselor, pastor and God to tease out the different strands of that knot of anger that is rooted in the past. That is where writing a letter is very useful. Below are a few fragments from a much longer letter that Luke wrote. He was struggling with depression when he came for counseling, and he tearfully told me about the relational dysfunction in his family that stretched back through two generations of missionaries and pastors. I encouraged him to express his unfiltered feelings about his father in a letter that would just be read to me.

Dear Dad,

This is a letter that I have wanted to write to you for some time. . . . I too am saddened by the shallowness of our father-and-son interaction, but I find the way forward to be difficult. There are a number of issues that I struggle with. . . .

Sure, you have told me that you are sorry for how your life affected mine, but always with the posture of a victim, never with the heart of someone who is ready to take responsibility for how their actions have affected others. You have basically repeatedly said, "I'm sorry . . . but it wasn't really my fault." You want to move forward in relationship without being willing to go back. But that is not possible! . . .

I say these things because I think they need to be said. I think that they are true, though I don't claim that my perspective is objective. I would be lying if I told you I wasn't angry about your response to the past. I think that your attitude toward these matters and your ability to act like we should live a fulfilled life, like you, when we are all reeling in emotional chaos is both sad and appalling! It is certainly hard to take. Sometimes I think you are in denial. . . .

My own experience of loss has been that I always wanted a man to look up to. Sure you taught me how to work hard, and you passed down your ability to fix things, for which I am grateful, but you couldn't teach me to be mature . . . to be a godly man. So I grew up as a fool, always hungry for direction, but always emotionally immature, sucking down any sin that might ease the pain. Christ has of course been very gracious to me, though I still struggle with insecurity and a lack of self-worth. I guess after all these years I still feel like saying to you, "When are you going to start acting like a man?" Why are we still playing the same games? How do you expect to have a relationship with someone you have hurt so deeply without seeking true repentance? You don't seem to take your betrayal seriously at all. You almost act aloof, like God will work everything out. . . . It is in his hands. Sometimes I wonder if you even live in reality.[6]

Luke's honesty about his anger and sadness is wonderful, because he wants to face reality. It is good to be honest about what is in our hearts and be open to examining whether we are angry with the right things, in the right way. King David found it was safe to have his outbursts in God's presence. In Psalm 55 he told God that he was very angry with his friends who had turned against him. In Psalm 13:1 he was grieved and angry with God, "Will you forget me forever? How long will you hide your face from me?" At other times he expressed his passionate hatred of injustice. When we are in emotional turmoil, it is a great comfort to find that David shared the same feelings and did not run from the pain, but he faced it squarely and brought it to God. One friend, in working through much deeply repressed anger when coming out of a time of depression, said that it was extremely helpful to write down exactly what she was feeling—swear words and all. "There was no need to reveal it. I could just tear it up because it was 'out' in words—on paper. It was out in the open, confessed to God."

As Luke and I discussed his story and his letter, he was able to see how deeply his father had been betrayed by his own father, a missionary who neglected his children for the sake of what he thought was a higher calling, preaching the gospel. Luke continued,

While I say all these things because I need to be honest, I also realize that you are a deeply wounded and hurting person. If my experience has left me guarded and, in many ways, unable to truly love others, then I can only imagine how deeply your experience has affected your ability to know and expose yourself. I also realize that it is extremely painful to go back and open up the past.

I think you want me to accept you, to love you, to tell you it is alright . . . but it is all too simplistic. Love is more complex. . . . It lives in the reality of hurt and loss. You want me to have compassion for your lifelong struggle, but are you willing to acknowledge the unthinkable . . . that you did to your children exactly what was done to you!

The truth of the matter is that I grew up in many ways without a father and I gave up hope that I would ever find one. I learned to try to cope on my own.

As a result of processing his feelings in the letter, Luke was able to be more open and gently but lovingly honest with his father on his next visit. Amazingly his father began to talk more about his own responsibility and seemed more open to hearing Luke's side of the story, and they are slowly moving toward forgiveness and reconciliation.

So often parents who have hurt us are only partially responsible for what they have done. They too may have been deeply wounded by others—often their own parents. This knowledge, hopefully, helps us to be more compassionate and eventually forgiving, without reducing the significance of their sin against us.

But then we have to face our own responsibility for how we have responded to their sin. Even as children we have some responsibility for how we react to situations. Sometimes we have to be boldly loving, make the first move and say we are sorry for what we have done, without demanding anything in return. If parents are able and willing to discuss and recognize wrong, there can be wonderful moments of reconciliation, but sadly, they may not understand at all, leaving us feeling hurt, rejected and even more angry. There are also some relationships in the past and present where we cannot set things right, either because the person involved has died or is unwilling to talk or perhaps has been severely abusive and does not admit this or desire to change, and these we can only leave with God and ask him to bring healing, to help us not hold onto resentment and bitterness. And that is where we move into the process of forgiveness.

FORGIVENESS

There is a natural connection between anger and forgiveness. It is interesting that there was very little mention of forgiveness in the psychotherapy literature until 30 years ago. Now, it is a very popular topic. We talk about the necessity for forgiveness but most of us find within ourselves a deep resistance to actually forgiving those who have wronged us.

Jesus taught his disciples a forgiveness 101 class and Paul clarified this for the early churches. The fundamental principle is "[forgive] each other, just as in Christ God forgave you" (Ephesians 4:32). The usual fallen reflex of revenge is to be replaced by the redemptive reflex of forgiveness. Jesus stressed this with the story of the unforgiving servant who, although he had been forgiven an impossibly huge debt failed to understand how enormous it was as he asked for more time to pay. Then he went out and demanded that the under-servant pay him back the few dollars he owed. He did not forgive because he failed to understand the seriousness of his sin and how much he had been forgiven (Matthew 18:21-35). In several places Jesus implies that if we continue to hate and withhold forgiveness, it may mean that we have not understood the gospel at all (Matthew 6:12-15; Luke 17:3-10). A fruit of the gospel taking root in our life is the willingness to forgive again and again, recognizing how much we need forgiveness and grace all the time.

On a day-to-day basis we should be practicing repentance and forgiveness with each other, taking sin seriously and not granting "forgiveness-lite." An apology is for accidental wrongs (like spilling coffee on your shirt). No need to ask forgiveness but it is necessary to say, "I am sorry." Where intentional wrong has been done, the sin should be named, repented of, forgiveness asked for and hopefully granted. It is a serious transaction. But since we sin against each other in all sorts of small ways all the time, there is a place to allow love to cover "a multitude of sins"(1 Peter 4:8) and sometimes it is "to one's glory to overlook an offense" (Proverbs 19:11). Major repetitive injuries cannot be "overlooked" in the same way.

These are basic general principles, but when in depression, there are often complex relationships and hurts that need careful application of further biblical wisdom. Erwin Lutzer writes in *Managing Your Emotions:*

> You may be one of those who has been rejected by your parents. In your heart you are saying, and you may well be saying it to your spouse, "I want to see my parents suffer for what they have done to me. No way am I going to let them off scot-free by forgiving them." You say that even though in your honest hours you admit they couldn't care less about whether you forgave them or not. They have rejected you— and they will continue to reject you. Your clearest response if you want to live by God's Word, must be "By God's grace I choose to forgive them." Don't wait until you feel like it— you never will.[7]

If no repentance? What if the person does not repent? What if they keep sinning against you and rejecting you? What if there is some injury in the past that still haunts you? When I am working with clients in counseling, I often find myself thinking about Romans 12:17-21, where Paul lays out a process of forgiveness with several principles. He explains what it means to "love your enemies"—especially individuals who may have done us harm. The first step in this process is to renounce revenge and to decide not to repay evil for evil (Romans 12:17, 19). Our desires for revenge are partly wanting to see the other person suffer and partly a good passion for justice, and this is where, in individual situations, we struggle toward the second step of leaving final justice to God. This is a major stumbling block for many.

I mentioned Sean in the last chapter in relation to PTSD. He came to see me with anxiety, nightmares and flashbacks of his time in Vietnam twenty-five years before. He walked me through that time, which was mostly boredom apart from two horrific battles in which he lost his two buddies. And then there was the rage! He told me how he had dreamed for years of all the horrible things he would like to do to the men in the White House at that time who had so badly let them down. He was convinced that if he did not get revenge, justice would not be done and those men would go free. I asked him if he had ever read Romans 12. He had, of course, but never made the connection to his situation. Gradually it dawned on him what it meant to trust that God would take care of this. He could leave justice in God's hands. Anger, tears, repentance and relief followed. The apostle Paul wrestled with this too when he wrote, "Alexander the metalworker did me a great deal of harm. The Lord will repay him for what he has done" (2 Timothy 4:14).

The third principle is to seek to live at peace with others—as far as it depends on us (Romans 12:18). Jesus taught that if we are going in to worship and we remember that someone has something against us—or that we have some grievance against somebody—we should take the initiative to seek forgiveness or forgive first (Matthew 5:23-24; Mark 11:25).

The fourth principle is to "overcome evil with good" (Romans 12:20-21), and by so doing, we "heap burning coals" on our neighbor's head! That sounds like practicing painful revenge but the intention is far from that; rather, it is to so surprise our enemy by our kindness that we provoke her conscience to repentance.

Sometimes overcoming evil with good in this way does not work and repentance may be sought by rebuke. Leviticus 19:17 says, "Rebuke your neighbor frankly so you will not share in his guilt." I like the ESV translation "reason frankly" instead of "rebuke." Jesus said, "If your brother sins, rebuke him, and if he repents, forgive him" (Luke 17:3-4). Such frank reasoning must be done with great humility and with a willingness to face our own sin, which may be even greater (Matthew 7:1-5). Such rebuking, whether on a personal one-to-one level or as part of church discipline, should lead to restoration. Paul writes: "If someone is caught in a sin, you who are spiritual should restore him gently. But watch yourself, or you also may be tempted. Carry each other's burdens. . . . If anyone thinks he is something when he is nothing, he deceives himself" (Galatians 6:1-3).

Is repentance necessary for forgiveness? At times the Bible calls us to forgiveness with no mention of repentance. At other times it says, "If he repents, forgive" (Luke 17:3). For our letter writer above, Luke moved toward his father with an attitude of forgiveness, so he gave up the right to revenge and trusted God that justice would be done. He sought to build a relationship with his father and overcame evil with good, but he also longed for more. He longed for repentance and reconciliation.

In his book *Bold Love*, Dan Allender tells a story that illustrates moving toward someone who has not repented with an attitude of forgiveness. For years Jane had been attacked by both her parents because they each believed that she was the other's favorite. She was shot at from both sides for anything that could be interpreted as loyalty to the other parent. This time she decided to take a bold but loving stand by deciding to stay away on an important national holiday, and as expected, this had caused trouble. Her father, blatantly ignoring her decision, called to see what time she would be arriving, and Jane laughed out loud as she responded:

JANE: Well, Dad, I can at least say it won't be in this calendar year.

DAD: What?! You know your mom is counting on you helping with the big Fourth of July party. She won't be able to do it without your help!

JANE: Oh, that's too bad, Dad. You know, a lot of catering firms do holiday spreads, and I bet there are some in your area.

DAD: Don't get cute with me. You know your mother wants you here, not a catering firm. Now let's get serious. You will be coming home.

JANE: Dad, do you recall the conversation a few nights ago when you yelled and called me some terrible names? Well, I told you then I would no longer allow you to sin against me or yourself by enduring your use of rage and shame. Before you get too much more intense, let me make it clear again: I will not stay on the phone if that is your manner of relating to me. Dad, are you willing to think with me about the way you deal with me and, frankly, almost everyone else in our family?

DAD: Well, fine! I'll tell your mother about your decision. And let me tell you I have no interest in being lectured by a kid who has no more sense than . . .

JANE: Dad, I will look forward to the day you do desire to interact, so I'll be talking with you soon. Bye, Dad.

This was a very significant event for Jane. This was the first time she was able to say such difficult things with grace and dignity. She trembled for hours afterward and told Dan, her therapist, that she felt as if she was "giving birth to evil incarnate one minute and to a totally new and wonderful life the next."[8]

Jane had given up the desire for revenge, was seeking to live at peace with her father and was building a bridge toward him—but, at the same time, she was setting a boundary so that she would not be abused again. She was also trying to overcome evil with good. However, the fullness and completion of forgiveness could not be experienced without her father's repentance.

Some years ago, Mindy came to stay with us at the L'Abri community where I worked at the time. She was struggling with depression and eventually told us about being a victim of sexual abuse by her father. Over the years she tried to confront him with this and he denied it completely. She nearly went "crazy," beginning to think she had imagined it and yet suffering with the memories and effects of what she thought he had done. We kept in touch by telephone and e-mail, and one year she told me she had had enough of trying to forgive and make peace with him. She was going to cut him off completely—not even a visit to the family at Thanksgiving or Christmas. I encouraged her, on the basis of Romans 12, to keep some minimal contact. Six months later she sent me this e-mail about her conversation with her Dad at an annual family event that she chose to attend:

> He was playing the piano when I asked if I could talk with him. He stopped playing and turned around to face me. I sat down.
>
> "Dad," I said, "We have all made mistakes, and we've all done things we wish we hadn't done. Some of the things you did to me when I was little have really made me feel like trash. I can forgive you and I have. It's my stuff now to deal with, and I will. But it would really help me if I knew that you were sorry for what you did and the effects it has had on me. Are you sorry?"

There was a long pause and then he said the most unexpected yet hoped for thing: "Am I sorry? Hell, yes, I'm sorry! A thousand times sorry! I am very sorry! There were times when I made mistakes. And there were other times when I didn't want to do something, I did it anyway and regretted immediately. I *am* sorry!"

I said, "Thanks, Dad, I needed to hear that. I love you." I gave him a hug. . . .

The validation of his acknowledging (by saying he is sorry) that he hurt me and that his actions have had horrible consequences, which I have to deal with, has been like a salve to my soul, pulling out bitterness. Somehow it helps heal my soul to know that the one who put those scars and welts there has deeply regretted it as he saw me struggling with their effects. Having extended forgiveness—and most importantly, having had that forgiveness be wanted—cleared away years and years of unsaid angers and sorrows.

I also think that since he has responded to this light, God will bring more light, more truth to him, and he might be more willing to accept it. I do hope so. I'd like to stand beside him at the cross, equally in need of the Savior's death.

I wish somewhat that he would have said what he had done, but I don't think he was capable of that then. However, his description of the sins that beset him pretty much supports my memories of his compulsive hatred and sexual abuse.

I am very glad I didn't send that letter, cutting off contact with him and dictating terms for resolution in such a way that it would have prevented his ever being able to acknowledge the truth like this—so simply and freely.[9]

Mindy renounced revenge, sought to live at peace with her father, overcame evil with good, and from time to time asked questions to provoke repentance. After her father's confession she could complete the process of forgiveness and begin to build trust again. Forgiveness did not mean that Mindy trusted her father immediately. That had to be earned over time. If this story gives the impression that her father's sin was dismissed lightly, it wasn't. This was not the only conversation they had about the seriousness of the damage her father had done and its very painful consequences. Sadly, though, many situations do not end as well as this—with repentance and reconciliation.

Forgiveness of deep and long-standing hurts is not easy. Often we feel that we are still in pain and cannot forgive. When that is the case, we can start by asking God to make us willing to begin the hard process that may have many layers and stages. Someone has said, "Refusal to forgive is a poison you take, hoping it will kill your enemy!" And that poison often results in depression.

QUESTIONS FOR REFLECTION AND DISCUSSION

1. What makes you angry?

2. What is your style of dealing with conflict—attack, avoid or something else?

3. What have you learned about dealing with anger from your parents and from your life experiences?

4. What have you learned from this chapter about how to deal with anger?

5. Is there someone you find it very hard to forgive?

6. How did this person hurt or offend you?

7. What stops you from being able to forgive them? How might you be able to begin the process of forgiveness?

8. Can you trust that justice will one day be done?

10

THE TANGLED WEB OF GUILT AND SHAME

You come of the Lord Adam and the Lady Eve, that is both honor enough to lift up the head of the poorest beggar, and shame enough to bow the shoulders of the greatest emperor on earth.

C. S. LEWIS, *PRINCE CASPIAN*

Macbeth, crazy with guilt and depression after murdering the king in order to take the throne himself, cried out, "Canst thou not minister to a mind diseased, pluck from the memory a rooted sorrow?" He longed to be able to undo the past. Both he and the doctor in the tragedy knew that medicine would not cure straightforward guilt: "Throw physic to the dogs—I'll have none of it." Macbeth was left to sort out his inner anguish alone, and the doctor, unable to cure Macbeth's distress, said, "Therein the patient must minister to himself."[1]

Guilt is another cause of depression. Like bitterness and resentment, guilt can eat into our hearts and cause physical and psychological problems. In Psalm 32, David described the physical and psychological effects of unconfessed sin:

> When I kept silent,
>   my bones wasted away

through my groaning all day long.
For day and night
    your hand was heavy upon me;
my strength was sapped
    as in the heat of summer.
Then I acknowledged my sin to you
    and did not cover up my iniquity.
I said, "I will confess
    my transgressions to the LORD"—
and you forgave
    the guilt of my sin. (Psalm 32:3-5)

Confession and forgiveness bring great relief.

REAL GUILT OR FALSE GUILT?

There are many people today who regard most guilt as neurotic, a product of a narrow-minded Christian heritage. They talk about getting rid of "guilt feelings" and rarely about the fact of real guilt. In a culture that has turned away from absolute moral values, it is hard to suggest that we may be offending some divine commands of a creator God. But if there is a God who has given us instructions about the best way to live in his world, then we will not be surprised if we feel guilty when we ignore the Maker's instructions. The rules are there for our good, and we suffer when we do not follow them. Guilt is not just a feeling; it is a moral reality. Thankfully, there is a remedy for sin and guilt. We are not left like Macbeth to minister to ourselves. God loves us so passionately that he sent his Son to rescue us from our predicament. Because Christ took the punishment for sin that we deserve, God offers us free forgiveness and cancellation of debts.

But what about those who feel guilt when they have not done anything wrong, like John? He was convinced he had cheated on his tax returns. His firm had been having financial difficulties for several years, and he had become progressively more depressed. He had a deep conviction that he had done something terribly wrong and that this depression was a punishment from God. On examination, his accounts were immaculate and there was no trace of any dishonesty to be found. He was a sensitive, perfection-istic man who tended to feel guilty about even the smallest things that went wrong in his life. For him, it was the state of depression that produced a false belief that he was guilty.

Dealing with guilt may be even more complex. Jeanette's parents were always arguing when she was small. Her father was very strict; her mother, a timid soul. Jeanette would try to make peace between them, and somehow always felt their quarrels were her fault. If she were a good girl, maybe her parents would be nice to each other. When she was nine years old, her father became ill with cancer and was obviously dying. He was often irrational, but she nursed him with devotion. However, sometimes he would try to stroke her body and touch her genitals, and in her silence, she would secretly wish that he were dead. Soon after, he died.

Some years later, she became a Christian but found it very difficult to believe that God could accept her as she was, to forgive her "evil" thoughts. She felt guilty because of her longing that her father would die, and she found it hard to believe that God was not like her own father and that he could really forgive her—even when she had such murderous thoughts.

Because of her parents' fights she was also very scared of arguments and felt guilty whenever she stood up for herself. Consequently she was very timid, and her desire to please meant that others took advantage of her kindness. She blamed herself for not resisting her father's sexual advances because she was afraid of making him angry. Any thought of sexual intimacy in marriage filled her with shame and disgust. Her mind and emotions were a tangle of anxiety, fear, shame, depression and guilt. Her conscience was scarred and confused.

CONSCIENCE: CREDIBLE OR CONFUSING?

So what is conscience? Some say it is an infallible guide to right and wrong, the inner voice of God?[2] It is the part of our being that makes us feel guilty or ashamed when we have done something wrong. It affirms our sense of acceptability and wholeness when we have done something right—a good or clear conscience (1 Timothy 1:5). The Greeks believed that the conscience was a totally reliable inner faculty: "There is no witness so terrible—no accuser so powerful—as conscience which dwells within us."[3]

Freud, however, questioned this view, suggesting that the over-scrupulous conscience (the tyrannical super-ego) might in fact be the product of one's upbringing. He believed that conscience was formed by a child's internal acceptance of parental values and cultural standards. For example, a child with a very strict father would have a very strict conscience. Freud recognized the need for some sort of restraints on the sexual and aggressive drives within us, but he certainly did not believe in God-given moral standards; therefore, guilt was only in relation to parental and societal values.

Seared or supersensitive? For someone who has been raised in a family where lying and deceit are the norm and promiscuous sex is accepted uncritically, guilt is a rare experience. Paul talks of those whose "consciences have been seared as with a hot iron" (1 Timothy 4:2). The image is of nerve endings in the superficial layers of the skin being burnt so that there is no longer any feeling. Then the conscience is insensitive to those things that really matter. It has become silenced by misuse or abuse. Paul also speaks of "minds and consciences [that] are corrupted" (Titus 1:15).

On the other hand, for someone who has grown up in a family where they have been constantly criticized and, as a result, have developed very high (perfectionistic) standards, a sense of guilt, shame and failure is a continual experience. Paul also speaks of those with an overactive, misguided or "weak conscience," those who did not believe it was right to eat the meat that had been offered to idols. He did not see the prohibition against eating that meat as an absolute moral law; therefore, while he encouraged the other Christians to respect such people, he implied that their consciences were oversensitive or a little too scrupulous (1 Corinthians 8). Because our consciences are imperfect, they need to be shaped by and tested against the Word of God.

In Psalm 51:5-6, David acknowledged that he needed truth and wisdom in the "inmost place" of his heart. In Psalm 119:9-11, he affirmed that it is God's word that is the ultimate standard—his conscience was not enough on its own: "How can a young man keep his way pure? By living according to your word . . . I have hidden your word in my heart that I might not sin against you." Or in Proverbs 14:12, "There is a way that seems right to a man, but in the end it leads to death." So inner guidance is neither automatically reliable nor responsible; it must be purified to conform to the will of God.

Before the Fall, Adam and Eve had the law of God in their hearts and naturally did what was right. After the Fall, they were (and we are) confused and broken in every area. Reason, will, emotions and conscience all swing between extremes and need some reference point. Our consciences need to be tested and adjusted, just as a sailor needs to have his compass checked against magnetic north. His compass is not automatically reliable, because it may have been thrown off by metal objects on the boat or by variations in the local magnetic field.

Our consciences are the result of an interaction between God's law, our parents' values and cultural values, and it is important to distinguish between false guilt feelings and real guilt, between an oversensitive conscience and a true sense of right and wrong. However, it is probably more common in this relativistic culture that young people do not have sensitive-enough consciences.

The "death of God" leads to the death of conscience, because without God, we lose any external reference point for reality and values, and many think that we are at liberty to redefine reality with ourselves at the center. *Conscience,* as a concept of absolute value, is a word that will probably remain alive only within the Christian culture. Thankfully, most caring humanists still have some vestiges of morality and will not take the "death of God" to its logical extreme because they still accept the golden rule—doing to others what you would like them to do to you.[4] But others are very selective, ultimately making decisions only on what is best for them and what they feel like doing.[5]

GETTING RID OF GUILT THE WRONG WAY

A sense of real guilt should prompt some response, but it may be handled in a number of unhelpful ways.

Ignoring and blame-shifting. Very often, it is swept under the carpet and suppressed, because it is painful and difficult to accept one's faults. Repressed guilt leads to self-justification and pride, blindness to our own faults. At the same time, there may be a deep awareness of something wrong, which may turn into irritation and anger—particularly directed at the person who stimulates the guilty feelings. This often involves shifting the blame, as Adam did to Eve in Genesis 3:12, "The woman you put here with me—she gave me some fruit." He was blaming Eve but also blaming God for giving him an imperfect companion!

Doing everything right. Some people attempt to get rid of guilt by subconsciously thinking that if they try to do everything right then they will make amends for what they have done wrong. This may develop into perfectionism, especially for those who are desperately afraid of losing control of themselves and are anxious to please others and God. These people may not be able to rest until their houses are spotless, their bodies beautiful, their performance perfect and their lives in immaculate order. This can also be a way of coping with not just guilt but all uncomfortable emotions—like anger, anxiety, shame or depression. In theological terms, people who live this way may be exhibiting an extreme form of living under law rather than grace.

Denying it exists. Another increasingly common way of getting rid of guilt is to deny failure and sin. Some therapists would say, after all, guilt and a belief in any absolute standards are only neurotic hang-ups from old-fashioned Christian ways. Freud's followers have tended to throw out the baby with the bathwater, the good conscience with the overscrupulous conscience, and without God, we alone are the judges of what is right and wrong.

Drowning it out. Conscience may also be simply deadened or drowned with drugs or alcohol. Or at the other extreme, guilt may become an obsession, a fixed belief that a person is too bad for anyone to forgive so she may wallow in a mire of self-recrimination.

GETTING RID OF GUILT THE RIGHT WAY

In contrast to these many unhelpful ways of dealing with guilt, health and sanity come from recognizing and acknowledging real guilt and appropriate guilt feelings. There is only one way of truly getting rid of guilt. The Bible tells us that if we think we have no sin then we are deceiving ourselves, but if we confess we will be forgiven (1 John 1:8-9). Because of Jesus' death for us, we can have confidence to "draw near to God with a sincere heart in full assurance of faith, having our hearts sprinkled to cleanse us from a guilty conscience" (Hebrews 10:22).

Pardon leads to peace, a refinement of conscience and increasing right sensitivity. As we soak ourselves in the Word of God, we will become more aware of our sin. The Sermon on the Mount underlines the fact that God is far more concerned about the attitude of our hearts than with our external actions.

By talking to ourselves, friends, God and, perhaps, a counselor, we can sort out the inappropriate guilt from the real guilt. The lies of a twisted conscience that produces false guilt feelings have to be countered with the truth about God's view of right and wrong.

It may take many months (or even years) of reminding ourselves of the truth about a situation to erase false guilt feelings. However, when false guilt is not recognized for what it is and we do not have a sense of innocence or forgiveness, the outraged conscience continues to demand some form of punishment and may extract it in the form of depression or psychosomatic illness. We may recognize pathological guilt underlying severe depression or in the person with an obsessive, perfectionistic personality.

Ultimately Jesus Christ alone can clear the guilty conscience. The Swiss psychiatrist Paul Tournier sums it up well:

> It is abundantly clear that no man lives free of guilt. Guilt is universal. But according as it is repressed or recognized, so it sets in motion one of two contradictory processes: repressed, it leads to anger, rebellion, fear and anxiety, a deadening of conscience, an increasing inability to recognize one's faults, and a growing dominance of aggressive tendencies.
>
> But consciously recognized . . . it leads to repentance, to the peace and security of divine pardon, and in that way to a progressive refinement of conscience and a steady weakening of aggressive impulses. . . . The enemy guilt becomes a friend because it leads to an experience of grace.[6]

SHAME

Shame is a much more complex experience than guilt and often drives anxiety, depression, anger and perfectionism. It is interwoven with guilt, and we need more help to identify it. If *guilt* is about what we have *done, shame* is about who we *are*. In his book *Beyond Identity*, Dick Keyes points out that guilt relates to morals and shame to models.[7] By *models* he means those people in our families or among our friends or in our society to whom we look for examples of how to live. For example, we may feel ashamed of our bodies, which is partly because of the self-consciousness that came after the Fall (before the Fall, Adam and Eve "were both naked, and they felt no shame"; Genesis 2:25) and partly because we do not measure up (or down!) to the bodies of the beautiful people of Hollywood and the advertisements in health and fashion magazines.

There is often shame in talking about shame, and shame may be an experience that many have not named. They may confuse it with guilt or it may be pushed below the level of awareness because it is too painful to feel. Not dealing with shame in a healthy way means that we often deny it or hide from it. It may surface as painful self-absorption and depression, when we want to withdraw and hide. Often it rears its head in vacillation between self-contempt and contempt toward others in our lives—especially those who cause us to feel ashamed!

Sometimes I feel a great surge of self-contempt when I don't live up to being the ideal husband, father, counselor or professor. Then I work hard to please and appease those around me. Other times I will find myself withdrawing and inwardly fuming; other times, I will be outwardly critical toward my wife for making some comment that questions my judgment or highlights my inadequacy and imperfection. Sometimes I am tempted to lash out and shame the person who I think is shaming me. So deep is our longing for significance and belonging that anything that makes us feel insignificant or rejected will trigger shame. Discovering the things that trigger our shame and finding healthier ways to deal with them makes us much less vulnerable to depression. Too easily I allow my models (or we could call them mini-idols) to rule my sense of value and, therefore, my sense of worth.

The Bible, however, clearly describes two polarities of experience: guilt and innocence, shame and honor. When we do something wrong, we usually feel guilt and shame—or, to use a more familiar and milder word for the latter, we may feel embarrassed. However, sometimes we may feel a sense of shame when we have not done anything morally wrong but when we have done something that we think makes us unacceptable to our friends—such as telling a joke at which nobody laughs or dressing inappropriately for a party.[8]

So shame is an experience of being a dishonorable, inferior or worthless person. It results from failing to live up to expectations—either our own, other people's or God's. It is usually triggered when we anticipate disapproval or rejection, and when our foolishness, weakness or sin is exposed. It is often experienced as loss of face. It may be accompanied by embarrassed blushing, a desire to avert one's eyes and avoid anyone's gaze.

The psalmist wrote, "My disgrace is before me all day long, and my face is covered with shame" (Psalm 44:15). Shame is the experience of *disgrace*. It is as if others can see right into our deficient souls and disapprove of what they see. Brene Brown, a research professor and author, summarizes her many years of research on shame with this definition: "Shame is the intensely painful feeling or experience of believing we are flawed and therefore unworthy of acceptance and belonging."[9]

Men and women experience shame for different things as they try to live up to the cultural expectations of body image, work and parenting, and how they handle emotions—the "shoulds" of life! Men *should* not be weak, emotional or incompetent. Women *should* be thin, beautiful, self-confident and sexy. Furthermore, what we feel shame for can vary by context. For example, in some schools a boy may feel ashamed if he does not get As on all his exams; in another school, where the few very bright students are mocked for being snobs, he may feel shame for getting As.

False shame. Many of our Christian young people know that sexual promiscuity is wrong, but most of their non-Christian friends think they are odd to be so old-fashioned. It will be hard for these young people not to feel ashamed for doing what is right. If they have the strength to stand out against their non-Christian friends, they may come to feel a sense of innocence (the opposite of guilt) and honor (the opposite of shame) in relation to God, their Christian friends and family, and themselves. However, because we all have a strong desire to be accepted by those around us, we may sometimes be ashamed of *doing* things that are morally *right*, and we may then be ashamed of *not* doing things that are morally *wrong*.[10]

Ideally our *morals* and *models* should coincide so that the people we look up to are the people who live with Christian values. The apostle Paul encouraged Christians to imitate him even as he imitated Christ. Dick Keyes encourages us to challenge and expose the false heroes and models of the day, and to recognize when our values are being shaped by them rather than by biblical values.

Separating shame from guilt. In the last chapter, I discussed untangling uncomfortable knots of righteous and unrighteous anger in our hearts, so also we have to learn to deal with the complex knots of guilt and shame. When we are confused about this, it is helpful to write down our thoughts or to talk with a friend to separate out the strands of false guilt from real guilt and appropriate shame from inappropriate shame. Those who do wrong *should* feel guilt and often do feel some shame.[11] If we are innocent we need not be ashamed.[12] Ideally real guilt and appropriate shame should go together, but in reality, guilt and shame are sometimes together,[13] sometimes separate and sometimes in conflict with each other. When we feel ashamed of doing what is right, or of being or doing something that is morally neutral (such as being the physical shape we inherited or wearing clothes we enjoy), then we need to remind ourselves of how God sees us and enjoy his acceptance in order to allow other people's disapproval (real or imaginary) to matter to us less and less.

If you have been raised by very critical parents or have experienced mental, physical or sexual abuse, you are likely dealing with a lot of shame. You wrongly feel responsible for things that happened to you through no fault of your own, and you feel ashamed that you are such a "bad" person. You may feel ashamed of your own God-given longings for connection and intimacy. You may have done wrong things in reaction to the wrong done against you, and for that you may feel real guilt, which can be confessed and forgiven. Research confirms that appropriate guilt is healthy and is associated with positive moods and relationships, but shame most often leads to unhealthy and destructive consequences.

Luke, who wrote the second letter about anger in the last chapter, grew up in a legalistic Christian family, where he often felt bad if he did not meet his parents' expectations. His father was a leader in the local Christian community, and Luke was a quiet, shy introvert who felt out of place and inferior. Most of the boys (and later, girls) in the neighborhood and at school teased him for being a geek. He was awarded a scholarship to a very good school where most of the other kids came from very affluent backgrounds, and there he was very ashamed of (among other things) the car in which he arrived at school each day. He remembers often sitting at home crying in a darkened room. Then there was a scandal in the church and community when his father's sexual sins were exposed to the world and he carried the shame of belonging to "that family." In college he gave up going to church, tried drugs, alcohol and sex to drown his pain, and found that no relationship lasted for long. This only compounded his depression and shame. To compensate, he would often fantasize about being a famous musician or doctor, imagining the admiring crowds or patients. Thankfully he became a Christian, married a woman who accepted and loved him well, had children, found a job where he could use his creativity, and began to care for others in an inner-city predominantly black neighborhood and church. All these things are helping him toward health and healing. Then he came for counseling and we have had to work through some painful things together as he has processed his depression and anger.

Shame arising from many years of abuse in childhood feels more like an indelible stain going through our whole being, staining our souls, defining our thoughts and feelings—even our core identity—as bad, disgusting, worthless and beyond redemption. How can those feelings and thoughts be healed? Only in the context of a relationship where we are told and shown repeatedly that what we learned as children is a lie, and that the reality is that we are loved and valued. Such a grace-filled relationship brings healing, and only God is big enough to do that perfectly—though others can help as the hands and feet of God. Do you remember how the prodigal son returned to his father after blowing his inheritance on fast-track living in the big city (Luke 15:11-32)? He repented and, in his shame, protested that he was not worthy to be a son anymore. His father could have disowned him and made him a servant; that would have been the cultural norm. But the father would have none of it. He accepted him back into the family with a magnificent welcome-home party.

So guilt leads to repentance and shame gives rise to deep sorrow over the effects of our own sin or the sin of others toward us. Acceptance and belonging are what gradually erode shame, and it takes time. We receive acceptance and grace from God, but we need to also receive it from people around us (friends, family, counselors, therapists, pastors), who have seen us at our weakest and most despicable, yet still love us and care enough to continue in relationship with us over many years.[14] Being able to share our stories of shame with another human being who listens well and does not shame us again is incredibly healing.[15]

ACCEPTING FORGIVENESS AND GRACE

You might think that accepting forgiveness and forgiving others who have wronged us should be easy, but many people find it very hard—and this is at the root of much insecurity and depression.

Why is it so hard? Francis Schaeffer never tired of saying that Christianity is the easiest religion in the world: we come to God with nothing in our hands to receive his free forgiveness and love. But it is also the hardest religion in the world *because* that is all we have to do!

There is a deep-seated pride in all of us that we can make ourselves good enough for God by our own efforts, or if some punishment is deserved for justice to be done, then we should take it ourselves. We think that we must make amends for our failures and imperfections. Some forms of perfectionism are driven by guilt and shame, by the sense that only when I am perfect or when I have pushed myself to the limits of endurance is acceptance possible. Accepting forgiveness and grace is especially difficult for those who have been heavily criticized as children and made to feel that there is little, if any, good in them. They may feel that they are unforgiveable and be left with a deep longing for, yet a distrust in, the possibility of acceptance and forgiveness.

At the other extreme, there are those who have been raised to have a high opinion of themselves—the self-made person who thinks of himself as a good person—who find the thought of needing to be forgiven insulting or even threatening, as if it undermines his whole identity and the basis for his sense of acceptance by others. These people rarely feel shame or guilt. They tend toward narcissism. In a similar way, some of these people accept forgiveness too lightly because they do not have a serious enough view of sin and of the greatness of God's love and mercy, while those mentioned in the previous paragraph will probably not accept forgiveness easily, because they do not see the greatness of God's love and mercy to cover what they believe are the most terrible sins.

The wonder is that God can and does forgive us as we accept him as Savior and Lord. Christ died to take the punishment we deserve. We can stand as Christian did in John Bunyan's *Pilgrim's*

Progress, at the foot of the cross, watching our burden of sin and guilt roll away down the hill and out of sight. Nothing that we can ever do is good enough to earn God's forgiveness. He offers it freely as we acknowledge our sin and begin to live for him. He accepts us with all our failings and weaknesses—and then begins the process of remaking us so that we, one day, will be without sin. "By one sacrifice," Christ has made us acceptable to God (Hebrews 10:14), and God will not remember our sins anymore. The guilt of the past is dealt with and can be put behind us; the future is secure because of his assurance of continuous acceptance and forgiveness. Our shame is wiped away and our honor as a child of God is restored.

The psychologist Carl Rogers discovered that the first step to helping people change is to accept them with all their hang-ups and problems. Even though he wrongly believed that we can find all the answers to our problems in ourselves, he was still discovering something of the way God has made us. When we are accepted as unique and valuable to someone, that gives us a measure of security to take risks and make changes. When we feel unacceptable to anyone, we are often so insecure that we retreat into a corner and build a wall around ourselves to reduce the risk of change. How much greater can be our freedom when we know we are loved, accepted and forgiven by our Creator, who adopts us into his family, offers us his friendship and gives us his Holy Spirit to help us daily to become more like him?

QUESTIONS FOR REFLECTION AND DISCUSSION

1. Are you aware of carrying a burden of guilt or shame?
2. Can you begin to tease out the different strands of guilt and shame in your thinking?
3. Have you recognized and named shame in your life before?
4. Where did your guilty or shame-filled feelings and thoughts

come from? Childhood? Past relationships? Past or present failures?

5. How do these feelings and thoughts make you sad, depressed, angry, contemptuous or confused?

6. What is the difference in the solution to shame and guilt?

7. What has been your experience of moving beyond feelings of guilt and shame?

8. How does the Spirit of God, through the Bible, speak to you about dealing with this?

11

REDUCING VULNERABILITY AND MOVING TOWARD HEALING

May . . . the God of peace, sanctify you through and through.

1 THESSALONIANS 5:23

He has sent me to bind up the brokenhearted,
to proclaim . . . release from darkness for the prisoners, . . .
to bestow on them . . . a garment of praise
instead of a spirit of despair.

ISAIAH 61:1, 3

We have looked at the biological, psychological and social factors that make us vulnerable to sinking into depression under the stresses and pressures of life. We do not have control over many of the things that happen to us, but we do have some control over how we react to them. We can push back against the different aspects of our fallen world—against our fallen bodies by learning good self-care and with the use of medication when necessary; against our fallen minds by learning healthier thought patterns and godly ways to deal with grief, anxiety, anger, guilt and shame; and against our fallen relationships by learning to share more honestly and deeply so that we might love better. Some things we can do on our own, but some need the help of another person. There are many aspects to this healing process. Ideally, we should all be building these habits of heart and life from an early age to help us on the road of sanctification, healing and the integration of the different parts of our brains. Unfortunately, most of us only begin to do this after things have gone wrong. Good parents and good churches teach and model these principles, thus doing a lot of preventive work.

PUSHING BACK AGAINST THE FALL

In order to push back against the Fall and reduce our vulnerability to depression, I will summarize some principles of good self-care, which are derived both from Scripture and from common-grace wisdom, and then I will walk us through a counseling situation where many of these are addressed. In severe depression, these will be hard to do, but in milder depression, they should help from going down further and, in recovery, will speed progress toward the light.

- Reflect on and be honest about what you are really feeling and thinking. It may take a while, and you may need help to name and own your feelings.

- Allow yourself to feel grief and sorrow in times of loss.

- Begin to identify unhealthy patterns of thinking, including for example, perfectionism, all-or-nothing thinking, pessimism, believing lies, deep fears or difficulty trusting.

- Reflect on how your life story has shaped your thinking and feeling about yourself, other people, God and life.

- Train your brain away from negative, pessimistic, all-or-nothing thinking. These thoughts and feelings have a habitual aspect to them. When you find yourself ruminating, call a friend or do something you enjoy to distract yourself.

- Examine your deepest longings, desires and expectations to try to discern which ones are God-given and good, and which are distorted by sin and evil.

- Be aware of the ways you feel and react when other people sin against you.

- Identify and name different aspects of that tangled knot of feelings in your heart—guilt, shame, sadness, anger and so on.

- Acknowledge and repent of sinful anger, envy, bitterness and other ways you have tried to dull pain, as well as any anger and disappointment with God.

- Recognize there are places that the devil has a foothold in your life and learn to resist him. These are often times when we experience frequent temptation or sin.

- Push yourself to get involved in some way with family, church and community. Don't remain isolated. Act as if you enjoy meeting people and gradually you will feel more like doing so. Social support reduces your vulnerability to depression.

- Do some things for fun.

- Eat healthy food, reduce or abstain from caffeine and alcohol intake, and take fish oil (combined EPA and DHA 2 g/day) and vitamin D (2000 IU/day) and perhaps folate (vitamin B_9).[1]

- Take regular exercise, listen to calming music, and learn breathing, relaxation[2] and mindfulness exercises.[3]

- When caught in the apathy and fatigue of depression, do small necessary tasks in brief (just a few minutes at first) episodes. Don't take on large (bound-to-fail) tasks.

- Practice thankfulness for the good things in your life. Keep a journal.[4]

- Meditate on beauty in nature and on the amazing stories, poetry, laments, prayers and teachings in the Bible.

- Care for others in some way—especially if they are less fortunate than you.

- Use medication if necessary and only with professional oversight. With your doctor, find the right antidepressant and dose with the least side effects. Be realistic about the need to be on medication for some time.

- Remember that change and recovery from depression often happen in slow and subtle shifts of thinking, feeling and doing.

- Talk to God in prayer. You can pour out your worst and most shameful feelings to him—knowing that he loves you, wants to know your heart and wants to help you out of the pit of depression.[5]

- Understand that you have great dignity and depravity, beauty and brokenness, because you are amazingly made in God's image but are deeply affected by the Fall and sin.

- Embrace the big picture with patience and hope, learning to "groan well" in a fallen world.

- Accept that life is full of sorrow and rejoicing. Have confidence that God is for you and not against you. Look forward to the day when there will be no more tears, depression, anxiety or pain.

Pastoral care, professional counseling and therapy are just a part of this. They can be very helpful to encourage all these steps, but they are most helpful in identifying unhealthy patterns of thinking and relating. To be honest, it is not easy to define what counseling or psychotherapy is, so I will describe how I approach counseling someone who struggles with depression and perfectionism.[6] I am inviting you into a therapy session in the hope that this will give you some understanding of how a therapist might approach such a problem. As I reflect on what happened with this one person, I will also reflect on other people and on the nature of the process of counseling. I describe six stages, but these do not necessarily follow in strict order. They often overlap and interweave with each other. Although built around Sarah's story, which is not her real name, it is a composite of several clients with similar issues.

A FRAMEWORK FOR COUNSELING IN THE KEY OF D

Drawing out her story. Sarah came to see me having heard a lecture that I gave on perfectionism, and she recognized that much of her own perfectionism was unhealthy. She also struggled with depression.[7] Initially I wanted to get to know her, build trust and to draw out her story. I did this by exploring her presenting problem in the context of her life story, in an atmosphere of genuineness, empathy and warmth.[8] This meant listening deeply and well. I needed to practice the art of asking good questions to help Sarah tell her story, to discover who and what had shaped her into the person she is today. Some people talk easily and need only to be guided by a few comments and questions; others need to be drawn out. I listened to Sarah's well-organized and systematic words, I heard her fearful, anxious and controlled emotions, I read her tense and inhibited body language, and I noted how I was reacting inside with empathy, parental protectiveness, warmth and curiosity.

Sarah, on the surface, was highly successful and much admired by others. She had been a leader of her Christian group in college, was good at sports and graduated summa cum laude. But the price she paid for her success was stress, anxiety, depression, shame and guilt for not living up to her own very high standards. None of these feelings were ever shared with anyone else, so she was regarded as someone who achieved very high standards with effortless ease. But her "imperfect" emotions had been held in check for a long time and were now beginning to find the cracks in her mask. She was finding it harder to fight back tears, to sleep well and to concentrate on her work, so she reluctantly sought help. She told me:

> Perfectionism pervades all areas of my life—daily routine, vocation and even relationships. I thrive on routine and familiar surroundings, because it helps me to be in control, feel competent and, ultimately, feel perfect. I do not like new roles and responsibilities, because there is room for incompetence. When I became a teaching assistant for the first time I felt that every lesson that I had to teach needed to be "perfect." This was almost debilitating. I would literally sit in my office for five hours and go through files and files on lessons and activities and would not find the "perfect" lesson to teach. I would just end up winging something last minute.

After most lessons she was full of self-contempt and was sometimes afraid that she might impulsively harm herself. To fail at anything meant that she was a worthless person in her mind.

Discovering dignity and depravity. As I go deep into my clients' stories, I discover the complex mixture of dignity (being created in the image of God) and depravity (being fallen and sinful), which is in all of our hearts. I am often reminded of C. S. Lewis's Prince Caspian: "You come of the Lord Adam and the Lady Eve, that is both honor enough to lift up the head of the poorest beggar, and shame enough to bow the shoulders of the greatest emperor on earth."

As I listened to the story of another client who was deeply mired in sexual addiction and depression, I found myself appalled at the depravity to which he had sunk. Then I discovered that he was also a very sensitive person, a gifted musician and artist with deep longings for affirmation and approval—a person who had been rejected by his father because art and music were "for sissies." I felt both admiration and sorrow for him as I caught a glimpse of his dignity.

Sarah's "depravity" was not immediately obvious because she has always been very obedient and successful. Everyone admired her for her maturity and willingness to help. However, her powerful people-pleasing tendencies and her pride were gradually exposed as methods of self-protection.

People usually come to counselors because their lives are in trouble and they need help, so we as therapists often hear stories of loss, depression, deceit, betrayal or addiction—stories of the darker side of life, of brokenness, of grief and, of course, depravity. Proverbs 20:5 wisely says, "The purposes of a person's heart are deep waters, but one who has insight draws them out." As humans, we don't know our own hearts very well, and we need others to help us to explore them—to sort out our good desires, dreams and motives from the bad ones. We need our gifts and dignity affirmed, as well as our bentness and depravity exposed. We need help to see how our legitimate God-given longings have turned to lust and our desires have mutated to demands. We need someone to draw out the damaging effect of ours and others' depravity, and we need this person to help us understand how this depravity has affected our hearts in good and bad ways. We need this person to be a gracious, accepting presence as we experience distress, despair, shame and godly sorrow at our wounds, deficiencies, folly and sin. In other words, this person needs to be a godly, gracious presence as we face ourselves more honestly. I think of Jesus and his heart-searching questions to the woman at the well (John 4:1-42).

Delighting in and dreaming of dignity. As I got to know Sarah over the first few weeks of therapy, I began to delight in and dream of her dignity as someone made in the image of God. I do not find it too difficult to focus on the dark side of life and on weaknesses because that is what people usually bring to counseling, but it is important for me to notice strengths and to affirm the gifts, resources and dignity of people made in the image of God. That image, although defaced and distorted by sin, is still very evident. We can see glimpses in their God-given beauty and dignity. From my time spent with Francis Schaeffer, I have his image of us as "glorious ruins" in my mind. I imagine what some ancient ruined castle or cathedral would be like if restored to its former glory.

I see dignity, for example, in artistic or musical creativity, in the ability to carefully organize and plan, and in sensitivity to other's pain. I found myself trying to envision Sarah with her God-given temperament and all her gifts being used to the full—with her sinful desires and patterns taken away. I asked myself, *What does God desire for Sarah now and in the future?* I tried to help her reframe her struggle and suffering to be able to see how God was using it to change her character to be more like Christ. Like most perfectionists, Sarah had high moral standards, a great work ethic and incredible integrity. Because she was eager to please, she was always extremely helpful to others. She desperately wanted to do what was right and good, so I could affirm and enjoy this good side of her perfectionism. It is part of the diversity of God's good creation that he has made some of us with a love for order, structure and high standards. These are character traits and virtues that are to be encouraged, but even these good traits can become distorted and exaggerated because some of the deeper roots and motives behind them are self-centered, self-protective and sinful—part of our depravity.

I wanted Sarah not only to understand her God-created dignity but also to understand how, as a believer, she had a new identity in Christ. She is a much-loved child of the King, her sin (or depravity) is covered with the righteousness of Christ, and the Spirit of God is working in her to change her.

Discerning the damage to her dignity. Before I moved to help Sarah see her own sin and depravity, I wanted to discern the damage to her dignity that had been done by others' sin. Sarah was, as counselor and author Michael Emlet points out, "saint, sufferer, and sinner" all at the same time.[9] But I wanted to know how she had been disappointed in her longings for love and acceptance from parents, siblings or friends. How had she been betrayed and damaged by physical, emotional or sexual abuse, leaving a proneness to shame, anxiety, fear, depression, anger and lack of trust? How had she been defiled by another's lusts and lies? Sometimes I weep openly, though more commonly it is inward, as I hear terrible stories of deception, betrayal, revenge, and loss of love and hope. I find comfort in knowing that God's heart is full of grief over the sin and brokenness of the world.[10] Entering God's grief and suffering over the world, as well as entering into the suffering of others, I find that "weep[ing] with those who weep" (Romans 12:15 ESV) is part of our calling. As I do this I have to face the inevitable questions from my clients: "Why is this happening to me?" "Where is God?" and "If there is a God, how can he be good and allow me to suffer in this way?"

Thankfully Sarah had not experienced sexual or physical abuse. However, she had perfectionist tendencies from an early age, and these were reinforced by her perfectionist culture (Korean American) and by her parents' focus on her faults and deficiencies rather than on the many things she did well. The latter were taken for granted! Sarah told me that Korean parents expect high, if not perfect, academic performance, and they will often hire tutors to help their children get As. Korean parents also want a perfect reputation: "Anything," Sarah said, "that is shameful is supposed to be hidden or swept under the rug."[11] She continued,

> I recall many times after I finished my chores, like sweeping the kitchen floor or vacuuming the carpet, I expected my mom to thank me or affirm me for doing my chores. However, instead of hearing words of encouragement, much to my dismay, she would say things like, "You missed a spot." This

little phrase really did impact me so that whenever I did the dishes or cleaned my room, I would make sure it was immaculate. Along with my mom, even though my dad is not a perfectionist, he has indirectly influenced me to become a perfectionist. I specifically remember a time when I wanted to arrange a delicious tray of food for him. Somehow my hands slipped and I managed to drop the tray. All the dishes and food came tumbling down with a loud clatter. Instead of asking if I was okay, I remember my dad scorning me for being clumsy. Since then I have felt the pressure to be "perfect" and "flawless."

After one of the sessions with Sarah, other clients who had initially sought my help for depression came to mind. John remembered his father as a workaholic and a hard taskmaster who expected his sons to mow the lawn and leave perfect lines as on a Wimbledon tennis court. Suzy remembered her father sexually abusing her when she was a child, and having to cover the sense of guilt and shame by pleasing everyone and being the brightest and most beautiful at school—lest anyone ever discovered her terrible secret. Michael remembered his parents' quarrels and the constant threats of divorce. In his insecurity he created his own very controlled world of symmetry, structure and order in his bedroom. David remembered his grandmother repeatedly holding him down in a bath of water to punish him for some minor mistake. Believing her lie that he was such a bad person, he worked incredibly hard to get straight As and dress perfectly so that the punishment would stop. It was counseling that helped them to understand the underlying cause of the depressive symptoms that drove them to seek help.

I often tell my students that we need to learn to be "good groaners" on this earth. We are called to rejoice in the hope of the gospel but also called to groan because we live with all the terrible effects of the Fall, others' sin and our own sin. Paul wrote that the "whole creation has been groaning. . . . Not only so, but we . . . groan" (Romans 8:22-23). Sarah needed permission to be sad, to grieve and to be angry. She had become so good at controlling her emotions that she needed help to connect her thoughts with her feelings, to sometimes stay with the feelings and recognize them. Often she would feel guilty and ashamed for feeling angry or sad. As a child she had been ignored or punished for showing such feelings. Her parents did not know how to deal with their own emotions, much less with hers. She was amazed one day when I was almost in tears as she told me the story of how, as an eight-year old, she had been left all alone, confused, very sad and with no one to talk to after her grandfather died in a very distressing and painful way. My sadness validated the normality of her own sadness and took away some of her shame. She had never had anyone help her to understand her emotions. She had come to believe that being needy was weak because expressing her own needs had always led to disappointment. No one would comfort her. So she had learned to be "strong," but in my presence, she learned that it was safe to be weak. She slowly learned to weep and groan well over her own story and over sin and evil in the world. She also learned to be righteously angry and appropriately assertive in relationships, as well as how to distinguish assertiveness from control.

As I enter deeply into the grief and loss of my clients, and empathize with the ways in which they have been wounded by the Fall and by others' sin, I find that a strange movement slowly occurs in their hearts as they begin to see more clearly how they have been sinned against—and also how they have contributed to their suffering and the pain of others by their own sin. It is often only after I have listened well to their stories and allowed trust between us to grow that I earn the right to ask difficult questions that may expose sinful attitudes of the heart. David, after telling me about his "evil" grandmother began to face his sadness, rage and desire that "she would burn in hell." Gradually he was able to move toward forgiveness, leaving justice in the hands of God. Having someone come alongside and tune in to our inner world and reflect with us on our life story is powerfully healing.

As trust grew in our relationship, I could sense that Sarah was becoming more and more dependent on me. She wanted me to tell her what to do and how to do it. She longed for a good protective parent. I felt the pull of what therapists call "countertransference."[12] In my desire to be that good parent, I also sometimes felt frustration at her dependence on me and with her unwillingness to take risks. She enjoyed the way I accepted her with all her imperfections exposed (her parents had not done that), but she was frustrated by my unwillingness to do what they did in giving very clear and rigid guidelines for behavior and life choices. I wanted her to move toward maturity in making her own decisions, being more independent herself and being dependent on God and his guidelines for her life. She was very stuck in all-or-nothing thinking and having a desire for complete control or no control at all. Also having recognized the downside of her perfectionism, she wanted to change but she still thought in very black-and-white ways, so change had to be completed tomorrow or not at all! She had little experience of living in the in-between world of little-by-little, day-by-day change, where most of life is lived.

Part of the healing in therapy came from recognizing how she transferred some of the old feelings toward her parents onto me and then having me be able to provide a corrective relational experience where I reacted (surprisingly to her) in different ways from her earlier childhood relationships. As I (and others around her) accepted her and showed grace with her now more-obvious imperfections—rather than responding with harsh, critical and legalistic expectations—her old patterns of relationship were disturbed and disrupted so new patterns could form.

Disturbing and disrupting depravity. In this stage, I am defining depravity as the damage, distortion and disorder resulting from Adam and Eve's original sin, followed by others' sin and our own sin, which affects every part of us—mind, emotions, will and body. God is at work in us by his Spirit, redeeming these aspects of our being, but he often uses or allows difficult circumstances to bring healing in our lives. Dan Allender writes: "God promises redemption, but his sacred path leads us away from safety, predictability and comfort."[13] When we are insecure, afraid and angry, our self-protective defense mechanisms and the idols that we cling to for comfort and help are exposed.

Psychologist Mark McMinn, in *Why Sin Matters*, discusses the research that painfully demonstrates how pride makes us terribly blind to our own sin.[14] He shows how we tend to see ourselves as more capable and better than we really are, how we tend to explain away our failures, taking credit when things go well and blaming others when things go badly. We don't see very clearly how prone we are to weakness and errors in our thinking. We tend to see evidence that confirms our beliefs and ignore contradictory evidence. It is not surprising, therefore, that we have a hard time taking responsibility for our own sin and folly. As T. S. Eliot said, "Humankind cannot bear very much reality."[15]

We can often see clearly how we have been hurt and betrayed, but it is much harder to see how we have damaged others and offended God by our sinful responses. Our sinful desires and dreams, our wrong thinking and feeling patterns, our self-protective style of relationships, our bitterness and desire for revenge, our avoidance of conflict and pain, and our idolatries are often painfully exposed in counseling. Thankfully this happens little by little. It would be too overwhelming all at once!

As Sarah and I talked, I would often point out examples of all-or-nothing thinking by asking if she noticed what she had just said. I would then ask what thoughts might be more reasonable to help her to live in that unfamiliar world between all-and-nothing, black-and-white. Slowly, she became able to identify the lies she had come to believe about herself and about God. Such a cognitive approach is the mainstay of disturbing and disrupting wrong thinking. Our minds need to be renewed (Romans 12:2).

The effects of the Fall may also be felt in the biological sphere. As we have seen, some people are vulnerable to a malfunction of brain cells and neurotransmitters causing depression, anxiety or, sometimes, frank psychosis. When life threatens to get out of control and we feel very insecure, our brain's alarm signals start firing and we may feel intense anxiety and depression. Medication may be necessary to disrupt and heal this part of our physical depravity. In fact, Sarah found antidepressants helpful over a two-year period when her perfectionism became more extreme and she became depressed, anxious, and obsessive in her thinking and behavior—though thankfully she was never suicidal. I also encouraged her to exercise regularly, eat a healthy diet, and practice breathing and relaxation techniques. She also learned to accept herself and her tendencies toward perfectionism while working against the unhealthy aspects of it.

I helped Sarah to recognize and resist the influence of Satan where he had obtained a "foothold" in her life (Ephesians 4:27). We can give Satan footholds in our lives in areas where our sinful nature is particularly weak—perhaps lust and pornography in one person, anger and loss of control in another. For Sarah, her temptation was strongest in her craving for approval and in her desire to be in control of her life. I was able to help her to recognize and ignore the devil's voice as he, the "father of lies" (John 8:44), whispered in her ear: "You'll never be good enough," "You should never make mistakes," "You can make sure you are in control in this situation to make sure you never experience anything that reminds you of that terrifying shame and humiliation again." Now admittedly, it is very hard to know the difference between the devil's voice, the ways we have been conditioned from childhood, and the thoughts that arise from our sinful nature. Paul does not have a neat formula for making this distinction. He knew that we are at war with the world, the flesh (sinful nature) and the devil, and that we need to learn to protect ourselves with godly armor (see Ephesians 6:10-18). Much counseling involves learning to distinguish between (and name) good and evil, truth and lies.

Probably the most powerful means of exposing heart attitudes is to ask good questions. Jesus would often tell stories or ask a question and then walk away! A good question often acts like a depth charge, or a delayed-action grenade: it sinks deep into the person's heart and explodes with some critical new awareness or perspective provoked by the question. God asked Adam and Eve in the Garden, after they had hidden from him in shame and guilt, "Where are you?" (Genesis 3:9). He knew where they were, but he wanted them to think about why they were hiding from him. Remember how Elijah ran from Jezebel in terror after his great victory over the prophets of Baal? He hid in a cave, and God asked him the same question twice: "What are you doing here, Elijah?" (1 Kings 19:9). The purpose of these questions is surely to provoke heart searching and self-reflection. It is to promote internal dialogue—rather than spoon-feeding a mini sermon with all the answers and what-to-dos neatly packaged for consumption! So it is a challenge for any counselor to be creative with such questions in helping people to examine their own hearts and expose their sin. Dan Allender writes: "My calling is to intrigue, disrupt and invite the other person to consider their own heart."[16]

Over the course of counseling with Sarah, whenever the context seemed appropriate, I asked questions to challenge her thinking. Below are some of the questions I would have asked. If they sound harsh, remember that I had waited to establish trust, and I did not ask them all at once—maybe only one or two in a session, and the more biblical ones came later in therapy. Read the following slowly to let them sink in:

- What are you afraid will happen if you do not get straight As?
- How will people think of you if you are not dressed immaculately and your skin is not flawless?
- How important to you is it that everyone likes you?
- Do you remember when you first felt shame like that?
- Can you really keep everything in your life under your control?
- What did Satan mean when he said that Adam and Eve would be like God if they ate the fruit?
- Have you ever felt that you are trying to be God?
- What do you think Jesus meant when he said "Be perfect" (Matthew 5:48), or "Unless your righteousness surpasses that of the Pharisees and the teachers of the law, you will certainly not enter the kingdom of heaven" (Matthew 5:20)?
- What do you think the apostle Peter meant when he wrote, "Your beauty should not come from outward adornment. . . . Instead, it should be that of your inner self, the unfading beauty of a gentle and quiet spirit" (1 Peter 3:3-4)? What is he saying about priorities?
- How does God see you? Is he punishing you? What do you think he thinks of your imperfections and failures?
- The Bible uses the language of idolatry a lot. That seems very distant to us today, but think with me about that and your dependence on other people's approval, your ambition to reach the perfect weight and to get straight A's. Could we call those forms of idolatry?[17]
- Can you imagine God delighting over you? (This is often a new concept for people, and they find it amazing, wonderful and a little disturbing.)

These questions were initially uncomfortable and challenging for Sarah, disturbing and disrupting her normal thought patterns, while sometimes confronting her with her own sin. However, as we discussed them in the context of her life story and unpacked the meaning of Scriptures that she had misunderstood, these questions had the effect of drawing and directing her toward a different perspective that offered freedom from the tyranny of unhealthy perfectionism. The truth was beginning to set her free from the lies she had believed about God and about herself. What was important was not just the "cognitive restructuring," rather it was the experience of grace in the counseling relationship, an imperfect model of God's gracious relationship with her. As another young woman said to me and to her community of believers: "You accepted me with the worst hanging out." Just as experiences of un-grace and shame so often lock in perfectionist patterns in the psyche, experiences of grace ultimately unlock the prison of neurotic perfectionism; for Sarah, she was able to respond to the difficult questions because she knew that I (and God) accepted her just as she was—flawed, foolish and fragile! At one point, I asked her to take time each day to meditate on Zephaniah 3:17: "The LORD your God is with you, he is mighty to save. He will take great delight in you, he will quiet you with his love, he will rejoice over you with singing."

Drawing and directing. Finally, I wanted to draw and direct[18] Sarah toward new perspectives and hope. From the very beginning of counseling, in how I drew out and understood her story to how I discovered her dignity and depravity, while discerning damage to that dignity, I was drawing her in a particular direction. We moved beyond talking about and grieving broken, unfulfilled and abandoned dreams to a positive dream of how God was shaping her and her life. The Bible speaks of the ultimate goal of being "sanctif[ied] . . . through and through" (1 Thessalonians 5:23), of becoming Christlike. This involves several things for Sarah, including sorrow and grief over the damage done by her parents' ignorance and sin, repentance and sorrow over her own sinful responses, and a growing understanding of herself and of the character of God. It also involved, in biblical language, working against her sinfulness and fallenness in every area of life, putting off her old nature and putting on the new (Ephesians 4:22-24), having her mind renewed (Romans 12:2), learning to love God and her neighbor more truly, and moving toward true humanness, wholeness and holiness.

I wanted to help Sarah to understand her own story in the light of God's big story of creation, fall, redemption and future glory. I wanted to draw and direct her away from the idols of appearance and performance and toward the true and living God, away from a life of frustration, despair, depression and legalism toward a vision of gradual change into who she was intended to be—toward love, faith, truth and hope, a transformation that will be completed in glory.

Along the way, I also shared with her a page from the story of *The Velveteen Rabbit* to illustrate how long, slow, deep and painful, but good, the transformation may be.

> "Real isn't how you are made," said the Skin Horse. "It's a thing that happens to you. When a child loves you for a long, long time, not just to play with, but REALLY loves you, then you become Real."
>
> "Does it hurt?" asked the Rabbit.
>
> "Sometimes," said the Skin Horse, for he was always truthful. "When you are Real you don't mind being hurt."
>
> "Does it happen all at once, like being wound up," he asked, "or bit by bit?"
>
> "It doesn't happen all at once," said the Skin Horse. "You become. It takes a long time. That's why it doesn't often happen to people who break easily, or have sharp edges, or

who have to be carefully kept. Generally, by the time you are Real, most of your hair has been loved off, and your eyes drop out and you get loose in the joints and very shabby. But these things don't matter at all, because once you are Real you can't be ugly, except to people who don't understand."[19]

In the context of God's love, we become more what he intended us to be, more human, more real—and God also uses other people to help bring about that healing.

THE HEALING POWER OF RELATIONSHIPS

As we talked about the practical ways in which change happens, I also showed her a humorous episode from the movie *Mostly Martha*[20] to illustrate some of the common and gracious ways that God disrupts our lives and pushes us out of our controlling, rigid ways into new and better patterns. Martha is a perfectionistic German chef in a high-class restaurant. She lives in a spotless apartment, works very hard and has few friends. One day her ordered life is disrupted when she gets the terrible news that her sister has been killed in a car accident, and her eight-year-old niece, Lina, is coming to live with her. The niece—grieving, angry and displaced—is a handful. At one point Martha says, "I wish I had a recipe for you." The second disruptive influence comes in the form of a very Italian sous chef, Mario. He is delightful, relaxed and playful, and he befriends Martha's niece who often comes to the restaurant in the evenings to do her homework. The two of them plan a surprise meal in Martha's apartment—cooked by them in her kitchen. We see the three of them eating a sumptuous meal on the living room floor, picnic style with no plates or cutlery. At the end of the meal, Martha walks into her kitchen to find a chaotic mess, and she starts hyperventilating with anxiety until Mario brings her a paper bag to breathe into! Eventually the relationship with these two people in her life becomes far more important than her perfectionist desire for control and order, and she begins to change.

I encouraged Sarah to get more involved in her local church, where she had been receiving good teaching but she needed to be part of a small community group in which she could hear other people's struggles and, hopefully, feel safe enough to share some of her own. This proved to be another context in which she experienced grace from other people.

Over the months of our conversations, and as a result of the other positive experiences in her life, Sarah began to understand the depths of God's grace toward her, and she started to let go of trying to control everything. Her fears of failure and rejection subsided, and the positive aspects of her perfectionism were more evident. She did not get depressed so deeply or so often. She learned to accept her own and others' imperfections—to be able to groan well about the fallenness of the world. She began to look forward to the day when everything will be renewed and when we will understand more fully God's purpose for us all. A glimpse of what is to come gave her much hope and anticipation. I wanted Sarah to understand that the remnants of glory in the glorious ruin that she is (and we all are) will be built on and restored, so that she will grow from one degree of glory to the next. We are reminded of this long view in the apostle Paul's writings: "Our present sufferings are not worth comparing with the glory that will be revealed in us" (Romans 8:18), and "We, who . . . reflect the Lord's glory, are being transformed into his likeness with ever-increasing glory" (2 Corinthians 3:18). I also gave her a paragraph from C. S. Lewis:

> The command Be ye perfect is not idealistic gas. Nor is it a command to do the impossible. He is going to make us into creatures that can obey that command. . . . He will make the feeblest and filthiest of us into a god or goddess, a dazzling,

radiant, immortal creature, pulsating all through with such energy and joy and wisdom and love as we cannot now imagine, a bright stainless mirror which reflects back to God perfectly (though, of course, on a smaller scale) His own boundless power and delight and goodness. The process will be long and in parts very painful; but that is what we are in for. Nothing less. He meant what He said.[21]

Eventually, Sarah and I spaced out our sessions from weekly to every other week to once a month and then to an occasional session to catch up and review. There will probably be times when the negative side of her perfectionism or depression will rear its head again, but she now has the tools and perspective to deal with that much more effectively. Her relationships to God, her family, her friends and her work are all, slowly but surely, being transformed.

Sarah understands more deeply that God loves her unconditionally, that she is a precious daughter of the King, a princess in the kingdom, and because he loves her that much, he does not want her to stay the same. Her motives for being and doing good have changed. No longer are they driven so much by fear of rejection by God or others; now they are more motivated by gratitude to God for his love and grace. Sarah has also experienced this reality in her marriage. Now a recovering perfectionist, she wrote,

I am slowly overcoming my unhealthy perfectionist tendencies through a very healthy marriage. My husband's unconditional love and constant affirmation have tremendously helped me to tackle my struggles with low self-esteem and an unhealthy desire to hide behind my "perfection." In the past, besides my family, I had a hard time opening up to people and being vulnerable. As a self-defense mechanism I tried to build a wall in many of my relationships so they would not see any flaws or imperfection. In short, even at the early stages of my marriage, I feel that I have been healed and freed from negative thinking and view of myself. I have been free to be myself—flawed and imperfect.[22]

QUESTIONS FOR REFLECTION AND DISCUSSION

1. Have you ever been to a counselor? Was it helpful? Why or why not?

2. Did you feel shame or embarrassment for going to counseling?

3. Can you see elements in your own experience of counseling of the patterns described in this chapter?

4. Are there things that irritate you in the description of these counseling sessions? What are they, and why? What are the things you like?

5. Do you think counseling can help people to grow and mature, reducing their overall vulnerability to depression?

12

HOPE AND LIGHT IN THE DARKNESS

The miserable have no other medicine but only hope.

WILLIAM SHAKESPEARE, *MEASURE FOR MEASURE*

I will . . . make the Valley of Achor [Trouble] a door of hope.

HOSEA 2:15

My God turns my darkness into light.

PSALM 18:28

God . . . made his light shine in our hearts.

2 CORINTHIANS 4:6

One of the first things counselors and therapists try to do is to help their depressed clients find some hope—hope that a marriage will improve, antidepressants will work, life can go on after losing someone very close or having to part with a precious dream—in short, find that life really is worth living. Sometimes hope is found in the small details of life; sometimes it is in the big picture. Over time in therapy it is important to help people make sense of their personal stories and connect them to a bigger life story that gives a deeper sense of hope and purpose. But how do we do this in an often overwhelmingly depressing world? Just look at headline news in recent years:

> A massive oil leak in the gulf . . . Six Afghan policemen be-headed by the Taliban . . . The body of an eleven-year-old girl found brutally raped and murdered . . . Wars . . . Hurricanes . . . 203 killed in plane crash . . . Earthquakes . . . Floods . . . Sexual slavery increasing around the world . . . Financial collapse of major banks . . . Stock market plunges . . . Pension funds decimated . . . National debt reaching record levels . . . Global warming . . . More species threatened!

The world has become a lot smaller and has more sophisticated technology, but it has not essentially changed much since biblical times. Paul lived under a Roman dictatorship with persecution, imprisonment and the constant threat of death—as do many Christians in the world today. Similarly, people have not changed much: our hearts are still infected with the same things that the Bible talks about—criticism, hatred, pride, selfishness and materialism. Some have experienced so much abuse and loss that it is too painful to hope, because it always seems to lead to more betrayal and disappointment. Life often seems, as Woody Allen says, "to be divided into the horrible and the miserable."[1] Most people cope by shutting out the bad news and hoping against hope that everything will turn out all right in the end. It is tempting to crawl into bed, take a few pills and be out of it all. In our darkest moments we wonder if God has given up on us too—or whether he is really even there at all.

But there is, of course, good news. Most people are not totally corrupt and, thankfully, people and the world have many beautiful and good things in them. We can find hope in the joy of a good marriage, the fun of family life, the good deed done for a neighbor, the glory of a beautiful sunset over the ocean or mountains, the delight in good food, a good movie, music or dance. It is good, as the old song goes, to "count our blessings, name them one by one" and to cultivate gratitude in order to maintain perspective and hope. But sometimes the bad seems to outweigh the good. Awful things happen to us, and our hope begins to shrivel and die.

Perspective on what is happening is vital to our sense of hope and on our will to live. So much depression arises because of a loss of perspective. We lose sight of the big picture, and lose our hold on truth and reality. Without realistic hope, all is lost. And when we become depressed, a vicious cycle takes over and things then look worse *because* we are depressed. It is as if depression darkens the lens of our view of the world.

NATHAN'S DESPAIR

Nathan, a good friend in England, overwhelmed with the seeming absurdity and pointlessness of life, set out to kill himself. A lonely corpse in the country and a bottle of sleeping pills—nobody would even notice his absence for a few days. For many months his mind had been in turmoil with questions, but now he knew it was a waste of time to even ask them. He had expected to find the answers in the great halls of learning at college, but he was amazed and disappointed that most other students and even his teachers did not want to take his questions seriously. His childhood in a country village had been happy, but now, at nineteen, he was facing a much bigger and more complicated world. After school, he had worked for a year as a gardener. It was there, working alone for many hours, that he began to think about the purpose of life. *Is there a God? Why is there so much suffering and evil? What does love mean?*

After a few months at school, he became progressively more

disillusioned. To fill his spare time and to distract himself from his own thoughts, he spent hours watching movies, but far from an escape, many of these movies only highlighted his dilemma as they vividly portrayed the pain and meaninglessness of life. The books he read and even the music he listened to only served to exaggerate his pessimistic mood.

On a clear, crisp January day, he set out to put an end to his struggle over a precipitous, rocky cliff not far away. The sun was shining and, fortunately, he was not past noticing the beauty of the fields and trees around him. His purposeful steps did not falter for some time, but after a while of walking, he hesitated. A flicker of doubt crept into his mind. *Perhaps there is something to live for,* he thought. *Maybe I should try just one more time before giving up completely.* Feeling rather cowardly he retraced his steps, not knowing where to look next.

He remained confused and depressed over the following weeks until he was invited by a friend to meet some people who took his questions seriously and seemed to understand his need for answers. His friend was part of a group of Christians who were discussing a book in which the writer seemed preoccupied with the same theme that had haunted him for the past few months: "Everything [is] meaningless, a chasing after the wind" (Ecclesiastes 2:11).

THE BIG QUESTIONS OF LIFE

The movie *Run Lola Run* opens with the narrator asking the same questions posed in the book of Ecclesiastes: "Who are we? Where do we come from? Where are we going? How do we know what we think we know? Why do we believe anything at all?"[2] In Shakespeare's *Macbeth* we hear an echo of the same theme:

Tomorrow, and tomorrow, and tomorrow,
Creeps in this petty pace from day to day. . . .

It is a tale
Told by an idiot, full of sound and fury,
Signifying nothing.[3]

Victor Frankl, an Austrian psychiatrist who survived the Holocaust, wrote that "more and more patients are crowding out clinics and consulting rooms, complaining of an inner emptiness, a sense of the total and ultimate meaninglessness of their lives."[4]

In deep depression, there is often a strong sense of the futility of life. Some psychiatrists believe that questions about the purpose of life are part of the neurotic ramblings of depression. Freud wrote in a letter to his friend Marie Bonaparte, "The moment a man raises the question of the meaning of life he is sick."[5] Certainly, some people who normally have a deep sense of purpose in life may express hopelessness when depressed because their perception of the world is so distorted. But loss of meaning is not only produced by depression, it may also be the primary reason for depression. Freud's hope was in psychoanalysis, but he was pessimistic about life and adopted a stoic attitude in the face of suffering. For him, hope in God was a foolish delusion, a projection of our needs for a comforting presence in a lonely world.

Carl Jung, in contrast to Freud, recognized the validity of the search for meaning. "Among all my patients in the second half of life—that is to say over thirty-five—there has not been one whose problem in the last resort was not that of finding a religious outlook on life."[6] Many people go through life avoiding such major questions about the ultimate purpose of existence, because they believe that there are no real answers. Only at times of major crisis might they face them for a while. When the crisis is past, the questions are usually forgotten. Some philosophers of the late nineteenth and early twentieth centuries (the existentialists) have been acutely aware of the way most people avoid facing the big questions about the purpose of life and the reality of their own death.

Ernest Becker highlighted this dilemma in his book *The Denial of Death*:

Man is literally split in two; he has an awareness of his own splendid uniqueness in that he sticks out of nature with a towering majesty, and yet he goes back into the ground a few feet in order blindly and dumbly to rot and disappear forever. It is a terrifying dilemma to be in and to have to live with.[7]

Becker saw many of life's activities as distractions from facing the reality of the ultimate meaningless of life. We cannot live for long with a conscious awareness of our situation, so we repress it and distract ourselves by endless activity: "Modern man is drinking and drugging himself out of awareness, or he spends his time shopping which is the same thing . . . or alternatively he buries himself in psychology in the belief that awareness all by itself will be some kind of magical cure for his problems."[8]

Victor Frankl, the existentialist psychiatrist above, described his terrible experiences in Nazi concentration camps in his book *Man's Search for Meaning*. He noted that only those who had some hope in life survived the camps. Without hope and meaning, people gave in to the physical and psychological horrors and died.[9] After World War II, millions were seduced by the Marxist utopian vision, but that fell with the Berlin wall in 1989. Marx accused the Christian hope of being the opium of the people—something that prevented them from dealing with their real situations.

Today, people usually find some sense of purpose in their career, possessions and families, as well as in the search for self-understanding, though some are preoccupied with just surviving another day. Since the Enlightenment began four centuries ago, many in Europe and the United States have tried to find *ultimate* hope outside Christianity in reason and science alone. As a culture, we have put our faith in progress, evolution, technology, psychology, material prosperity, democracy and medicine—anything that will give us hope, happiness and meaning in life. And some people even reduce hope to biology and evolution: "Thinking rosy futures is as biological as sexual fantasy; optimistically calculating the odds as basic as seeking food when hungry. . . . Perhaps the promises of Marx, Mohammed, Jefferson, and Jesus are engraved not on stone but in chemistry."[10]

These were sources of hope in modernism (the belief that science and reason would find a solution), and many still cling to them. Others have embraced postmodernism, claiming that there are no authoritative or conclusive answers to the big questions of life, an outlook that some have described as cynicism with a smile. Often they will live for any temporary experience that gives them a sense of meaning and pleasure.

For some, like Nathan, who dare to face these questions about the reality of the world we live in and questions of where our values come from, there may be a major crisis in their lives. If the normal distractions of job, family and friends do not prove enough, anxiety and despair may lead to deep depression. Unlike their strictly Freudian, behavioral or biological predecessors, many contemporary therapists find themselves more in tune with Jung and the existentialists in recognizing the importance of spirituality, meaning and hope, but they find these important things in different stories that give reasons for our existence—whether evolutionary psychology or some form of Eastern or Western spirituality.

KAREN'S SEARCH

For Karen, a courageous search for answers led through the valley of depression and hopelessness to a whole new perspective on the meaning of life. She had coped pretty well with life until recently. After breaking up with her boyfriend, she had become preoccupied with the futility of life. While she had always accepted what she had learned in high school, now it was all coming back to her as if she was seeing it for the first time: human beings, she had been taught, are just the product of millions of years of chance speeding through space on a microscopic planet in one of millions of galaxies in the universe. She began to wonder if we are really so utterly insignificant. Her mind was full of questions: *Is there anything beyond death? Is there a God? How do I know I'm not just dreaming—perhaps my life is all a terrible nightmare? How do I know what's right and wrong? What's the point of it all?*

Her friends told her not to be so neurotic. "Enjoy yourself," they said. "None of us knows the answers to those questions. Nobody really does." But Karen was too desperate to be able to switch off the incessant searching of her mind. She turned to yoga to try to relax and was told that she was thinking too much. They said she had to learn to see reality differently; really there are no problems, and it is just our minds that think there are. While meditating she had some experiences of real peace, and the questions became less insistent for a while. But eventually her depression overwhelmed her, and she was admitted to a psychiatric hospital because she was suicidal. Antidepressants helped her to think more clearly and rationally, and the psychologist talked about her problems with her parents, who had both struggled with alcoholism and anger, and about the breakup with her boyfriend. However, the psychologist seemed to ignore the bigger questions buzzing in her mind, and one doctor even told her that those questions about the meaning of life wouldn't worry her so much once she was better.

But after she left hospital, she continued her search. She met some friends who were Christians and spent many hours talking with them. Gradually she began to see that if there really was a God who had created her, loved her and wanted to have a relationship with her, then that made sense of her deep longings for meaning, love and a sense of what was ultimately right or wrong— because God had made her that way.

Somehow it took less "faith" for her to believe in that—in fact, it seemed more reasonable—than in the idea that there is no God and that we are no more than highly evolved animals who have no sure idea of why we are here or where we are going. Belief in God explained the amazing beauty, design and variety in the world around her, and it did not ignore the ugliness and suffering. Rather, this belief system recognized that such pain was a result of human beings trying to live without God. She began to see that however anti-religious or irreligious people claim to be, they normally have to put their faith in something—whether it is evolution, science, an optimism that says it will all work out alright in the end, or even some sort of mystical belief in the oneness of everything.

It also seemed to her that it took more faith to believe in the atheistic prophets of the nineteenth century, such as Freud, Marx and Darwin, who had their own explanations of man's nature and purpose, than it did to believe Jesus' view. As she read the Bible, she realized that she had to come to terms with all that Jesus did and said. Was he crazy, power-hungry and out to deceive people, or was he speaking the truth? He claimed to be the Son of God—God come in human form, to make it possible for people who had tried to live without him to come back into a relationship with their Creator.

So who should she believe? Should she remain on the fence, agnostic and finding ultimate meaning in the search itself? Should she become a cynic—not believing that there are any answers? Should she join her friends and hide her head in the sand? It became increasingly clear to her that Christianity was not just a prop to help her whistle in the dark, but it was a way of seeing things that really made sense of the world she lived in. It was the truth about reality. It involved not just a belief that the Christian understanding of the world is true but it took her into a relationship with the living, personal God in whom she found a deep sense of forgiveness, love, purpose, significance and hope.

A BASIS FOR REAL HOPE

The Concise Oxford Dictionary defines *hope* as "expectation and desire combined."[11] We use the word with varying degrees of expectation, and in our culture, it has become a tentative feeling-oriented verb. We say, "I hope that everything will work out all right," without much certainty that it will. Perhaps our use of the word not only reflects a culture that lives more on feelings than facts but also reflects the uncertainty of the world in general. The prophets of doom and gloom in the economic, social and ecological disciplines, together with the daily newscasts of wars and murders (not to mention our own family and personal problems), have undermined our illusions of a happy future.

In contrast to that, however, biblical writers used the word *hope* to mean a strong desire joined with a deep conviction and expectation that what they desired would actually happen. They *had* hope. It is used as a noun, not just a verb. It is solid and objective, not just a subjective longing.[12] Their hope was not based on speculation or circumstances, but it was based on belief in God and in what he had revealed about himself. For David and Jeremiah, this was the key to the door out of the blackness of depression and despair when circumstances were very hard. Indeed, Jeremiah wrote:

> I remember my affliction and my wandering,
>   the bitterness and the gall.
> I well remember them,
>   and my soul is downcast within me.
> Yet this I call to mind
>   and therefore I have hope:

> Because of the LORD's great love we are not consumed,
>   for his compassions never fail.
> They are new every morning;
>   great is your faithfulness. . . .

It is good to wait quietly
  for the salvation of the LORD. . . .
For he does not willingly bring affliction
  or grief to anyone.
(Lamentations 3:19-23, 26, 33)

And David:

Why, my soul, are you downcast?
Why so disturbed within me?
Put your hope in God,
  for I will yet praise him,
  my Savior and my God. (Psalm 42:11)

When they were down in the depths, they talked to themselves, reminding themselves of the true perspective on life. When everything seemed to be going against them and they could not see things very clearly, they clung to the One who they had seen, in easier times, to be the real source of hope—the only One who had a true perspective on the situation: God. They found hope in their knowledge of him and by trusting that he is ultimately in control, even if he did not immediately take away their confusion and suffering.

Jeremiah reminded himself of God's character—that God is loving, faithful and just. David based his hope on God's Word (Psalm 119:74, 81). In the Torah (which is probably all that David had of the Scriptures), he found an explanation of the purpose of his life—where he had come from and why he had been created. He also knew of God's love, faithfulness and forgiveness, and as he delighted in and obeyed God's Word, he knew he would be living the way God intended him to live and would be most fulfilled.

In the New Testament the same themes recur in more detail. Again and again the theme of hope is sounded in the context of encouragement in trial and difficulty. As we read it today, we are encouraged repeatedly to renew our perspective, to look up and beyond the immediate situation, to see the forest from the trees. We easily lose sight of reality and fall prey to cynicism and despair—or we become unrealistically idealistic. But the apostle Paul, in the middle of all his hardships and troubles, said that he was "sorrowful, yet always rejoicing" (2 Corinthians 6:10).

In this broken world we may often experience two emotions at once: sadness at sin and evil but joy at what God is doing in us and in the world—and at what he is going to do in the future. Rejoicing, like Paul, does not always mean happiness; rather, it is an attitude of mind that may bring a feeling of happiness. As the preacher and author Martin Lloyd-Jones wrote, "Seek happiness and you will never find it. Seek for righteousness and you will find you are happy."[13] Likewise, Paul encourages the Philippians to hang onto their new perspective of life and to learn contentment (1 Timothy 6:6) and joy (Philippians 4:4).

Both David and Paul knew that it was not enough to talk to themselves about having a right perspective when they were down, but they also needed to bring all their anxieties and fears to God. As we daily remind ourselves of who God is and what he is doing in us, we will know something of "the peace of God," which "will guard [our] hearts and minds" (Philippians 4:4-7). Even though we still experience the ups and downs of life, the more we see things from God's point of view, the more we will know his peace—a peace that can set a wall around our minds and emotions, protecting us from the extremes of depression and anxiety.

THE BIGGER PICTURE: WHY DO WE SUFFER?

When we are depressed, we struggle to make sense of our pain, and I find it helpful, in order to keep perspective and have my mind renewed, to think through (and we often need help from others with this) and summarize the different aspects of human suffering.

First, we are caught up in a fallen world and deeply affected by it. All sorts of bad things may happen to good people through no choice of their own. Our bodies are subject to disease and decay. Our brains do not work in the integrated and harmonious ways that they should.

Second, we live with the effects of others' sins and their rebellion against God. Parents' neglect or abuse, accidents caused by drunk drivers, poverty, crime, racism, and the horrors of torture or rape, imprisonment and war may leave scars and wounds on our brains, hearts and bodies.

Third, our own sinful nature with its strong bias toward independence, codependence and rebellion against God may bring suffering through our own choices. For example, selfishness in marriage or sexual unfaithfulness may lead to divorce and to depression—bringing not only problems for us but for our own children, and perhaps their children too. We may bring suffering to ourselves by neglecting the principles God has given us in the Bible.

But, fourth, we are also told "our struggle is not against flesh and blood, but against the rulers, against the authorities, against the powers of this dark world" (Ephesians 6:12). We do not fully understand this aspect of the battle, but we have glimpses of it all through Scripture. We pray for protection and trust the One who said, "He will not let you be tempted beyond what you can bear. But . . . will also provide a way out so that you can stand up under it" (1 Corinthians 10:13). That way is sometimes not easy to see, and it may feel as if there is no escape except giving in. It takes courage, self-discipline and trust that Christ came into the world to destroy the work of Satan (1 John 3:8; see more on spiritual warfare in the appendix).

Fifth, a final reason we may suffer is God's discipline. When we struggle with sin and experience the consequences of giving in to that sin, God uses this to discipline us and teach us something new. His desire is for us to turn back to him in repentance. The writer to the Hebrews reminds us that we should not lose heart, because God's discipline (or discipling us) is a sign that God loves us and is working even our disobedience toward making us more like him (Hebrews 12:4-13). Martin Lloyd-Jones wrote, "God's great concern for us primarily is not our happiness but our holiness."[14] Our difficulties and suffering allow us to face our wrong and unhealthy attitudes, values and goals in life. Indeed, times of loss or frustration may open a door to times of change and growth.

Overall, sometimes we can see a simple reason for depression, but often there are several of those factors interwoven together.

LIVING IN A FALLEN WORLD WITH HOPE

The psychologist Larry Crabb writes about "false hope" among believers:

> Modern Christianity, in dramatic reversal of its biblical form, promises to relieve the pain of living in a fallen world. The message, whether it's from fundamentalists requiring us to live by a favored set of rules or from charismatics urging a deeper surrender to the Spirit's power, is too often the same: The promise of bliss is for *now*! Complete satisfaction can be ours this side of heaven. . . .
>
> An inexpressible joy is available which, rather than *supporting* us through hard times, can actually *eliminate* pressure, worry, and pain from our experience.[15]

Contrary to this view, for the apostle Paul, the Christian life was no bed of roses: he suffered troubles, hardships, distresses, beatings, imprisonments, riots, hard work, sleepless nights and hunger. He concluded that he was "sorrowful, yet always rejoicing; poor, yet making many rich; having nothing, and yet possessing everything" (2 Corinthians 6:4-10, especially v. 10). Struggles, pains and battles mixed with contentment, joy and peace. Again and again in the New Testament, Paul gives the basis for hope and endurance as being in our relationship to Christ—knowing we are accepted and loved by him. He prays "that the eyes of your heart may be enlightened in order that you may know *the hope to which he has called you,* the riches of his glorious inheritance in the saints, and his incomparably great power for us who believe" (Ephesians 1:18-19, italics added). When we are in the depths of depression, this all seems like super-spiritual mumbo-jumbo. We can see no light at the end of the tunnel, but as we go further through the tunnel, we may catch a glimpse of light in the distance that slowly gets bigger.

We may experience the beginning of this glorious inheritance now, but we will be given it completely when we are with the Lord in eternity. Meanwhile his power is at work and he uses suffering to mysteriously bring about change in us to be more like him. We *are* being changed. There *is* purpose in it all. God *does* bring good out of the apparent chaos of this fallen world. In us the image of God is being restored.

Many of us may have to fight against particular weaknesses, vulnerabilities or "thorns in the flesh" (see 2 Corinthians 12:7) for many months or years, but we do so in the confidence that we are being changed. We long for the process of sanctification to be complete. We long to be free from all that holds us back. But we need patience, and that is why Paul so often talks of hope when he is encouraging the Christians in times of trouble. Peter writes of the same hope:

> Praise be to the God and Father of our Lord Jesus Christ! In his great mercy he has given us new birth into *a living hope* through the resurrection of Jesus Christ from the dead, and into an inheritance that can never perish, spoil or fade— kept in heaven for you, who through faith are shielded by God's power until the coming of the salvation that is ready to be revealed in the last time. In this you greatly rejoice, though now for a little while you may have had to suffer grief in all kinds of trials. (1 Peter 1:3-6, italics added)

Because we have Christ in us by his Spirit, we are being changed and will go through death (if he does not come back before that time) into eternal life and the glory of his presence. There we, with the whole creation, will be renewed and restored and there will be no more death, mourning, crying or pain. This is our "living hope."

In the meantime, we long for freedom from struggle, and we ache for the day of Christ's return. Paul speaks of "endurance inspired by hope" (1 Thessalonians 1:3) and of the need for patience when struggling against our sinful nature (Romans 8:25; Colossians 1:11). Larry Crabb writes:

> Beneath the surface of everyone's life, especially the more mature, is an ache that will not go away. It can be ignored, disguised, mislabeled, or submerged by a torrent of activity, but it will not disappear. And for good reason. We were designed to enjoy a better world than this. And until that better world comes along, we will groan for what we do not have. *An aching soul is evidence not of neurosis or spiritual immaturity, but of realism.*[16]

A door, a helmet and an anchor. There are three beautiful images linked to the theme of hope in Scripture. First, God says to his people, "I will . . . make the Valley of Achor [Trouble] a door of hope. There she will sing as in the days of her youth" (Hosea 2:15). Hope is seen here as a door out of a valley (for some a deep canyon!) of darkness, discouragement and depression. Second, Paul writes that we should put "on faith and love as a breastplate, and the hope of salvation as a helmet" (1 Thessalonians 5:8). The hope of salvation from sin and suffering is our helmet, protecting our minds from despair. Third, we read, "We have this hope as an anchor for the soul, firm and secure" (Hebrews 6:19). For a sailor, a safe anchorage in stormy weather brings incredible peace. Hope, as an anchor, gives us a deep security and prevents us from drifting onto the rocks of doubt, depression and hopelessness.

Wonderful Counselor. In the middle of suffering, we know that Jesus promised that he would send a "Counselor," the Holy Spirit, to be with us to encourage, comfort, challenge and change us (John 14:16-26; 15:26). We can find solace in the knowledge that Christ himself has been through more suffering than we will know. On the cross, in a way that our finite minds cannot fully understand, he bore the agony of the consequences of our sin. He not only suffered a painful and shameful physical death but he also experienced the judgment that we deserve for our self-centeredness and sin. In our deepest depression we can remember that he cried out from the cross, "My God, my God, why have you forsaken me?" (Matthew 27:46). So when we walk through the valley of the shadow of depression and even death, we know that he has been that way before us. He is able "to sympathize with our weaknesses" because he "has been tempted in every way, just as we are" (Hebrews 4:15). So we can come to him "with confidence" and "receive mercy and find grace to help us in our time of need" (Hebrews 4:16).

MINDS AND EMOTIONS RENEWED

As we are daily tempted to slip back into the world's way of seeing, we need to be "transformed by the renewing of your mind" (Romans 12:2) with this broad perspective of what God is doing in the world and in us. The beginning of this renewal is a new identity based on the significance, security, acceptance and hope that we receive in our relationship with God and with other Christians in the family of God. As we begin to see things from his point of view, we realize more and more that our self-esteem cannot depend entirely on what other people think of us. It must be rooted in God's view of us. When we feel like saying, "I'm a useless failure," we remind ourselves that this is a lie; the reality is that we are loved and accepted with all our failings. As we expose ourselves to the truth of God's Word, our thoughts and attitudes are continuously challenged and renewed. We begin to have a new understanding of our value, purpose and place in the universe. Modern neuroscience affirms the biblical reality that this renewal and reintegration process begins as we open ourselves to relationships with people with whom we can share our life stories, becoming able to experience and understand our inner emotional life and our habitual responses to ourselves, to people around us and to God.[17]

We begin to have new attitudes toward ourselves (right self-acceptance), toward others, and toward the details and difficulties of our lives. Emotions begin to be stabilized as we are not blown around so much by circumstances or by other people's attitudes toward us. We learn how to handle anger, guilt, shame, fear, anxiety and depression more appropriately and sensitively, so that we do not have to be ruled by our runaway emotions or extreme thoughts.

Our consciences too are cleansed as we are forgiven for sin. Consciences that have been made insensitive by constant abuse are renewed by the Holy Spirit and by a growing awareness of God's standards revealed in Scripture. Consciences that are weak, either under- or oversensitive, are refined, strengthened and made more accurate. The false shaping of our consciences by parents and others is gradually undone as we come to see things more often from God's point of view.

As we daily, hourly, minute-by-minute affirm God's truth about ourselves and our situations, our emotions will become more truly sensitive and appropriate, and less the dominating and controlling factors in our lives—mind and emotions will work together in harmony rather than at odds with each other, moving toward full integration of brain, body, mind and heart. Our confidence is in the fact that, when we are with him and see him face to face, this integration and healing will be complete.

SOMETHING TO CELEBRATE

Christians through the ages have, in the shadow of the suffering of the world and in the light of the hope of redemption, celebrated the great historical moments of Christmas and Easter, which stand to remind us what God has done and is doing in the world and in us. Just as Moses often had to remind the doubting and grumbling Israelites to remember how God has delivered them, so we need to have feast days, not only to praise God but to remind ourselves and our children, so that we do not lose hope.

As I write this final chapter, it is almost Christmas and my thoughts have been playing over some of the great promises of Christ's first coming. I was struck by how little difference there is between our culture with its faith in human beings, with its famines and wars, with its economic crises, with its fascination with psychic powers and with its growing cynicism, and the people to whom the prophet Isaiah spoke, contrasting the eventual darkness of unbelief with faith in the coming Messiah:

> When men tell you to consult mediums and spiritists . . . should not a people inquire of their God? . . . Distressed and hungry, they will roam through the land; when they are famished, they will become enraged and, looking upward, will curse their king and their God. Then they will look toward the earth and see only distress and darkness and fearful gloom. . . .
>
> Nevertheless there will be no more gloom for those who were in distress. . . .
>
> The people walking in darkness
>   have seen a great light;
> on those living in the land of the shadow of death
>   a light has dawned. . . .
>
> For to us a child is born,
>   to us a son is given,

and the government will be on his shoulders.
And he will be called
   Wonderful Counselor, Mighty God,
   Everlasting Father, Prince of Peace. (Isaiah 8:19; 8:21–9:3, 6)

These feast days not only remind us of what God has done but also of what he is doing to to deliver us from darkness. So Paul, while encouraging us to rejoice in all circumstances, also recognizes the pain of giving birth to new life: "We know that the whole creation has been groaning as in the pains of childbirth right up to the present time. Not only so, but we ourselves, who have the firstfruits of the Spirit, groan inwardly as we wait eagerly for our adoption as sons, the redemption of our bodies. For in this hope we were saved" (Romans 8:22-24).

What a great image of childbirth! Women endure the pain of labor with the hope that it will end in rejoicing as the child is born. At times we are overwhelmed with the pain and groaning of this broken world, at other times we can rise above it in the knowledge of our great hope. Sorrow without celebration leads to hopelessness. Celebration without sorrow is out of touch with reality. Groaning without the hope of glory leads to despair. Christ, the light of the world, came to dispel darkness in all its forms. For now we endure the valleys, shadows and dark nights with our hope in the day when Christ returns. Then the darkness will never fall again.

QUESTIONS FOR REFLECTION AND DISCUSSION

1. If you were to go out on the street and ask people what they put their hope in, what do you think their answers would be?

2. Describe a time when you felt hopeless and without meaning or purpose.

3. How do you use the word *hope* in your day-to-day conversations?

4. What are your long-term hopes?

5. How did the biblical writers use the word *hope*? In what do they encourage us to put our hope?

6. Do you think hope is important in order to counter depression?

7. How can you help someone who is depressed to find hope?

8. What do the images of darkness and light point to in Scripture?

ARE DARKER FORCES
AT WORK IN DEPRESSION?

On Spiritual Warfare

The devil is the author of confusion.

ROBERT BURTON, *THE ANATOMY OF MELANCHOLY*

There are two equal and opposite errors into which our race can fall about the devils. One is to disbelieve in their existence. And the other is to believe, and to feel an excessive and unhealthy interest in them. They themselves are equally pleased by both errors.

C. S. LEWIS, *THE SCREWTAPE LETTERS*

Imagine your house burning down with your children and all your possessions, or a hurricane sweeping through and destroying your home and neighborhood. Jerry Sittser, in his book *A Grace Disguised: How the Soul Grows Through Loss,* tells the moving story of his dark hours in terrible grief after his wife of twenty years, his mother and his daughter were killed in a car accident. Almost everything he cherished was swept away in an instant.

That initial deluge of loss slowly gave way over the next months to the steady seepage of pain that comes when grief, the floodwaters refusing to subside, finds every crack and crevice of the human spirit to enter and erode. I thought that I was going to lose my mind. I was overwhelmed with depression. The foundation of my life was close to caving in.

Life was chaotic. My children too experienced intense grief and fear. John was seriously injured. . . . People from everywhere called on the telephone, sent letters, and reached out to help and mourn. Responsibilities at home and work accumulated like trash on a vacant lot, threatening to push me toward collapse. I remember sinking into my favorite chair night after night, feeling so exhausted and anguished that I wondered whether I could survive another day, whether I *wanted* to survive another day. I felt punished by simply being alive and thought death would bring welcomed relief.

I remember counting the consecutive days in which I cried. Tears came for forty days, and then they stopped, at least for a few days. . . . It was only *after* those forty days that my mourning became too deep for tears.[1]

Jerry is a modern-day Job. Many of us know Job's dramatic and painful story. We are told that he was a prosperous, upright, God-fearing man who shunned evil (Job 1:8). Then disaster struck. Marauding enemy tribes, a lightning strike, a tornado; his children, grandchildren, servants and animals were all killed. On a psychological stress scale, Job would be way over the top in a cumulative score of negative life events.[2]

In desperate grief and distress, Job did what most men would have done in that culture; he tore his robe and shaved his head to show his grief, but then did a most unexpected thing—he expressed his deep trust in the providence of God: "The LORD gave and the LORD has taken away; may the name of the LORD be praised" (Job 1:21). Years of relationship with God had partially prepared him for this moment, and amazingly, Job did not blame God for all that had happened to him and his family.

But then comes the next traumatic and testing event in Job's life: sickness. We find him sitting on the ash heap amidst the ruins of his family and his property, using a piece of broken pottery to scrape the festering, smelly sores that covered him "from the soles of his feet to the top of his head" (Job 2:7). On the stage of this drama, his wife appears, his first counselor, but she too is desperate and in need of comfort and counsel. It seems her numbness is wearing off. She is a mother who has lost all her children, and not surprisingly, she is beginning to feel bitterness, resentment and rage rising in her soul. "How can God be good to allow all this?" we imagine her saying. "It is stupid of you, Job, to trust him. Obviously you have been living in an illusion. Your view of God is all twisted and warped. You think he is good, but look what he has done to us, you fool. Just curse God and die" (my paraphrase of Job 2:9). She holds no pretense, there is just utter honesty, and we can admire her for that. She blurts it all out, but Job, holding onto his trust for dear life though probably swaying in the wind of his wife's cynicism, rebukes her for her foolishness (Job 2:10).

Then his three friends arrive. Do they come with a message like "Cheer up, Job, God has a wonderful plan for your life"? Thankfully no. Perhaps the best bit of their counsel in the whole book is that they sit for seven days in silence, weeping with the one who was in such distress because "they saw how great his suffering was" (Job 2:13).

Soon, though, it is Job's numbness that begins to wear off. We have seen how, after unanticipated loss, people very often feel numb for a few days or weeks, and then the pain begins to come in waves. For Job, the turmoil begins to bubble up in his heart and mind, and he breaks the silence in a desperate lament:

May the day of my birth perish,
  and the night that said, "A boy is conceived!"
That day—may it turn to darkness; . . .
Why did I not perish at birth,
  and die as I came from the womb?
Why were there knees to receive me
  and breasts that I might be nursed? . . .
Why was I not hidden in the ground like a stillborn child?
    (Job 3:3-4, 11-12, 16)

Today he might have said, "Why didn't my mother get an abortion? I long to be dead." Job goes on to ask why (Job 3:20-23). "I have no peace, no quietness," he says. "I have no rest, but only turmoil" (Job 3:26), and "I loathe my very life" (Job 10:1). For thirty-five long chapters of painful dialogue, we hear Job's lament—working through the pain. *What is God up to? Is he really good? Can I trust him in all this grief and pain and confusion?*

When God finally answers, he is firm and sharp. Maybe he knows that it is the time for Job to move on; he is stuck in a groove of going over and over these issues, and he needs to be jolted back to a bigger reality. Maybe Job was getting too uppity in his questioning of God. God, the wonderful Counselor, responds with questions to expose Job's soul. There is almost a touch of humor in the way God questions him to help him laugh at himself and restore his perspective.

The LORD spoke to Job out of the storm. He said:

"Who is this that obscures my plans
  with words without knowledge?
Brace yourself like a man;
  I will question you." (Job 38:1-3)

God seemed to say, "Job, you have done enough questioning; the time has come for you to be quiet and listen." With that, the

Creator of the universe embarked on a wonderful (and lengthy) description of all he had made. What an answer to someone who is suffering: "Look at the hippopotamus, look at the crocodile!" (see Job 40:15; 41:1). God was saying, "Trust me, I am in control of it all, even though it sometimes seems to you as if I'm not!" Finally Job bowed in humble repentance, submission and trust. God comforted him, and he provided for him once more through his extended family and friends, giving him more children and restoring his fortunes.

SATANIC INFLUENCE

Loss and tragedy can easily push us to the point of hopelessness and despair of life. But there is an additional important factor here that even Job never saw. The reason these disasters came is revealed to the reader but not to him: glimpsing behind the curtain into the supernatural realm, we see that Satan was given permission by God to test Job's faith but not to take his life. We can see in Job's story the overwhelming loss and tragedy that may come to any one of us in life because we live in a fallen world— where disasters happen through no fault of our own and we have to work through the grief and the many why questions. For Job, there were things going on that he never knew. Although he must have been aware of the reality of evil, he had not so personally experienced Satan's desire to destroy what is good or seen God's ultimate control over Satan. When disaster strikes, there may be things happening in heavenly places that we will never know about and that we may only discover when we are with the Lord in glory.

To many of us, it may seem very strange to believe in demonic influence in the midst of our scientific, enlightened world. Because this is a topic that is confusing and difficult for all of us, I might be tempted to omit its discussion in this book, but that would leave out an important factor in the darkness of depression, hopelessness and suicide. We are all involved in spiritual warfare all the time. To one degree or another, we all have been damaged and deceived by the influence of evil, and many of us are not consciously aware of this. However, much counseling involves the painful discovery of the dark footprints of evil in the lies we have come to believe about ourselves, about the people who love us and even about God himself. Counseling also helps us to see good and evil more clearly when our sensibilities have been dulled by constant exposure to, and immersion in, the mixture of good and evil in the culture around us. We know the reality of pride, envy, lust and hatred in our own hearts, and we see greed, materialism, envy, selfishness, lust, sexual slavery, racial prejudice and other evidences of darkness all around us in our culture. Satan hates goodness, beauty and truth. But evil is, perhaps, seen most starkly in countries that experience genocide and civil war with the horrors of systematic rape, torture and killing. Nearer to home, we know of many situations where children and teens have been horribly sexually abused and suffer terrible emotional and physical damage. The effects may last many years and span the generations—with depression, anxiety, PTSD, alcoholism and suicide. Satan is having a field day in such places.

But we often think of spiritual warfare in more limited terms in relation to some who have dabbled on the edge of demonic influence and who know the power that it has over them. For example, Margaret came from a churchgoing family. But the Sunday formality had little relationship to the rest of her life. In her mid-teens she rebelled against anything to do with the church and later became involved with friends who regularly smoked marijuana and occasionally used LSD. Gradually she became fascinated with the occult world of mediums and séances, finally deciding to become an active member of a Satanist church. Soon after this, she began to be haunted by deep fears and became increasingly depressed and suicidal. She felt trapped and unable to extricate herself from her decision. Finally, she left the country to get away from her new friends, but the torment continued and she eventually sought help from Christians. The urge to kill herself or run away increased, but after a great struggle, she was able to confess to God what she had done and pray for deliverance from satanic influence.

In a similar way Fiona, the only child of middle-class non-Christian parents, drifted into the drug culture. Often on her drug trips she saw a figure in white that kept turning toward her but she never saw a face. She presumed it was God and felt encouraged to continue these trips. However she became increasingly haunted by fears, depression and an urge to destroy herself—by jumping from a high window or throwing herself in front of a car. On one occasion she asked the figure to turn around, and she said, "I saw it was Satan and was terrified." She phoned the only Christian she knew who had previously been involved with drugs, tarot cards and séances. Her friend took her to a Christian counselor and, in the context of dealing with a number of problems in her life, she prayed for forgiveness and protection from the evil one. As she moved into her new life as a Christian she was increasingly free from fear and depression.

We could travel to Brazil, Ethiopia, West Africa and India and find more dramatic stories of such oppression, and we would also find stories of Christians challenging Satan's power and seeing Christ's victory over evil. The Lausanne Movement has many helpful resources on this topic from all over the world.[3] We could even visit Western Pentecostal churches in London, New York or St. Louis and find similar power encounters with evil forces.

Many of us have stories of strange experiences of haunted rooms, dark figures, overwhelming temptations, hearing voices, and feelings of being choked or suffocating. Many also have stories of people who have been delivered in some dramatic way from what seems like personal forces of evil.

Of skeptics and spirits. Does it seem ridiculous to believe in the devil in our enlightened, scientific age? Many would say that Satan is just a symbol of evil, but in the United States, approximately 25 percent believe he is a real figure or spirit. Certainly many psychiatrists would not take the reality of a demonic influence seriously because it cannot be proved "scientifically," and perhaps more importantly, because it is too unbelievable it is not even worth considering. Freud explained that what men once called "demonic" or "evil spirits" were actually "base and evil wishes," deriving from "impulses which have been rejected and repressed" in one's personality.[4] Carl Jung implied that the demonic is the area of "autonomous complexes," the parts of our personalities that we have difficulty admitting to ourselves.[5]

For those who have abandoned the supernatural reality of God and Satan, explanations for disturbed behavior have now to be found only within nature itself: in our genes, our biochemistry and our childhood. Dissociative Identity Disorder (the new name for Multiple Personality Disorder), schizophrenia and hysteria are the common labels used to identify what once might have been described as "demon possession"—and, to be sure, most people who have been given one of these diagnoses are more likely suffering from mental illness than demon possession.

But still there are many Christians who believe that many psychological problems are caused by demons, and there have been times in history when this belief has given rise to "witch hunts." And even now, in some churches, spirits of depression, anxiety, loneliness, lust and alcohol are seen as needing to be exorcised or bound. People are viewed as a battleground of divine and satanic forces, and little significance is given to their own good or bad choices. In addition, little emphasis is placed on the fact that Satan's destructive influence in the world is far wider than his effect on individual people.

While some people put all their faith in science—in what can be observed and measured—and do not believe in a supernatural world, others explain most physical and psychological problems as spiritual and demonic. However, in between there are varying degrees of belief in natural and supernatural causes.

In the last fifty years we have seen a resurgence of interest in the mystical, the supernatural and the occult. Many movies, TV shows, video games, novels and, especially, young people's comic books feature stories about the use of supernatural or occult power. It is a common leisure activity to dabble in astrology, séances, spiritual healing, parapsychology and magic. The supernatural has become commonplace and cool. It is often portrayed as harmless and fun; therefore, it raises less anxiety than it did many years ago.

Furthermore, major bookstores have large sections on the occult—sometimes bigger than the sections on Christianity. In addition, interest in witchcraft and pagan spirituality has grown enormously, more in Europe than in the United States. Still, the American Religious Identification Survey found that Wiccans grew from 8,000 members in 1990 to an estimated 134,000 in 2001 and 800,000 by 2006; and Spiritualists grew from 116,000 in 2001 to 426,000 in 2006.[6] The Roman Catholic Church is deeply concerned about these trends, especially in Italy, and has greatly increased the numbers of exorcists.[7] The Anglican Church in the United Kingdom has developed teams to deliver people and places that seem to have fallen prey to dark forces.

Meanwhile, many are growing up without any knowledge of traditional religion or Christianity. They are schooled in a skeptical, scientific worldview and acculturated in a postmodern climate that has no answers to the deeper questions of meaning and purpose. So where do they turn with those questions? Not to old-fashioned, orthodox Christianity but to the intriguing and fascinating world of the supernatural and the ancient pagan traditions of mystery and sacred ritual. Young people are often hungry for meaning in a world that tells them that they are ultimately no more significant than a monkey or a machine. Care for our planet is rightly a high priority for many, but some environmentalism has pantheistic and occult undertones. Respected public figures, such as National Public Radio journalist and Wiccan priestess Margot Adler embrace ancient paganism and help bring it into mainstream culture.[8]

THE WILES OF THE DEVIL

When we turn to the Bible to discover who or what Satan really is, we find hints that he was once an important angel who rebelled against God, took other angels with him (now demons), later tempted Adam and Eve to question God's goodness and sin, and since then, has been doing all he can to destroy the people and the kingdom of God.[9]

Most people are well acquainted with *The Lord of the Rings*, and many have read *Paradise Lost* by John Milton. Hundreds of years ago Milton, and more recently Tolkien in *The Silmarillion,* used his artistic imagination to describe the creation of the world and the origin of Satan in stories based on the scriptural account. We do not know exactly how Satan came to be, but we can speculate with these creative Christian writers.

In *The Silmarillion,* Iluvatar (God) made Ainur (the angels) who "were with him before ought was made . . . and they sang before him, and he was glad." God told them something of the glory of what he was doing and gave them the power to adorn the harmony of the music they were making with their own "thoughts and devices." So the Ainur used their voices and instruments "to fashion the theme of Iluvatar to a great music; and a sound arose of endless interchanging melodies woven in harmony. . . . Iluvatar sat and hearkened, and for a great while it seemed good to him, for in the music there were no flaws."

But one of the angels, Melkor, began to

interweave matters of his own imagining that were not in accord with the theme of Iluvatar; for he sought therein to increase the power and glory of the part assigned to himself. To Melkor among the Ainur had been given the greatest gift of power and knowledge . . . desire grew hot within him to bring into being things of his own.

He was impatient with God and began to think different thoughts.

Some of these thoughts he now wove into his music, and straightway discord arose about him, and many that sang nigh him grew despondent, and their thought was disturbed and their music faltered; but some began to attune their music to his rather than to the thought which they had at first. Then the discord of Melkor spread ever wider, and the melodies which had been heard before foundered in a sea of turbulent sound.[10]

Here is a picture of a created being rebelling against his Creator and wanting to do things his own way, bringing confusion and chaos, deception and darkness through his temptation of Adam and Eve.

DEPRESSION, DISEASE OR DEMON?

So how does all of this relate to those who are depressed? There are some Christian counselors who would say that, because a depressed person finds it hard to pray and read the Bible and because he doubts his own salvation and feels his heart is hard toward God (even to the point of being tempted with blasphemous thoughts), then these must be signs of demonic activity. The easily swayed person who is so depressed may actually believe that he is possessed by the devil. But these morbid thoughts are characteristic of severe depression. Often people with morbid, delusional beliefs have other false ideas as well—for example, that they are suffering from cancer, are completely poverty stricken, are being persecuted by the police or foreign powers, or that they have committed the unforgiveable sin. Difficulty with sleeping, weight loss or gain, tearfulness, agitation or fatigue are also usually present in depression. Suicidal thoughts may result from the belief that he is a burden to everyone and has committed terrible sins.

It is cruel and very harmful to tell someone in the depths of depression that she is possessed by an evil spirit—unless there is obvious evidence of such activity. Unfortunately, such simple-minded formulations are often used in the church today, which is probably the result of several factors. First, there is the temptation in some churches to define anything psychological that is not understood as being demonic. There is a common human desire for simple answers to complex problems. Then there is an inadequate understanding of the radical nature of the Fall and its repercussions in every area of life. Third, fear of feeling helpless and useless in the face of obvious suffering is also common among those dealing with the psychologically disturbed, and there is a strong temptation to want to be seen to have power and authority as a Christian healer and leader.

One situation that often causes confusion for well-meaning Christians is what is called Multiple Personality Disorder (MPD) or Dissociative Identity Disorder (DID), where the person feels as if they are controlled by two or more separate personalities and they also have extensive memory lapses. There may also be depression, flashbacks, physical symptoms, anxiety, paranoia and hearing voices. Because of the voices and different personalities, this may well be erroneously identified as demonic influence or possession.[11]

However, in those cases, there is often a history of early childhood, life-threatening events or abuse that has resulted in PTSD and DID. One young woman told me how she had an out-of-body experience as she watched her father raping her own four-year-old body. The memories of the event were too terrifying to keep in her conscious awareness, and they emerged later in life when she felt safe enough to face them. This also resulted for her in different voices and personalities—one eager to please and fearful and another aggressive and threatening. She felt possessed, but in reality, the personalities were just different aspects of one person, and she needed professional help for these parts of herself to be reintegrated.[12]

OPPRESSION, POSSESSION OR DEPRESSION?

So how are Christians affected by demonic forces? It is important to note that the Greek word for *possession* simply means "demonized," so this can include what we commonly call oppression as well. In the thirteen instances where the word *possession* or *demonized* occurs in the New Testament, it implies varying degrees of control by evil spirits. So I certainly believe that a Christian can be "demonized" and harassed by demons or Satan in some way (*oppressed*) but not completely taken over, controlled and *possessed*.

Apart from Satan's general deceptive and destructive influence in the world, there appear to be two types of particular satanic influence. First, there are those who are oppressed or possessed involuntarily, without knowingly inviting it—and this seems to have been the fate of some of the people healed by Jesus in the Gospel accounts. Second, there are those who are possessed voluntarily. They have openly sold themselves to Satan and have willingly been involved in occult activity.

The Bible does not imply that a Christian can be possessed by the devil or evil spirits, but it seems that Christians who have been involved in some way with the occult are particularly sensitive to Satan's activity and may be more vulnerable to "oppression" or demonization. Many would say that someone who has a family history of involvement in the occult (for example, a grandmother who was a medium or witch) or has been involved in activities including astrology, séances or spiritualism, should be careful to renounce very specifically all curses, connections and claims of Satan over their life. It is wise to destroy any charms, amulets, tarot cards, letters or books that have any association with such activity. The Christian should also ask forgiveness for their own dabbling in such things and renew their commitment to Jesus Christ, asking for his protection in the future. David Appleby, a contemporary Protestant deliverance minister and author of *It's Only a Demon: A Model of Christian Deliverance,* has extensive experience of dealing with demonic activity. He believes, as have many writers on this topic before him,[13] that there are particular doorways or points of entry for demonic activity. hereditary curses and afflictions, occult involvement, trauma and victimization, and long-term sin and disobedience to God.[14]

As an example, here is the story of Peter. He came for counseling because he was in constant torment—depressed, withdrawn, often thinking of suicide and terrified that he would murder someone. From time to time he would have "this red flash in my head," which was accompanied by an obsessive drive to kill someone or something. As he talked, it emerged that he had an extraordinary family history, including a great-grandmother who had been hanged as a witch in Spain. Furthermore, his grandmother and mother were active mediums, and several members of the family had shown signs of pathological depression and violence, while some had died by suicide.

After Peter renounced his own dabbling with the occult and prayed for deliverance and protection from any satanic influence from his ancestors and relatives, he gradually began to lose his fears of the "red flash" returning and was freed from depression. However, he did also need help in sorting out his relationship with his parents, and he found his sense of self-worth increasing as he realized that God loved him and that other Christians accepted him as he was.

I do not believe that the three people I have described in this chapter (Margaret, Fiona and Peter) were "possessed," but they were certainly "oppressed." I think that possession of non-Christians is still rare in this country, and there are probably more cases of possession in countries where satanic forces are openly embraced and where Christianity has not had its historic restraining influence. Perhaps Satan is happy to have us in our materialism, in North America and Europe, more possessed by our possessions, as well as other idols, so he does not need to be so obvious in his activities.

In my own years of experience in psychiatry, counseling and pastoral care in the United Kingdom and the United States, I have only met a few people I thought might have been possessed. One was a young man of West Indian origin, whose parents had been very heavily involved in voodoo. However, much of his strange behavior could be explained on the basis of the extraordinary relationships within his family and by his paranoid psychosis. But how can one tell? So often the psychological, physical and spiritual factors are woven together. Sometimes those who are psychologically disturbed are attracted by the occult, so it is difficult to tell which is cause and which is effect. I have certainly met people with severe depression or schizophrenia who have the delusional belief that they are possessed by the devil or are being influenced by evil forces in some way when, in fact, that belief is a symptom of their psychosis.

Some years ago, the Anglican priest, John Richards, in his book *But Deliver Us from Evil*—an introduction to the demonic dimension in pastoral care—summarized the common themes of those Christians who had written about the diagnosis of demon possession.[15] There may be a change of personality with variable character, intelligence, demeanor or appearance. There may be physical symptoms, such as extraordinary strength, epileptic-like seizures, catatonic postures, falling, clouding of consciousness, anesthesia to pain and changed voice. Mental changes may occur, such as speaking in tongues, understanding unknown languages or experiencing psychic powers, including telepathy and clairvoyance. There is usually a reaction of fear or blasphemy to the name of Christ, and deliverance may be performed in the name of Jesus. Many of these symptoms and signs may occur for other reasons, and it is certainly rare to see them all together in one person—so a diagnosis of possession is not easy.

One factor that we seriously underestimate is the power of suggestion in our lives. Hypnotism and much so-called spiritual healing demonstrate that the human mind will believe whatever a person who wields power and authority suggests to it. Any system of explanation is willingly accepted to make sense of inner confusion. A person in distress who is seeking relief, if told that she is possessed, will increasingly behave as if this is in fact the case, and may show all the signs of relief and healing when it is suggested that the spirit is gone. Therefore, we need great discernment in this area where there is such confusion.

WANTED: A SPIRIT OF DISCERNMENT

There are few places in the Old Testament where Satan or evil spirits are mentioned.[16] We have already seen, perhaps, the most significant one where we get a glimpse behind the scenes of Job's suffering and discover that Satan was allowed to test him in all sorts of psychological and physical ways, though his power was limited since he was not allowed to take Job's life. The Bible does not define in precise detail how the devil influences the world, but it gives a number of principles to help us understand something of his activity in relation to psychological problems.

First, in the New Testament, illness is clearly distinguished from demon possession.[17] Those who were not demon-possessed were not healed by exorcism or binding of spirits. The Bible makes a distinction between natural and supernatural causes of disease.

Ultimately, in tempting Adam and Eve to disobey God, Satan is partly responsible for the entry of even what we call natural disease, disharmony and death in the world. But the result of the Fall of Adam and Eve in history is not the same as direct possession by an evil spirit in the present.

Second, we can and do sin without Satan's assistance! "Each one is tempted when, by his own evil desire, he is dragged away and enticed" (James 1:14).[18] Our sinful nature leads us to sin. While acknowledging the reality of Satan's activity and power, there is a great danger in some churches today of explaining too much abnormal behavior in terms of demonic forces. This removes our responsibility for recognizing and confessing our own sinfulness. Paul describes the acts of the sinful nature: "sexual immorality, impurity . . . jealousy, fits of rage, selfish ambition" (Galatians 5:19-20). He exhorts the Christians not to "indulge the sinful nature" (Galatians 5:13).

Satan is not mentioned in these verses, so "the devil made me do it" won't work as an excuse. If we only see ourselves as passive victims caught up in a battle between the forces of good and evil, there is little incentive for us to make any change in our lives because we think our own actions against sin have little significance—we are but pawns in the cosmic drama of spiritual warfare. However, Paul gives a good example of the usual relationship between our sinful nature and Satan when he talks about anger. He does not say, "cast out a *spirit* of anger," but he writes of the acts of the sinful nature as being hatred and fits of rage (Galatians 5:19-29). We are responsible for our actions, even when he warns, "In your anger do not sin. . . . Do not give the devil a foothold" (Ephesians 4:26-27).

Many cases of suicide are associated with anger, frustration, bitterness, and a desire for revenge or escape. When we feel angry with God, with others and with ourselves, the seemingly logical end point is self-destruction. But Paul warns us not to listen to the devil's urgings. The devil is described as the deceiver and the destroyer, and he will do all he can to find chinks in the armor of the Christian to exacerbate bitterness or despair in order to push us over the edge!

Third, Satan does tempt us directly. He tempted Christ himself (Matthew 4:1), and he is active in trying to destroy our faith and hope (as he was with Job). He will take advantage of our points of vulnerability and weakness. We must constantly pray for protection from the evil one ("deliver us from the evil one," Matthew 6:13), as he "prowls around like a roaring lion looking for someone to devour" (1 Peter 5:8). He will enslave, steal, oppress, tempt, torment, sift, accuse, depress, deceive, cause dissension and promote injustice.[19] Sometimes he will even disguise himself as "an angel of light" (2 Corinthians 11:14) to beguile us, as he did with Fiona. Satan is described as being granted considerable freedom to deceive and destroy, to create havoc in the church now, but ultimately he is destined for complete destruction (Revelation 20:10).

Until that day, Paul reminds us of the spiritual battle in which we are involved and the need for protection: "Finally, be strong in the Lord and in his mighty power. Put on the full armor of God so that you can take your stand against the devil's schemes. For our struggle is not against flesh and blood, but against the rulers, against the authorities, against the powers of this dark world and against the spiritual forces of evil in the heavenly realms" (Ephesians 6:10-12). It seems that demonic activity increased greatly in the presence of Christ and continues to do so whenever there are particular expansions of the kingdom of God. There are a few major and dramatic exorcisms in the Gospels and many instances of Jesus and the apostles healing and driving out demons by a simple word of command.[20] But only one of Jesus' post-resurrection commissions mentions exorcism and healing, and that is contained in the dubious section of the manuscript at the end of the Gospel of Mark.[21]

Sydney Page helpfully notes that

the gospels and Acts represent demon possession as a condition in which one or more demons indwell an individual
in such a way that the person's personality is suppressed
and an alien personality speaks and acts through him or
her. . . . The New Testament does not discuss how possession was diagnosed.[22]

He goes on to show how there were a variety of mental and physical
symptoms. Exorcisms were most often performed by a word of
command. There was no laying on of hands or incantations or
rituals and very little conversation with demons. People who were
possessed are treated as unfortunate sufferers and treated with
compassion, not held responsible. None were accused of sin or
letting themselves be possessed. Deliverance was related not to the
faith of the possessed but sometimes related to the faith of others.

We are all caught up in spiritual warfare every day,[23] and the
biblical weapons are prayer, discerning good from evil and truth
from lies, immersion in biblical reality, putting on the whole armor
of God, and living in constant obedience. As we do this, the forces
of evil retreat and are restrained, and we can be confident that the
Spirit of God is stronger than any spirit of the evil one.

One day Satan's power over us will be destroyed completely
(Revelation 20:10). J. R. R. Tolkien catches the amazing, dawning
awareness of that freedom from darkness and depression at the
end of *The Return of the King* when Sam asks Gandalf, "Is everything sad going to come untrue? What's happened to the world?"

"A great Shadow has departed," said Gandalf, and then he
laughed, and the sound was like music, or like water in a
parched land; and as he listened the thought came to Sam
that he had not heard laughter, the pure sound of merriment,
for days upon days without count.

QUESTIONS FOR REFLECTION AND DISCUSSION

1. Have you ever had an experience of demonic influence and/or deliverance from it?

   Do you know of others who have? What was your experience or theirs?

2. What have you been taught about the devil and evil spirits in church?

3. Do you think that interest in alternative spirituality opens people up to demonic influence? Why or why not?

4. Do you think the current interest in magic, spiritual powers and occult arts in games, TV shows and movies is a reflection of the culture—or a cause of change in the culture?

5. In what ways can you seek protection from the influence of Satan?

NOTES

Introduction

[1] Richard Winter, *The Roots of Sorrow: Reflections on Depression and Hope* (Basingstoke, U.K.: Marshall Pickering, 1986).

[2] You may note that I frequently refer to "counseling" or "psychotherapy," and though I see them as being on a continuum, I distinguish between counseling on the one end as including supportive lay counseling (including discipleship, mentoring, spiritual guidance and personal coaching) from in-depth professional psychotherapy on the other end (which has the aim of substantial change in a person's way of coping with life and relationships).

[3] I have written on the important question of the relationship between biblical wisdom and secular wisdom in my article "The Search for Truth in Psychology and Counseling," *Presbyterion* 31, no. 1 (Spring 2005): 18-36. The article is posted at <http://richardwinter.org>.

Chapter 1: Falling into Darkness

[1] Kay Redfield Jamison, *An Unquiet Mind: A Memoir of Moods and Madness* (New York: Random House, 1995), p. 110.

[2] William Styron, *Darkness Visible* (New York: Random House, 1990), pp. 16, 38.

[3] Tony Lewis, *The Guardian*, May 5, 1982.

[4] Mayo Clinic staff, "Depression in Women: Understanding the Gender Gap," the website of the Mayo Clinic <www.mayoclinic.com/health/de pression/MH00035>. Different studies will give different statistics, and these often depend on the definition of depression that is being used.

[5] Mark Olfson and Steven Marcus, "National Patterns in Antidepressant Medication Treatment," *Archives of General Psychiatry* 66, no. 8 (2009): 848-56.

[6] Peter Kramer, *Against Depression* (London: Penguin, 2005); see also *Listening to Prozac* (New York: Penguin, 1997).

[7] "Suicide in the U.S.: Statistics and Prevention," the website of the National Institute of Mental Health <www.nimh.nih.gov/health/publications/ suicide-in-the-us-statistics-and-prevention/index.shtml>.

[8]Charles Barber, "The Medicated Americans," *Scientific American Mind*, February/March 2008, p. 49.

[9]Ibid., p. 46.

[10]Sylvia Plath, *The Bell Jar* (New York: Faber & Faber, 1963), pp. 2-3. Some of Plath's life and suicide is portrayed in the 2003 movie *Sylvia*.

[11]William Cowper, "Letter to Lady Hesketh, October 1978," *Letters of William Cowper*, ed. William Hadley (London: J. M. Dent & Sons, 1925).

[12]John Colquhoun, "Nature and the Signs of Melancholy in a True Christian: Spiritual Depressions," *Banner of Truth Magazine*, no. 96 (September 1971): 33.

[13]William Cowper, "Letter to William Hayley," *William Cowper's Letters*, ed. E. V. Lucas (Oxford: Oxford University Press, 1908).

[14]Styron, *Darkness Visible*, pp. 48-49.

[15]"Psychotic Depression," WebMD.com, reviewed March 1, 2010 <www.webmd.com/depression/guide/psychotic-depression>.

[16]Used courtesy of the writer.

[17]Styron, *Darkness Visible*, p. 16.

[18]Andrew Solomon, "Anatomy of Melancholy," *The New Yorker*, January 12, 1998, pp. 48-49.

[19]For more firsthand descriptions of the experience of serious depression, watch the PBS home video *Depression: Out of the Shadows* (Arlington, Va.: Twin Cities Public Television and WGBM Boston, 2008).

[20]U. Halbreich and L. S. Kahn, "Role of Estrogen in the Aetiology and Treatment of Mood Disorders," *CNS Drugs* 15, no. 10 (2001): 797-817.

[21]J. Wang et al., "Gender Differences in Neural Response to Psychological Stress," *Social Cognitive and Affective Neuroscience* 2, no. 3 (2007): 227-39.

[22]Colquhoun, "Nature and Signs of Melancholy," p. 33.

[23]Major depression is defined in *The Diagnostic and Statistical Manual of Mental Disorders*, called the *DSM*, and this manual is the authoritative reference book for making diagnostic decisions in the field of psychology and psychiatry. It is revised and updated every few years.

[24]Peter Whybrow, *A Mood Apart: Depression, Mania and Other Afflictions of the Self* (New York: Basic Books, 1997), p. 15.

[25]In *Darkness Visible*, Styron lists many who have died by suicide, including van Gogh, Virginia Woolf, Sylvia Plath, John Berryman, Jack London and Ernest Hemingway (pp. 35-36). In *Night Falls Fast*, Kay Redfield Jamison lists writers and artists who attempted suicide: Joseph Conrad, F. Scott Fitzgerald, Graham Greene, Edgar Allan Poe, Evelyn Waugh and Paul Gauguin, among others. See also Albert Y. Hsu, *Grieving a Suicide* (Downers Grove, Ill.: InterVarsity Press, 2002), pp. 83-85.

Chapter 2: Rising into Light

[1]The symptoms of mania are memorably captured for medical students with the mnemonic DIGFAST: distractibility, indiscretion, grandiosity, flight of ideas, activity increase, sleep deficit and talkativeness.

[2]Kay Redfield Jamison, *Exuberance: The Passion for Life* (New York: Random House, 2004), p. 121.

[3]Kay Redfield Jamison, *An Unquiet Mind: A Memoir of Moods and Madness* (New York: Random House, 1995), pp. 36-37.

[4]Ibid., p. 38.

[5]Jamison, *Exuberance*, p. 183.

[6]Kay Redfield Jamison, *Touched by Fire: Manic-Depressive Illness and the Artistic Temperament* (New York: Simon & Schuster, 2003).

[7]There has also been an increase in the number of adults diagnosed with bipolar disorder in this same timeframe, although the increase has been much less. One survey suggests that another 2.4 percent of the adult population have a sub-threshold form of bipolar disorder, like the more minor but still impairing forms of depression. This same study commented that only a small proportion of these people are getting adequate help and treatment. Kathleen R. Merikangas et al., "Lifetime and 12-Month Prevalence of Bipolar Spectrum Disorder in the National Comorbidity Survey Replication," *Archives of General Psychiatry* 64, no. 5 (May 2007): 543-52.

[8]The most likely reason for this incredible increase and for the possible over-diagnosis is the widening description of bipolar disorder in popular books such as *The Bipolar Child* by Demitri and Janice Papolos, first published in 1999. Additionally, some child-psychiatry teams are ready to make a diagnosis of bipolar if the predominant mood is irritability—even if the mood is not elevated. This widening of the diagnosis for bipolar disorder has permitted children with difficult, aggressive and moody behaviors—who have not responded to treatment for ADHD—to try mood stabilizers.

[9]I *do* think that bipolar disorder exists in children. However, many of the children who were diagnosed with it between 1993 and 2003 have not gone on to show the typical mood swings of bipolar disorder as they have grown into their late teens and early twenties. But some were correctly diagnosed, and it seems that with careful family interviews the typical highs and lows of mania (or hypomania) can be recognized in children and young adults—although it seems to be rare below the age of ten ("When Children with Bipolar Disorder Grow Up," *Harvard Mental Health Letter*, February 2009, p. 6).

[10]Mihaly Csikszentmihalyi, "If We Are So Rich, Why Aren't We Happy?" *The American Psychologist* 54, no. 10 (1999): 821-27, esp. p. 826.

[11]Mihaly Csikszentmihalyi, *Flow: The Psychology of Optimal Experience* (New York: Harper Perennial, 1991), p. 45.
[12]Ibid., p. 3.
[13]Ibid., p. xi.
[14]Ibid., p. 53.
[15]Ibid., p. 159.

Chapter 3: A Mind Diseased

[1]Klaus P. Ebmeier, Claire Donaghey and J. Douglas Steele, "Recent Developments and Current Controversies in Depression," *Lancet* 367 (January 14, 2006): 153-67.
[2]Douglas F. Levinson and Walter E. Nichols, "Major Depression and Genetics," Stanford School of Medicine Genetics of Brain Function website <http://depressiongenetics.stanford.edu/mddandgenes.html>.
[3]"Breaking Ground, Breaking Through: The Strategic Plan for Mood Disorders Research," National Institute of Mental Health, July 2002 <www.nimh.nih.gov/about/strategic-planning-reports/breaking-ground-breaking-through--the-strategic-plan-for-mood-disorders-research.pdf>.
[4]Placebos are pills that look and taste the same as the real ones but have no active chemical in them.
[5]Jay Fournier et al., "Antidepressant Drug Effects and Depression Severity," *Journal of the American Medical Association* 303, no. 1 (2010): 47-53, and Irving Kirsch, *The Emperor's New Drugs: Exploding the Antidepressant Myth* (New York: Basic Books, 2010). Note that in the studies reported by Kirsch, only one antidepressant was compared with a placebo, and the patients included in the studies were not representative of those most therapists see. Also, most studies only covered six weeks of treatment.
[6]It is now claimed that placebos are working almost as well as the real thing in *mild* and *moderate* depression.
[7]See Kirsch, *The Emperor's New Drugs*.
[8]Karen Swartz, "Depression and Anxiety," *Johns Hopkins White Papers*, 2011, p. 19.
[9]See Peter Kramer, "In Defense of Antidepressants," *The New York Times*, July 10, 2011, Sunday Review, pp. 1, 6.
[10]The largest study to date of the effect of antidepressants with the kind of patients commonly seen in practice was the STAR-D study (Sequential Treatment Alternatives to Relieve Depression) done by the National Institute of Mental Health in 2006. Nearly 3,000 patients with major depression were treated with an antidepressant. Thirty percent recovered by seven weeks, and for the rest, another antidepressant was added or they

were switched to a different one. Another 25 percent recovered in phase two. Other changes were made in phase three, and the final outcome was that 67 percent recovered fully. This was not a double bind study, and there was no placebo control, but it demonstrates the complexity of treatment and the value of trying different medications. See www.nimh.nih.gov/trials/practical/stard/allmedicationlevels.shtml.

[11]Neuroleptic literally means "affecting the nerves."

[12]Kay Redfield Jamison, *An Unquiet Mind: A Memoir of Moods and Madness* (New York: Random House, 1995), p. 88.

[13]Ebmeier, Donaghey and Steele, "Recent Developments and Current Controversies," pp. 153-67.

[14]Helen S. Mayberg, J. Arturo Silva et al., "The Functional Neuroanatomy of the Placebo Effect," *American Journal of Psychiatry* 159, no. 5 (May 2002): 728-37.

[15]Helen S. Mayberg et al., "Modulation of Cortical-Limbic Pathways in Major Depression: Treatment Specific Effects of CBT," *Archives of General Psychiatry* 61 (1951): 34-41.

[16]Jessica E. Malberg, Amelia J. Eisch, Eric J. Nestler and Ronald S. Duman, "Chronic Antidepressant Treatment Increases Neurogenesis in Adult Rat Hippocampus," *Journal of Neuroscience* 20, no. 24 (December 15, 2000): 9104-10.

[17]E. Slater, "Evaluation of Electric Convulsion Therapy as Compared with Conservative Methods of Treatment in Depressive States," *Journal of Mental Science* 97 (1951): 567-69.

[18]Transcranial magnetic stimulation (TMS) is a treatment where the brain is stimulated by electromagnetic waves. There is no need for anesthesia or muscle relaxants, since the patient is fully conscious and sitting upright in a comfortable chair. The only sensation is a pounding vibration from magnetic pulses, as no machinery touches the body or head of the patient. There are very few side effects and, at the moment, mixed results for the treatment of depression.

Vagus nerve stimulation (VNS) is when a small electrical pulse generator (like a pacemaker) is connected to a wire implanted in a person's chest. This sends signals along the vagus nerve, which runs through the chest into the neck and brain, connecting the heart and stomach to the mood centers in the brain. VNS is recommended for some cases of severe or chronic depression. Though early evidence for its effectiveness is not conclusive, that may be because treatment was only given for eight weeks. More recent research has shown good treatment response at three to six months of treatment.

Deep brain stimulation (DBS) is used in a few people with severe, unremitting depression. There have been reports of amazing, rapid and sustained relief when a very fine wire is carefully inserted into a particular area of the brain that is associated with mood (area 25). An electric current is then passed to this overactive part of the brain to block it or, in a few people who have chosen this, destroy the overactive cells. This is an experimental treatment of last resort. The people who underwent this treatment had tried every other form of treatment for their desperate and often suicidal depression. Results after three to six years show one third of people experienced complete relief, one third showed partial relief, and one third showed no improvement or got worse. A more recent study comparing sham stimulation with active stimulation found distinct sustained improvement in those with active treatment (P. E. Holtzheimeer et al., "Subcallosal Cingulate Deep Brain Stimulation of Resistant Unipolar and Bipolar Depression," *Archive of General Psychiatry* 69 [2012]: 150).

[19]Used courtesy of the writer.

[20]Used courtesy of the writer.

Chapter 4: Some Rooted Sorrows

[1]Martin Luther, *Table Talk*, trans. William Hazlitt (London: G. Bell & Sons, 1909), p. 317.

[2]Hippocrates, *Aphorisms*, sec. 6.23.

[3]J. L. Gibson, *John Cassian: Conferences*, ed. H. Wace and P. Schaff, Nicene and Post-Nicene Fathers Series, series 2, vol. 11 (Oxford: Oxford University Press, 1894), pp. 343-44.

[4]Don Duarte, *Leal Consulheiro*, p. 22, quoted in F. J. Roberts, "Depression: A Linguistic, Historical and Philosophical Exploration" (M.D. thesis, University of Bristol, 1973), p. 57.

[5]Algis Valiunas, "Melancholy's Whole Physician," *The New Atlantis*, no. 17 (Summer 2007): pp. 53-69 <www.thenewatlantis.com/publications/melancholys-whole-physician>.

[6]Richard Baxter, "The Causes and Cure of Melancholy," in *The Cure of Melancholy and Overmuch Sorrow, by Faith*, p. 7 <www.puritansermons.com/baxter/baxter25.htm#sec2>.

[7]John Colquhoun, *Spiritual Comfort* (Morgan, Penn.: Soli Deo Gloria Publications, 1998), p. 147.

[8]Thomas Brooks, *The Complete Works of Thomas Brooks*, ed. Alexander Grosart, vols. 1-6 (New York: AMS Press, 1978), 4:260.

[9]John Bowlby, *Attachment and Loss* (Harmondsworth, U.K.: Pelican Books, 1983). See also Bowlby, *A Secure Base* (New York: Basic Books, 1988).

[10]Mary D. Salter Ainsworth, Mary C. Blehar, Everett Waters and Sally Wall,

Patterns of Attachment (Hillsdale, N.J.: Lawrence Erlbaum, 1978).

[11]Dan Siegel, *Mindsight: The New Science of Personal Transformation* (New York: Bantam Books, 2010), p. 170. See also Curt Thompson, *Anatomy of the Soul* (Wheaton, Ill.: Tyndale House Publishers, 2010), pp. 113-34.

[12]M. Main, E. Hesse, and N. Kaplan, "Predictability of Attachment Behavior and Representational Processes at 1, 6, and 19 Years of Age: The Berkeley Longitudinal Study," in *Attachment from Infancy to Adulthood*, ed. K. E. Grossmann, K. Grossmann and E. Waters (New York: Guilford Press, 2005), pp. 245-304.

[13]Jerome Kagan and Nancy Snidman, *The Long Shadow of Temperament* (Cambridge, Mass.: Belknap Press, 2004).

[14]Used courtesy of the writer.

[15]Aaron Beck, *Cognitive Therapy and the Emotional Disorders* (New York: Meridian, 1976), pp. 29-46. See also his *Cognitive Theory of Depression*, The Guilford Clinical Psychology and Psychopathology Series (New York: Guilford Press, 1987).

[16]Richard Winter, *Perfecting Ourselves to Death: The Pursuit of Excellence and the Perils of Perfectionism* (Downers Grove, Ill.: InterVarsity Press, 2005).

[17]Alec Roy, "Vulnerability Factors and Depression in Men," *British Journal of Psychology* 138 (January 1981): 75-77.

[18]George W. Brown and Tirril Harris, *Social Origins of Depression: A Study of Psychiatric Disorder in Women* (New York: Routledge, 2001).

[19]C. Tennant et al., "The Relationship of Childhood Separation Experiences to Adult Depressive and Anxiety States," *British Journal of Psychiatry* 141 (1982): 475.

[20]This separation will usually mean that the person is away from home completely, but it may also apply if a parent is severely depressed and is so emotionally withdrawn from the children that they experience a sense of emptiness in the relationship.

[21]Lord David Cecil, *William Cowper: The Stricken Deer* (London: Constable, 1929), p. 172.

[22]Aaron Beck, Brad Alford and David Clark, *Scientific Foundations of Cognitive Theory of Depression* (Hoboken, N.J.: John Wiley & Sons, 1999), p. 52.

[23]Aaron Beck, *Depression: Clinical Experimental and Theoretical Aspects* (London: Staples Press, 1967), p. 277.

[24]When much of the research quoted above was done there was no diagnostic category that included "complicated grief," which we have today. There is considerable overlap between complicated grief and depression, and some have suggested that early loss of a parent may predispose children to complicated grief more than depression. This would explain why more recent studies have

not found a clear relationship between early parent loss and later depression.
[25]Ian H. Gotlib and Constance L. Hammen, *Psychological Aspects of Depression: Toward a Cognitive-Interpersonal Integration* (New York: Wiley, 1992).
[26]"An Estimated 1 in 10 U.S. Adults Report Depression," Centers for Disease Control and Prevention website <www.cdc.gov/features/dsdepression/>.
[27]Stephen E. Gilman et al., "Socioeconomic Status in Childhood and the Lifetime Risk of Major Depression," *International Journal of Epidemiology* 31, no. 2 (2002): 359-67; Vijaya Murali and Femi Oyebode, "Poverty, Social Inequality and Mental Health," *Advances in Psychiatric Treatment* (2004): 10:216-24; Catherine Ross, "Neighbourhood Disadvantage and Adult Depression," *Journal of Mental Health and Social Behavior* 41, no. 2 (June 2009): 177-87.
[28]Ruth Lanius, Eric Vermetten and Clare Pain, eds., *The Impact of Early Life Trauma on Health and Disease. The Hidden Epidemic* (Cambridge: Cambridge University Press, 2010). See also ACE (Adverse Childhood Experiences) Study, 1995-1997 <www.acestudy.org> and <www.cdc.gov/ace/index.htm>.
[29]M. E. P. Seligman, *Helplessness: On Depression, Development and Death* (San Francisco: W. H. Freeman, 1975).

Chapter 5: Loss, Sorrow and Grief
[1]Used courtesy of the writer.
[2]Joseph Nowinski, "The New Grief," *Psychotherapy Networker*, July/August 2011, pp. 21-27, 52. Nowinski describes the stages of this roller coaster process for a couple where the wife has stage 3 ovarian cancer.
[3]See Rob Moll, *The Art of Dying* (Downers Grove, Ill.: InterVarsity Press, 2010).
[4]C. S. Lewis, *A Grief Observed* (London: Faber and Faber, 1961), p. 47.
[5]C. Everett Koop and Elizabeth Koop, *Sometimes Mountains Move* (Wheaton, Ill.: Tyndale House, 1979), p. 11.
[6]Colin Murray Parkes, *Bereavement: Studies of Grief in Adult Life* (Gretna, La.: Pelican, 1975), p. 79.
[7]George Bonanno, *The Other Side of Sadness: What the New Science of Bereavement Tells Us About Life After Loss* (New York: Basic Books, 2009). p. 39.
[8]Anne Lamott, *Traveling Mercies: Some Thoughts on Faith* (New York: Anchor Books, 1999), pp. 70, 72.
[9]Parkes, *Bereavement*, p. 79.
[10]Michelle Magorian, *Goodnight Mister Tom* (London: Puffin Books, 1983), pp. 287-88. Some parts are not suitable for very young children.
[11]See Albert Y. Hsu, *Grieving a Suicide* (Downers Grove, Ill.: InterVarsity Press, 2002).

[12] Bonanno, *Other Side of Sadness*.

[13] George A. Bonanno, "Loss, Trauma and Human Resilience," *American Psychologist* 59, no. 1 (January 2004): 20-28.

[14] K. Boerner, C. B. Wortman and G. A . Bonanno, "Resilient or At Risk? A Four-Year Study of Older Adults Who Initially Showed High or Low Distress Following Conjugal Loss," *Journal of Gerontology: Psychological Science* 60B (2005): 67-73. See also <www.cloc.isr.umich.edu/papers/boerner.pdf>.

[15] Martin Luther, *Table Talk*, ed. Will Hazlitt (London: G. Bell & Sons, 1909), p. 277.

[16] Henri J. M. Nouwen, *Out of Solitude: Three Meditations on the Christian Life* (Notre Dame, Ind.: Ave Maria Press, 2004), p. 38.

[17] Bonanno, *Other Side of Sadness*, p. 75.

[18] The kinsman redeemer is a family member who has responsibility to help with financial hardship and to father a son to carry on Naomi's husband's name. This usually involved some sacrifice and cost for the relative who was the kinsman redeemer. But there was a problem for Ruth. There was another closer relative who had the first choice, but after deliberation, he did not want to take the responsibility. So Boaz went beyond the call of duty and the law, and he married Ruth out of love and kindness, redeeming an outcast and bringing her into the fellowship of God's people.

Chapter 6: Suicide

[1] John Berryman, *Eleven Addresses to the Lord from Love and Fame* (New York: Farrar, Straus and Giroux, 1972).

[2] Preliminary data for 2009 shows a rising rate overall to a total of 36,547 suicides.

[3] "Suicide in the U.S.: Statistics and Prevention," NIH Publication No. 06-4594, National Institute of Mental Health <www.nimh.nih.gov/health/publications/suicide-in-the-us-statistics-and-prevention/index.shtml>.

[4] See American Foundation for Suicide Prevention <www.afsp.org> and The National Institute of Mental Health <www.nimh.nih.gov/health/publications/suicide-in-the-us-statistics-and-prevention/index.shtml>.

[5] Scott Anderson, "The Urge to End It All," *The New York Times Magazine,* July 6, 2008 <www.nytimes.com/2008/07/06/magazine/06suicide-t.html?pagewanted=all>.

[6] Ibid., p. 38.

Chapter 7: Breaking Points and Suicidal Saints

[1] Another example of this is David's honesty with God in the Psalms. It is the

key to his security in the midst of tremendous ups and downs of mood in reaction both to his own sin and folly and to other people's sins against him. [2]How we react to pressure and stressful circumstances is certainly affected by our individual personalities, and perfectionists are particularly prone to self-doubt, fear of failure, a desire to please everyone, an inability to share weaknesses with others and high expectations of themselves. There is often deep frustration with being an imperfect person in an imperfect world. Moses, in his desire to serve God well, shows some streaks of perfectionism in his character.

[3]I am grateful to my colleague Brian Aucker, professor of Old Testament, for sharing his sermon "Spelunking with Elijah" (given at Covenant Presbyterian Church, St. Louis, MO, on July 4, 2004), from which this sentence is taken.

[4]Terry Cooper, *Sin, Pride and Self Acceptance: The Problem of Identity in Theology and Psychology* (Downers Grove, Ill.: InterVarsity Press, 2003), p. 166.

Chapter 8: Coping with Anxiety, Worry and Fear

[1]See Isaiah 41:10, 13; Matthew 6:25; Psalm 37:1, 7-8; 2 Timothy 1:7; and Philippians 4:6.

[2]Jerome Kagan, "Bringing Up Baby," *Psychotherapy Networker* (March/April 2011), p. 33.

[3]Jerome Kagan, *Unstable Ideas: Temperament, Cognition and Self* (Cambridge, Mass.: Harvard University Press, 1989).

[4]John Bunyan, *Grace Abounding to the Chief of Sinners* (London: Oxford University Press, 1966), p. 33.

[5]George Bonanno et al., *The Other Side of Sadness: What the New Science of Bereavement Tells Us About Life After Loss* (New York: Basic Books, 2009), p. 60.

[6]Ibid., p. 61.

[7]Ibid., p. 62.

[8]Daniel Siegel, *Mindsight* (New York: Bantam Books, 2010), p. 138.

[9]For example, EMDR (Eye Movement Desensitization and Reprocessing) and exercises that teach relaxation, breathing, writing and drawing the story, body awareness and emotional regulation.

[10]In this context *fear* means to lovingly revere, bow before and trust God as Creator, Sustainer, Savior and Judge of the universe.

[11]CBT has been shown to be very effective and is widely used. Depressed and anxious people tend to have a "cognitive bias" toward pessimistic thinking and often have deeply embedded expectations ("negative schemas") about life that need to be exposed and changed.

[12]Common grace is an expression used by theologians to describe the good things God gives to both Christians and non-Christians, such as enabling

non-Christian scientists (and artists and writers) to discover and describe things that are true, even if they don't believe in the God behind these truths (see Matthew 5:45 and Romans 1:19-20). I have written on the important question of the relationship between biblical wisdom and "secular" wisdom in "The Search for Truth in Psychology and Counseling," *Presbyterion* 31, no. 1 (Spring 2005), pp. 18-36, available at <http://richardwinter .org>. See also Lydia C. W. Kim-van Daalen, "The Holy Spirit, Common Grace, and Secular Psychotherapy," *Journal of Psychology and Theology*, in press.

[13]Although mindfulness techniques originated in Buddhist meditation, there are some helpful common-grace insights and practices for learning emotional regulation that can be carefully used within a Christian worldview.

Chapter 9: Anger and the Struggle to Forgive

[1]Used courtesy of the writer.

[2]D. A. Carson, *The Gospel According to John* (Grand Rapids: Eerdmans, 1991), p. 415.

[3]Curt Thompson, *Anatomy of the Soul: Surprising Connections Between Neuroscience and Spiritual Practices That Can Transform Your Life and Relationships* (Wheaton, Ill.: Tyndale House, 2010), pp. 157-65.

[4]Anthony Storr, *The Art of Psychotherapy* (London: Secker and Warburg/ Heinemann, 1979), pp. 101-2.

[5]Most of us need restraint, and there are many verses about this in the Bible that I will summarize these under seven headings: (1) Don't hate or treat with contempt—Leviticus 19:17; 1 John 2:11; 3:15; (2) don't lose control— Proverbs 17:14; 19:19; 25:28; Galatians 5:19-20; Ephesians 4:31; (3) be gentle, patient and kind—Proverbs 15:1; 1 Corinthians 13:4-7; Ephesians 4:32; (4) don't be bitter—Ephesians 4:26; Hebrews 12:15; (5) don't pretend you are not angry when you are—Psalm 55:21; Proverbs 10:18; (6) speak the truth with love—Ephesians 4:15, 25; and (7) forgive—Matthew 6:12-15; 18:21-35; Romans 12:17-21; Ephesians 4:32.

[6]Used courtesy of the writer.

[7]Erwin Lutzer, *Managing Your Emotions* (Eastbourne, U.K.: Kingsway Publishers, 1981), p. 144.

[8]Dan B. Allender and Tremper Longman III, *Bold Love* (Colorado Springs: NavPress, 1992), pp. 247-48.

[9]Used courtesy of the writer.

Chapter 10: The Tangled Web of Guilt and Shame

[1]Shakespeare *Macbeth* 5.3.

[2]Tyron Edwards, C. N. Catrevas, Jonathan Edwards and Ralph Emerson Browns, *The New Dictionary of Thoughts* (New York: Standard Book Company, 1960), p. 104.

[3]Edwards et al., "Sophocles," *New Dictionary of Thoughts,* p. 105.

[4]In contrast to Freud, the existentialist psychotherapists recognize certain guilt feelings are not just the products of parental and social conditioning, which should then be removed by psychoanalysis. Rather, they see us as genuinely guilty in failing to fulfill all the possibilities of being human. This is close to the Christian view of guilt, but the existentialist's solution is to try harder to live up to his potential. There is no grace or forgiveness.

[5]If guilt can be gotten rid of by throwing out the values that give rise to the guilt, then a closely related view takes this process one step further. In some forms of Eastern mysticism, especially the teachings popularized in the West, reality is redefined to where we are already perfect. It has been reported that Maharishi Mahesh Yogi said, "The answer to all your problems is that there is no problem." Apparently, if we can only realize it ("enlightenment"), there is no suffering, no sin, because all is one. I cannot harm anyone else because, in reality, I am that person too. Guilt is an illusion, and we move beyond the Western categories of right and wrong.

[6]Paul Tournier, *Guilt and Grace* (London: Hodder & Stoughton, 1974), p. 152.

[7]Dick Keyes, *Beyond Identity: Finding Your Way in the Image and Character of God* (Eugene, Ore.: Wipf and Stock, 2003), pp. 32-57.

[8]I have explored this in more detail in my book *Perfecting Ourselves to Death: The Pursuit of Excellence and the Perils of Perfectionism* (Downers Grove, Ill.: IVP Books, 2005), pp. 89-97.

[9]Brene Brown, *I Thought It Was Just Me (But It Isn't)* (New York: Gotham Books, 2007), p. 5.

[10]Many of us feel ashamed when explaining why we are Christians because it seems too uncool, old-fashioned and out-of-touch with contemporary culture.

[11]"Those who trust in idols, who say to images, 'You are our gods,' will be turned back in utter shame" (Isaiah 42:17).

[12]"May my heart be blameless toward your decrees, that I may not be put to shame" (Psalm 119:80).

[13]After the Fall, Adam and Eve felt shame, guilt and fear and tried to hide from God.

[14]In counseling and psychotherapy language, this is called a "corrective emotional experience."

[15]Brene Brown, in *I Thought It Was Just Me (But It Isn't),* uses the very helpful concept of "shame resilience," p. 31. She develops this in relation to our need for "courage, compassion and connection," p. xxiii.

Chapter 11: Reducing Vulnerability and Moving Toward Healing

[1]Taking fish oil, vitamin D and folate should be done in consultation with your doctor. There is suggestive but as yet inconclusive evidence that these supplements help relieve or prevent depression and may enhance the effect of antidepressants. I recommend Andrew Weil, M.D., *Spontaneous Happiness* (New York: Little, Brown, 2011). Even though he comes from a Buddhist and secular spirituality, his holistic understanding of depression is very helpful, and his recommendations for vitamins and supplements and many other practical aspects of decreasing vulnerability to depression are well researched and explained. His book is common-grace wisdom while missing the core human problem of rebellion and alienation from God.

[2]Here is a helpful website of a psychologist colleague, Len Matheson, who explains how he approaches relaxation and breathing exercises and then helps you learn how to do those exercises: www.epicrehab.com/clients/resources/ppr_0_stress_and_distress.

[3]In Mindfulness-Based Cognitive Therapy you can learn to accept undesired feelings and thoughts, and let them come and then go without trying to wrestle with them. This helps people to focus on the present, rather than on anxiety about the future or on regrets from the past.

[4]Some research shows that practicing gratitude raises one's happiness set point by as much as 25 percent! See Weil, *Spontaneous Happiness*, p. 190.

[5]I strongly recommend my friend Scotty Smith's wonderful daily prayers, based on biblical texts, as models of heart-felt prayer on many aspects of life. I sometimes email an appropriate one to my clients. See *Everyday Prayers: 365 Days to Gospel-Centered Faith* (Grand Rapids: Baker Books, 2011). See also his website: http://scottysmith.org.

[6]The original version of this case study was published in *Edification: The Journal of the Society for Christian Psychology* 2, no. 2 (2008): 31-38. Used with permission.

[7]In this section I acknowledge a debt to the writings and friendship of Dan Allender, especially for *The Wounded Heart* (Colorado Springs: NavPress, 1990); and *The Healing Path* (Colorado Springs: Waterbrook Press, 1999).

[8]Carl Rogers described these qualities as essential for counseling. They reflect an attitude of compassion, commitment and care.

[9]Michael Emlet, *Crosstalk: Where Life and Scripture Meet* (Greensboro, N.C.: New Growth Press, 2009), p. 181.

[10]"The LORD saw how great man's wickedness . . . had become. . . . The LORD was grieved . . . and his heart was filled with pain" (Genesis 6:5-6).

[11]See Nikki Toyama's chapter on perfectionism in Nikki Toyama and Tracey Gee, eds., *More Than Serving Tea: Asian American Women on Expectations, Relation-*

ships, Leadership and Faith (Downers Grove, Ill.: IVP Books, 2006), pp. 50-68.

[12]*Transference* is used to describe the client's feelings from early relationships that are now "transferred" to the therapist. *Countertransference* means feelings the therapist has toward the client.

[13]Allender, *Healing Path*, p. 19.

[14]Mark McMinn, *Why Sin Matters* (Wheaton, Ill.: Tyndale House, 2004), pp. 63-67.

[15]T. S. Eliot, *The Complete Poems and Plays, 1909-1950* (New York: Harcourt, Brace and World, 1952), p. 118.

[16]Allender, *Healing Path*, p. 235.

[17]For further exploration of this theme, when the person is ready, I might point them to the sermons and writing of Tim Keller, *Counterfeit Gods* (New York: Penguin Group, 2009).

[18]Allender, *Healing Path*, pp. 200-202.

[19]Margery Williams, *The Velveteen Rabbit* (New York: Avon Books, 1975), pp. 16-17.

[20]*Mostly Martha*, directed by S. Nettelbeck (Hollywood: Paramount Classics, 2002).

[21]C. S. Lewis, *Mere Christianity* (New York: Macmillan, 1960), p. 160.

[22]Used courtesy of the writer.

Chapter 12: Hope and Light in the Darkness

[1]*Annie Hall* (Hollywood: MGM Studios, Inc., 1977).

[2]*Run Lola Run*, written and directed by Tom Tykwer (New York: Sony Picture Classics, 1998).

[3]Shakespeare, *Macbeth* 5.5.

[4]Mary Harrington Hall, "A Conversation with Victor Frankl of Vienna," *Psychology Today* 1, no. 9 (February 1968): 56-63.

[5]Sigmund Freud, quoted in Hall, "Conversation with Victor Frankl," pp. 56-63.

[6]Carl G. Jung, *Modern Man in Search of a Soul* (New York: Harcourt Brace, 1933), p. 229.

[7]Ernest Becker, *The Denial of Death* (New York: Free Press, 1973), p. 26.

[8]Ibid., p. 284.

[9]Victor Frankl, *Man's Search for Meaning* (London: Hodder & Stoughton, 1974), pp. 104-5.

[10]Lionel Tiger, "Optimism: The Biological Roots of Hope," *Psychology Today*, January 1979, p. 18. See also Anthony Scioli and Henry B. Biller, *Hope in the Age of Anxiety: A Guide to Understanding and Strengthening Our Most Important Virtue* (New York: Oxford University Press, 2009), p. 42.

[11]*The Concise Oxford Dictionary*, 7th ed., s.v. "hope."

[12]See Albert Y. Hsu, *Grieving a Suicide* (Downers Grove, Ill.: InterVarsity Press, 2002), p. 134.

[13]Martin Lloyd-Jones, *Spiritual Depression: Its Causes and Cure* (London: Pickering and Inglis, 1965), p. 117.

[14]Ibid., p. 235. See also Ephesians 1:4 and 1 Thessalonians 4:3.

[15]Larry Crabb, *Inside Out* (Colorado Springs: NavPress, 1988), p. 13.

[16]Ibid., p. 14.

[17]See Dan Siegel, *Mindsight: The New Science of Personal Transformation* (New York: Bantam Books, 2010). See also a wonderful Christian exploration of Siegel's ideas by psychiatrist Curt Thompson in *Anatomy of the Soul: Surprising Connections Between Neuroscience and Spiritual Practices That Can Transform Your Life and Relationships* (Wheaton, Ill.: Tyndale House, 2010).

Appendix

[1]Gerald Sittser, *A Grace Disguised: How the Soul Grows Through Loss* (Grand Rapids: Zondervan, 2004), pp. 27-28.

[2]See the Holmes and Rahe Stress scale at <www.mindtools.com/pages/article/newTCS_82.htm>.

[3]Also known as the Lausanne Committee for World Evangelization. See Paul Hiebert, "Spiritual Warfare and Worldview" (Nairobi: The Lausanne Movement, 2000), <www.lausanne.org/all-documents/spiritual-warfare-and-worldview.html>. This writing on spiritual warfare includes case studies from different countries around the world.

[4]Sigmund Freud, "A Neurosis of Demoniacal Possession in the Seventeenth Century," in *Collected Papers* (London: Hogarth Press, 1957), p. 437; and Sigmund Freud, *Totem and Taboo: The Basic Writings of Sigmund Freud* (New York: Random House, 1938), pp. 854, 856.

[5]Carl G. Jung, *Jung on Evil*, ed. Murray Stein (Princeton, N.J.: Princeton University Press, 1996), p. 7.

[6]Barry A. Kosmin and Ariela Keysar, "American Religious Identification Survey (Aris 2008) Summary Report" (Hartford, Conn.: Institute for the Study of Secularism in Society and Culture, 2009) <http://commons.trincoll.edu/aris/publications/aris-2008-summary-report/>.

[7]See Matt Baglio, *The Rite: The Making of a Modern Exorcist* (New York: Random House, 2009).

[8]Margot Adler, *Drawing Down the Moon: Witches, Druids, Goddess Worshippers and Other Pagans in America* (New York: Penguin Books, 2006).

[9]See Genesis 3; 1 Chronicles 21:1; Job 1; and Zechariah 3:1-2.

[10]J. R. R. Tolkien, *The Silmarillion* (London: Unwin Paperbacks, 1979), pp. 15-16.

[11]It is sometimes possible for both to occur together.

[12]For more helpful analysis see Jerry Mugadze, "Spiritual Conflict in Light of Psychology and Medicine," (Nairobi: Lausanne Documents, 2000) <www .lausanne.org/all-documents/psychology-and-medicine.html>.

[13]R. K. Bufford, *Counseling and the Demonic* (Dallas: Word Publishing, 1988); C. F. Dickason, *Demon Possession and the Christian: A New Perspective* (Wheaton, Ill.: Crossway, 1989); Derek Prince, *They Shall Expel Demons: What You Need to Know About Demons—Your Invisible Enemy* (Tarrytown, N.Y.: Chosen Books, 1998); Merrill Unger, *What Demons Can Do to Saints* (Chicago: Moody Press, 1991).

[14]David Appleby, *It's Only a Demon: A Model of Christian Deliverance* (Winona Lake, Ind.: BMH Books, 2009). This book is a careful biblical explanation of the work of Satan and demons, a practical manual for doing deliverance, and a compilation of extensive and impressive personal testimonies from Christians who have experienced "demonization" and deliverance. It is nonsensational and a testimony to the need for discernment and gifting in this area of much confusion in the church.

[15]John Richards, *But Deliver Us from Evil* (London: Darton, Longman & Todd, 1974), p. 156.

[16]See Judges 9:23; 1 Samuel 16:13-23; 28:3-25; 1 Kings 22:6-28.

[17]See Matthew 4:24; Mark 6:13; Luke 6:17-19; Acts 19:11-12.

[18]See also Jeremiah 17:9 and Mark 7:20-21.

[19]Here is one reference for each of the ways I have described Satan's activity: Luke 13:16; 8:12-15; Acts 10:38; 1 Corinthians 7:5; 2 Corinthians 12:7; Luke 22:31-32; Revelation 12:9-10; John 8:44; Romans 16:17-20; Ephesians 6:12.

[20]A helpful resource is David Powlison, *Power Encounters: Reclaiming Spiritual Warfare* (Grand Rapids: Baker Books, 1995).

[21]It is dubious because it is not in the older and more reliable Greek manuscripts and, where it is, there are stylistic and vocabulary differences from the rest of Mark's Gospel. See *ESV Study Bible* (Wheaton, Ill.: Crossway Bibles, 2008) note on Mark 16:9-20.

[22]Sydney Page, *Powers of Evil: A Biblical Study of Satan and Demons* (Grand Rapids: Baker Books, 1995), pp. 178-79.

[23]See also C. S. Lewis, *The Screwtape Letters* (New York: HarperCollins, 2001) for helpful images of Satan's ordinary day-to-day activity.

[24]J. R. R. Tolkien, *The Lord of the Rings: The Return of the King* (London: George Allen and Unwin, 1968), p. 988.

Name Index

Subject Index

Scripture Index